W9-DBI-233

Landmarks in Modern American Business

MAGILL'S CHOICE

Landmarks in Modern American Business

Volume 1

1897–1942

Edited by

The Editors of Salem Press

SALEM PRESS, INC.
Pasadena, California
Hackensack, New Jersey

Essays originally appeared in *Great Events from History II: Business and Commerce*, 1994; new material has been added.

∞ The paper used in these volumes conforms to the American National Standard for Permanence of Paper for Printed Library Materials, Z39.48-1992 (R1997).

Library of Congress Cataloging-in-Publication Data

Landmarks in modern American business / edited by the editors of Salem Press

    p.   cm. — (Magill's choice)

Includes bibliographical references and index.

    ISBN 0-89356-135-5 (set : alk. paper). — ISBN 0-89356-139-8 (v. 1 : alk. paper). — ISBN 0-89356-143-6 (v. 2 : alk. paper). — ISBN 0-89356-149-5 (v. 3 : alk. paper)

    1. United States — Commerce — History — 20th century — Chronology. 2. Industries — United States — History — 20th century — Chronology. 3. Corporations — United States — History — 20th century — Chronology. 4. Commercial law — United States — History — 20th century — Chronology. I. Series.

HF3021 .L36 2000

338.0973—dc21

00-032962

First Printing

Publisher's Note

Landmarks in Modern American Business is the first Magill's Choice title to draw on Salem Press's popular *Great Events from History II* books. That series was designed to provide students and general readers with insights into important historical subjects by supplying information in a quickly retrievable format and easy-to-understand style. All but six articles in *Landmarks in Modern American Business* are taken from *Great Events from History II: Business and Commerce*, a five-volume set published in 1994. That set contained 374 articles on important businesss-related events and developments that occurrred throughout the world during the twentieth century. In selecting which articles to use in the present set, our first decision was to restrict coverage to the United States. The next decision was to identify articles covering the most significant events—those representing major turning points, or landmarks, in American business and commercial history.

Articles in *Landmarks in Modern American Business* focus on key developments in the evolution of American business and commerce—from the creation of the Dow Jones Industrial Average at the very end of the nineteenth century to the much-anticipated "Y2K" crisis of January 1, 2000, and the court-ordered breakup of Microsoft in mid-2000.

Throughout these three volumes, business is defined broadly to include any activity concerned with the production of goods or with the rendering of financial or other services. Commerce involves the exchange of commodities or services. The stages of these activities can be seen as a cycle, from the creation of products or services through marketing, distribution, and sales; and back to investment in product creation, expansion of businesses that produce them, or genesis of new businesses or products.

Reflecting the rapidly growing importance of computerization and electronic communications, this set also contains entirely new articles on the addition of Microsoft and Intel to the Dow Jones Industrials in 1999, cable television's challenge to network television, and the impact of the Internet and World Wide Web on American business. The final article addresses the crisis that was expected to occur when the world's computer's shifted over to January 1, 2000.

After being bombarded with dire warnings of eminent disaster during the late 1990's, many people expected that government and commercial mayhem would erupt when millions of unprepared computer clocks throughout the world confronted the year 2000 and did not know what to do with a date not starting with "19." A new article in *Landmarks in Modern American Business*, "The Y2K Crisis Finally Arrives," explains what actually happened.

The history of American business and commerce provides a unique perspective on history as a whole, showing how economic forces have shaped the nation and the lives of its citizens. Most of the events covered in these volumes had political or cultural, as well as economic, repercussions. Virtually every essay in this set touches on a wide variety of issues.

Landmarks in Modern American Business follows the general arrangement and format of the Great Events II series. Articles are arranged chronologically, by event. Ranging in length from 2,000 to 2,500 words, each of them opens with ready-reference top matter listing the *category* of the event discussed—from advertising to transportation; the *time* the event occurred; the *locale* where it occurred; a brief *summary* of its significance in the history of business and commerce; and descriptions of *principal personages* who were key players in the event. The main text that follows is divided into two subsections: *Summary of Event* describes the event itself and the circumstances leading up to it, and *Impact of Event*. The latter section analyzes the influence of the event on such issues as the evolution of business practices, the growth of an industry, or national politics—in both the short and long runs.

Every article has an annotated and updated *Bibliography* listing important publications relating to the essay topic. Titles of these publications are chosen for their relevance to the topic in question and their accessibility through to target readers. Finally, each article ends with a list of *Cross-References*, identifying other articles in this set on related or similar subjects.

At the back of volume 3 of *Landmarks in Modern American Business* readers will find a variety of indexes that will help them find the articles and information they seek. These include a Chronological List of Events, an Alphabetical List of Events, a Category Index, an index of Principal Personages, and a general Subject Index.

All the articles in this set are written and signed by experts in the various fields of business and economics; most contributors are academicians in these fields. A list of the contributors, along with their affiliations, follows this note. Once again, we gratefully acknowledge their participation and thank them for making their expert knowledge accessible to general readers.

Contributors

Christina Ashton
Independent Scholar

Siva Balasubramanian
*Southern Illinois
University at Carbondale*

Richard Barrett
Elmira College

Jonathan Bean
Ohio State University

Bruce Andre Beaubouef
University of Houston

Jack Blicksilver
Georgia State University

John Braeman
*University of Nebraska
at Lincoln*

Anthony Branch
Golden Gate University

Carmi Brandis
Independent Scholar

Jon R. Carpenter
*University of South
Dakota*

Brian J. Carroll
*California Baptist
College*

Elisabeth A. Cawthon
*University of Texas at
Arlington*

Edward J. Davies II
University of Utah

Jennifer Davis
Independent Scholar

Bill Delaney
Independent Scholar

Satch Ejike
Independent Scholar

Eric Elder
Northwestern College

Corinne Elliott
Independent Scholar

Loring Emery
Independent Scholar

Chiarella Esposito
University of Mississippi

Daniel C. Falkowski
Canisius College

John L. Farbo
University of Idaho

John C. Foltz
University of Idaho

Andrew M. Forman
Hofstra University

Eugene Garaventa
*College of Staten Island
of the City University of
New York*

Elizabeth Gaydou
Jordan College

Richard Goedde
St. Olaf College

Nancy M. Gordon
Independent Scholar

Sam Ramsey Hakim
University of Nebraska

Mark D. Hanna
Miami University

Baban Hasnat
*State University of New
York College at Brockport*

Sarah Holmes
University of Connecticut

Frederick B. Hoyt
*Illinois Wesleyan
University*

Jeffry Jensen
Independent Scholar

Rajiv Kalra
*Moorhead State
University*

Dan Kennedy
Independent Scholar

Benjamin J. Klebaner
*City College of the City
University of New York*

Theodore P. Kovaleff
*Center for Study of the
Presidency*

Mitchell Langbert
Clarkson University

Victor J. LaPorte, Jr.
*University of Central
Florida*

Martin J. Lecker
*Rockland Community
College*

Daniel Y. Lee
Shippensburg University

Jim Lee
*Fort Hays State
University*

Jose C. de Leon
*Society for Technical
Communication*

Marie McKendall
*Grand Valley State
University*

Lewis Mandell
University of Connecticut

S. A. Marino
*Westchester Community
College*

James D. Matthews
Lynn University

Patricia C. Matthews
Mount Union College

Andre Millard
*University of Alabama at
Birmingham*

Jay Nathan
St. John's University

Anthony Patrick O'Brien
Lehigh University

John F. O'Connell
College of the Holy Cross

Virginia Ann Paulins
Ohio University

Iris A. Pirozzoli
University of Wisconsin

Patrick D. Reagan
*Tennessee Technological
University*

Betty Richardson
*Southern Illinois
University at
Edwardsville*

Joseph R. Rudolph, Jr.
Towson State University

Larry Schweikart
University of Dayton

Arthur G. Sharp
Independent Scholar

Elaine Sherman
Hofstra University

Roger Smith
Independent Scholar

A. J. Sobczak
Independent Scholar

Robert Sobel
Hofstra University

Alene Staley
Saint Joseph's College

Timothy E. Sullivan
Towson State University

Kambiz Tabibzadeh
*Eastern Kentucky
University*

John R. Tate
*New Jersey Institute of
Technology*

Paul B. Trescott
*Southern Illinois
University*

Sharon C. Wagner
*Missouri Western State
College*

M. Mark Walker
University of Mississippi

William J. Wallace
Monmouth College

Theodore O. Wallin
Syracuse University

William C. Ward III
Kent State University

Rowena Wildin
Independent Scholar

Clifton K. Yearley
*State University of New
York at Buffalo*

Charles Zelden
*University of Texas at
Arlington*

Contents

Volume 1

Landmarks in Modern American Business

THE WALL STREET JOURNAL PRINTS THE DOW JONES INDUSTRIAL AVERAGE

CATEGORY OF EVENT: Finance
TIME: 1897
LOCALE: New York, New York

Dow, Jones and Company began publishing its Dow Jones Industrial Average, a measure of the stock prices of important industrial companies, in The Wall Street Journal

Principal personages:
CHARLES HENRY DOW (1851-1902), a financial analyst and reporter
EDWARD DAVIS JONES (1856-1920), a reporter and businessperson
CHARLES MILFORD BERGSTRESSER (b. 1858?), a partner in Dow, Jones and Company

Summary of Event

Charles Dow, a financial analyst, thought it important that members of the financial community have access to a summary measure of prices on the New York Stock Exchange. He believed that such a measure would aid in predicting financial trends. As cofounder of Dow, Jones and Company (the comma was later dropped from the company name) and cofounder and editor of *The Wall Street Journal*, he was able to publish various indices and promote his own theories of the behavior of the stock market.

At its founding in 1882, Dow, Jones and Company was a news-gathering organization focused on and located in New York City. The company soon expanded its focus to include any major news that would affect the business

1

community. Coverage of financial news certainly was not new; various publications had discussed the New York Stock Exchange (NYSE) and news connected with it since its founding in 1792. Soon after the founding of that stock market, James Oram began publishing *The Shipping and Commercial List and New York Prices Current*, stating the facts and news that affected shipping, finance, and commerce in the region. By 1825, this newspaper had been taken over by the *Journal of Commerce*, which was still being published in 1993. New York had established itself as the financial center of the young nation, and financial news was both created there and disseminated from there.

Early business reporting was filled with speculation and rumors. The few hard facts that were available were valuable to investors, and reporters were sometimes paid for delivering information in advance of publication or for holding back information. John J. Kiernan saw a need for speedy and accurate business reporting. He borrowed funds from family and friends and started the Kiernan News Agency, offering subscribers hand-delivered newsletters containing up-to-date information on all aspects of business. Charles Dow began working for the agency in 1880. Several months later, Dow recommended Edward Jones to fill another reportorial position.

By 1882, Dow and Jones had struck out on their own, forming Dow, Jones and Company. The new enterprise had a total of six employees and was located at the back of a candy store. In 1883, the company began publishing *Customers' Afternoon Letter*, a daily newspaper of two pages. The workload soon became overwhelming, and the company added Charles Milford Bergstresser as a third partner, though his name was not added to the company's name.

By 1889, Dow, Jones and Company had a staff of about fifty, including its first out-of-town reporter, stationed in Boston. The partners realized that their two-page newspaper could not hold all the information that the company gathered; they reorganized the publication as *The Wall Street Journal* in that year. The paper stated that it aimed to give full and fair information regarding fluctuations in the prices of stocks, bonds, and some commodities and was intended to be a paper of news rather than of opinions. A policy statement further explained that the paper would "give a good deal of news not found in other publications, and will present . . . a faithful picture of the rapidly shifting panorama of the Street."

One of the main ideas developed by Dow and Jones was a composite list of major stocks and an index of their prices. Company publications began carrying lists as early as 1884. The Dow Jones Industrial Average (DJIA), one version of these lists, is generally recognized as having first been published in 1897. That first DJIA averaged the prices of twelve major companies. The list was expanded to twenty companies in 1916 and to thirty in 1928. The companies included have changed over time, reflecting mergers and dissolutions, but the DJIA is adjusted for such changes so that the index number has the same meaning, with no jumps in its value because of such changes.

Charles Dow thought that such an index would be useful as an indicator, or even predictor, of general trends in the market. He promoted the Dow theory of market behavior, which identified primary trends in stock prices and identified types of market fluctuations. Daily fluctuations in a market price index had no significance other than as part of a primary upward or downward trend, or as part of a reaction (a temporary reversal in an upward trend) or rally (a temporary reversal in a downward trend). In identifying primary trends, the theory looks for the market index to move outside (or "break out") of a set of upper and lower boundaries. The trend continues until a secondary movement confirms that it has ended, as when the bottom of a reaction falls below the level of the previous reaction or the peak of a rally rises above the peak of the previous rally.

Dow's theories found wide followings and were discussed in books by various market theoreticians. The Dow theory was first labeled as such in book form in Samuel Armstrong Nelson's *The ABC of Speculation* (1902). After Dow's death in 1902, William Peter Hamilton, who had worked under Dow, continued to promote the Dow theory. In 1922, his book titled *The Stock Market Barometer: A Study of Its Forecast Value Based on Charles H. Dow's Theory of the Price Movement* assessed how the Dow theory had performed since 1897. Robert Rhea later promoted the theory, enlarging its scope to incorporate information on the number of shares traded daily. He emphasized, as had Dow, that the theory was designed as one tool to help read the marketplace, to be used in combination with other indicators and theories rather than on its own.

Jones sold out his share of Dow, Jones and Company to his partners in 1899; they sold the company in 1902 to Clarence Barron. *The Wall Street Journal* continued as primarily a financial newspaper until 1941, when a new managing editor, Bernard Kilgore, broadened the paper's coverage to major news events and in-depth articles on business.

Impact of Event

The growth of Dow, Jones and Company, from a two-man organization to a corporation ranked in 1990 among the largest five hundred in the United States and the thousand largest in the world, involved expansion of the firm's basic business of providing news of the marketplace. Even though the company underwent changes of ownership and expanded its scope, provision of accurate, timely financial news remained an important part of the company. In a contemporary world filled with different stock markets and theories of them, the DJIA is the most recognizable index of market performance. News of movements in the DJIA is enough to affect prices in markets other than the NYSE, which is the only market measured by the DJIA.

The company is best known as publisher of *The Wall Street Journal*, which branched out into European and Asian editions. The firm's business publications division also produced *Barron's*, a respected business magazine, and the *National Business Employment Weekly*, among other publications. Business publications, however, accounted for less than half the company's revenues by 1989. Various information services, including the Dow Jones News/Retrieval on-line computer service and Telerate, an international supplier of up-to-the-minute market data, accounted for most of the remainder. In 1990, for the seventh year in a row, *Fortune* magazine ranked Dow Jones first in its industry for quality of products and services.

Other industrial nations have developed stock markets, and stock market indicators, of their own. The DJIA is unusual in being based on only thirty stocks, with adjustments made when an included company announces a stock split (changing the price of the stock) or when one company's stock is substituted for that of another, which becomes necessary when companies dissolve. The Japanese stock market is measured by the widely reported Nikkei index. Canada has several different stock markets. The Vancouver market concentrates on mining stocks, while the Toronto exchange closely resembles the NYSE. Even within the United States, several different indices and markets exist. The Standard & Poor's S&P 500 index, for example, measures the average price level of five hundred individual stocks, thus providing a broader base than does the DJIA. Regional markets such as the Pacific Stock Exchange and the Philadelphia Stock Exchange allow traders to work in cities other than New York, and specialized markets such as NASDAQ (National Association of Securities Dealers Automated Quotations) and the American Stock Exchange allow national trading in stocks not carried on the NYSE. The advent of computerized trading has allowed investors to trade worldwide and around the clock, making the Dow Jones product of current, accurate information all the more important.

Stock traders have become increasingly sophisticated, using increasing numbers of tools and amounts of data to make their trading decisions. The Dow theory still forms the background for many theories, and many theories use movements in the DJIA as a predictor of stock market price changes. The NYSE has grown tremendously, making information concerning it meaningful to many more people. During the 1920's, perhaps five million shares would change hands on a busy day. By the 1990's, trading of two hundred million shares daily was common, and many more individuals had entered the market to buy small amounts of stock. Indicators of the markets assumed prominence and even became the subjects of trading. Markets developed for the combinations of stocks on which various indices were based; investors thus could place bets on which direction they thought the market as a whole would move. Advances in the level of the DJIA and other market indices offered data to support the theory that over the long term (depending on the precise period measured), the U.S. stock market usually offered a rate of return on investment higher than rates offered on most alternative investments.

The DJIA has attained stature, as have other stock market indices to a lesser degree, as a measure of overall economic activity, something for which it was not intended. Financial writers commonly make reference to the level of the DJIA when referring to future economic prospects or past performance. Although there is a link between stock prices and economic activity—stocks tend to be worth more when companies are profitable, which occurs when business activity is at a high level and unemployment rates are low—the link is far from perfect. The DJIA, however, has become recognized as an important measurement even by those who know almost nothing about financial markets.

Bibliography

Neilson, Winthrop, and Frances Neilson. *What's News: Dow Jones*. Radnor, Pa.: Chilton Book Company, 1973. Provides a history of *The Wall Street Journal* and the involvement of various individuals in its publication. Discusses content of the newspaper during different eras as well as describing innovations made by the paper.

Pierce, Phyllis S., ed. *The Dow Jones Averages, 1895-1995*. Chicago: Irwin Professional Publications, 1996. Comprehensive history of the DJIA.

Rosenberg, Jerry M. *Inside The Wall Street Journal*. New York: Macmillan, 1982. Gives the newspaper's history and describes its impact. Shows the evolution of the paper from a two-page newsletter through its ownership by Clarence Barron and beyond, discussing various advances and difficulties.

Seligman, Joel. *The Transformation of Wall Street*. New York: Houghton Mifflin, 1982. Describes the changes that have occurred since the advent of the Securities and Exchange Commission in the 1930's. More generally discusses the evolution of the financial markets on Wall Street.

Stillman, Richard J. *Dow Jones Industrial Average*. Homewood, Ill.: Dow Jones-Irwin, 1986. A history, with pictures, of Dow, Jones and Company, focusing on the DJIA. Discusses how the DJIA is computed and describes the contributions of various people to its development and use.

Wendt, Lloyd. *The Wall Street Journal.* Chicago: Rand McNally, 1982. A history of the newspaper and those who headed it at different times. Good on the origins of the paper and its original publishers as well as on the transformation from a New York to a national publication.

Carmi Brandis

Cross-References

The U.S. Stock Market Crashes on Black Tuesday (1929); The Securities Exchange Act Establishes the SEC (1934); Insider Trading Scandals Mar the Emerging Junk Bond Market (1986); The U.S. Stock Market Crashes on 1987's "Black Monday" (1987).

DISCOVERY OF OIL AT SPINDLETOP TRANSFORMS THE OIL INDUSTRY

CATEGORY OF EVENT: New products
TIME: January 10, 1901
LOCALE: Texas

The discovery of oil at the Spindletop field was the beginning of the Texas oil boom and led to the growth of a number of important present-day oil corporations

Principal personages:
PATILLO HIGGINS (1862-1955), a Beaumont resident, the first to find evidence of petroleum reserves in the area
ANTHONY F. LUCAS (1855-1921), an Austrian geologist and engineer, the first to act upon the theory that salt domes in the Gulf Coastal Plains were associated with petroleum reservoirs
JAMES M. GUFFEY (1839-1930), the head of the J. M. Guffey Petroleum Company
JOHN H. GALEY (1840-1918), the partner of Guffey
WILLIAM L. MELLON (1868-1949), an investment banker who helped finance Guffey
JOSEPH S. CULLINAN (1860-1937), a manager of a Standard Oil subsidiary who formed the Texas Fuel Company from discoveries made at Spindletop
JOHN D. ROCKEFELLER (1839-1937), the head of Standard Oil Company

Summary of Event
On January 10, 1901, at 10:30 A.M., the first major "gusher" came in at the Spindletop oil field. Spindletop was named for the salt dome known as

7

the "Big Hill," just south of Beaumont in southeastern Texas. This first major oil well at Spindletop at first produced 75,000 to 100,000 barrels per day, approximately 800,000 barrels before it was brought under control nine days after oil was struck. This dramatic discovery made the Spindletop area the first major oil "boom town" of Texas and shifted the focus of petroleum entrepreneurs to Texas. Texas was the leading petroleum producing state in the United States for much of the twentieth century and was one of the fastest-growing areas in terms of population. The Spindletop discovery also led to the formation and development of a number of important oil corporations.

Prior to the discovery of oil in Texas, the primary and best-known oil fields were in Pennsylvania. Officials of the Standard Oil Company believed that there were few, if any, productive oil fields west of the Mississippi River. By 1890, however, there was evidence of petroleum in Texas, primarily in Corsicana, just south of Dallas. The opportunity to develop the Corsicana oil fields brought two Pennsylvania wildcatters, James M. Guffey and John H. Galey, to Corsicana. The need to provide pipeline transportation facilities in the area also brought Joseph S. Cullinan of Pennsylvania, head of one of Standard Oil's pipeline subsidiaries, to Corsicana. The Spindletop discovery, which would dwarf the production at Corsicana, brought these three men and many others to the oil fields of southeastern Texas. These three would form the oil-producing and refining companies that would become Gulf Oil Company and the Texas Company (Texaco).

Patillo Higgins, a Beaumont resident, was the first to find evidence of petroleum reserves at the Spindletop salt dome. Higgins, despite receiving ridicule for believing that there were commercial quantities of petroleum in the Spindletop hill, formed the Gladys City Oil, Gas, and Manufacturing Company in 1892 to exploit the oil and gas reserves. Higgins ran out of funds before he had drilled deep enough to reach the oil. In 1899, he placed an advertisement in a trade journal to lease the field. Anthony F. Lucas, an Austrian mining engineer and consultant, answered the advertisement. In his work as a consultant, Lucas had traveled through the Texas and Louisiana Gulf Coast Plains. He often found seepages of petroleum in and around the salt dome formations that occurred throughout the region. Lucas contended that these salt domes were associated with vast reservoirs of petroleum.

Lucas drilled a well on Spindletop in 1899. Although he reached some crude oil, he too ran out of funds for the project. Lucas had difficulty obtaining additional financial backing because there was no proof in any of the other oil fields of the world to back up his contention that salt domes were associated with petroleum reservoirs. Through associates in the University of Texas geology department, Lucas came into contact with John H. Galey, a partner in the J. M. Guffey Petroleum Company of Pittsburgh. With $400,000 borrowed from the Mellon Bank of Pittsburgh, Guffey, Galey, and Lucas renewed efforts to find oil at Spindletop.

On January 10, 1901, these efforts reached fruition. After weeks of continual drilling problems, the drilling crew reached a depth of 1,160 feet. At 10:30 A.M., an oil gusher that could be seen three miles away erupted. In contrast to the first major oil discovery in Pennsylvania in 1859, which flowed at 20 barrels per day with the aid of a pump, the first Spindletop gusher spewed 75,000 to 100,000 barrels per day. In 1902, the Spindletop field produced more than eighteen million barrels of crude oil, which amounted to 20 percent of the production of the United States. This was 93 percent of the year's national increase in production. By the end of 1902, almost four hundred wells were bunched together at Spindletop. By 1904, that number had reached nearly twelve hundred.

The fist six oil wells drilled at Spindletop accounted for more oil than all the other oil wells in the world at that time. Such rapid and massive exploitation of the Spindletop's petroleum resources, accompanied often by extravagant waste, meant that the petroleum reservoirs in the Spindletop field were rapidly depleted between 1902 and 1904. Such exhaustion of petroleum resources, at Spindletop and later elsewhere in Texas and throughout the nation, would lead to concerns about conservation. In the very early twentieth century, however, at a time of economic opportunity and prosperity, concerns about conservation were rare.

William L. Mellon, whose family bank had substantially funded the Guffey operations at Spindletop, soon realized that a greater level of financial and personal involvement was necessary to maintaining profitability and expansion. The Mellons bought out Guffey's interests and in 1907 removed Guffey as president of the J. M. Guffey Petroleum Company. William L. Mellon was subsequently named president, and the company was renamed the Gulf Oil Company.

Cullinan also realized that the opportunities at Spindletop were much greater than at Corsicana. In January, 1902, Cullinan formed the Texas Fuel Company, an organization designed to refine and market the vast amounts of crude oil being produced in the area. Cullinan also formed the Producers Oil Company to ensure his company a continual source of supply. The Texas Fuel Company proved too small to meet the increasingly immense task of refining all the crude produced, and in March, 1902, its assets were transferred to a new corporation, the Texas Company, capitalized at three million dollars. Cullinan's renown from his days with Standard Oil led to the continual growth and success of the Texas Company at a time when approximately two hundred competitors and other entrepreneurs at Spindletop were failing.

Other major petroleum corporations were born or grew stronger at Spindletop. Shell Oil Company had its origins at Spindletop. The Shell Transport and Trading Company of London had signed a twenty-year contract in which Guffey's operations would produce oil for the British Navy. Shell's petroleum transportation investments later led it to engage in the other major functions of the oil industry. The Sun Oil Company, another Pennsylvania organization, grew much stronger at Spindletop. The Magnolia Oil Company, a Standard Oil affiliate, had its origins at Spindletop. It later became part of the Mobil Oil Company. The group of Texas oilmen that ultimately became the Humble Oil and Refining Company individually got their starts at Spindletop. After the Humble Oil and Refining Company merged with Standard Oil of New Jersey, the Humble organization later became the Texas branch of Exxon, a Standard Oil subsidiary.

Impact of Event

The discovery of oil at Spindletop had a number of important long-run consequences. It proved that there were vast reservoirs of petroleum reserves west of the Mississippi River and that petroleum was not limited to the eastern half of the United States. The discovery of oil at Spindletop spurred other research and discoveries in the Texas and Louisiana salt dome fields, establishing the area as an oil region of permanent importance. This new research in turn propelled further oil-seeking activities and development of oil fields in northern and western Texas, making Texas the leading petroleum state in the union for much of the twentieth century. By 1929, Texas was the leading producer of petroleum in the United States, producing 35 to 45 percent of the national total, and it became one of the leading oil-producing areas in the world. Texas held the position of the top-producing state in the union until the 1970's, when Alaska and Texas each produced approximately 30 percent of the national total.

The progress of the oil industry in Texas led to rapid growth of highly lucrative associated industries. In their very first oil strike at Spindletop, Lucas and his team used new techniques such as rotary drilling, drilling mud, and airlift of oil that afterward became standard operating procedure for oil producers. All these methods created a demand for an industry to produce drill bits and other tools and supplies. The most prominent of the companies supplying this equipment was the Hughes Tool Company, the source of the initial fortune of Howard Hughes. The growth of petroleum transportation pipelines created a demand for firms to service and supply them. These organizations, growing in a symbiotic relationship with the large oil corporations and many other smaller independent oil-producing organizations, were all crucial to the rapid growth of Texas beginning especially in the 1920's and continuing into the 1950's and 1960's. Urban areas such as Houston and the Spindletop-Beaumont-Port Arthur-Orange complex, with ports giving access to the Gulf of Mexico, became the sites of many large refining and petrochemical plants. Because of its location on the Trinity River and its proximity to the highly productive fields of northern Texas, the Dallas-Fort Worth area grew dramatically beginning in the middle of the twentieth century.

The Spindletop discovery opened up economic opportunity in an industry that had been monopolized by John D. Rockefeller's Standard Oil Company. The Texas Company, Gulf Oil Company, and Shell Oil Company were born at Spindletop, and the Sun Oil Company grew stronger at Spindletop. All of these would later provide competition to Standard Oil. Although all these growing oil companies remained independent of Standard Oil, practically all had ties to that company, whether selling crude oil to be refined or refined oil to be marketed and sold to the general public. The growth of these corporations would, however, transform the oil industry from one characterized by monopoly (Standard Oil) to one that was more oligopolistic in nature.

The dramatic discovery at Spindletop, by proving that there were major untapped areas of petroleum in the United States, opened the door for other opportunistic, risk-taking entrepreneurs and organizations. This led to the formation of the aforementioned major corporations as well as many smaller independents that helped boost the economy of Texas and the Gulf Coast region.

Bibliography

Clark, James A., and Michel T. Halbouty. *Spindletop*. New York: Random House, 1952. Written in a popular style, without footnotes or documentation. Effectively captures the drama and impact of the birth of the Texas oil industry at Spindletop. Good for those seeking an introduction to the Spindletop discovery and the early Texas oil industry.

Goodwyn, Lawrence. *Texas Oil, American Dreams: A Study of the Texas Independent Producers and Royalty Owners Association*. Austin, Tex.: Center for American History, 1996.

King, John O. *Joseph Stephen Cullinan: A Study of Leadership in the Texas Petroleum Industry, 1897-1937*. Nashville, Tenn.: Vanderbilt University Press, 1970. Gives an excellent account of Cullinan's life, his establishment of the Texas Company, and the early Texas oil industry in general.

Larson, Henrietta M., and Kenneth Wiggins Porter. *History of Humble Oil and Refining Company: A Study in Industrial Growth.* New York: Harper, 1959. A thorough, encyclopedic study of a small Texas company whose founders started at Spindletop and later merged with Standard Oil of New Jersey. Excellent in its analysis of intraindustry relationships.

Melosi, Martin V. "Oil Strike! The Birth of the Petroleum Industry." In *Coping with Abundance: Energy and Environment in Industrial America.* Philadelphia, Pa.: Temple University Press, 1985. Concisely details the events and impact of Spindletop as well as the early oil industry in Pennsylvania and California. The book as a whole is an excellent study of industrial-governmental relationships in the twentieth century United States.

Pratt, Joseph A. *The Growth of a Refining Region.* Greenwich, Conn.: JAI Press, 1980. A good comprehensive study of the growth of the oil organizations in the Texas-Louisiana Gulf Coast region.

_____. "The Petroleum Industry in Transition: Antitrust and the Decline of Monopoly Control in Oil." *Journal of Economic History* 40 (December, 1980): 815-837. A very good, concise analysis of the growth of the oil firms at Spindletop that challenged Standard Oil's control of the oil industry.

Bruce Andre Beaubouef

Cross-References

The Supreme Court Decides to Break Up Standard Oil (1911); The Teapot Dome Scandal Prompts Reforms in the Oil Industry (1924); Atlantic Richfield Discovers Oil at Prudhoe Bay, Alaska (1967); Arab Oil Producers Curtail Oil Shipments to Industrial States (1973); The United States Plans to Cut Dependence on Foreign Oil (1974); The Alaskan Oil Pipeline Opens (1977).

CHAMPION V. AMES UPHOLDS FEDERAL POWERS TO REGULATE COMMERCE

CATEGORY OF EVENT: Retailing
TIME: 1903
LOCALE: Washington, D.C.

The U.S. Supreme Court, through its broad interpretation of the commerce clause in Champion v. Ames, *sustained federal powers to prohibit and regulate commerce*

Principal personages:
MELVILLE W. FULLER (1833-1910), the Chief Justice of the United States, 1888-1910
JOHN MARSHALL HARLAN (1833-1911), an associate justice of the U.S. Supreme Court, 1877-1911
JOHN MARSHALL (1755-1835), the Chief Justice of the United States, 1801-1835
ALBERT J. BEVERIDGE (1862-1927), a U.S. senator, 1899-1911, influential in passage of the Meat Inspection Amendment

Summary of Event

In 1903, the U.S. Supreme Court upheld the federal government's potential to prohibit or restrict commerce. The case of *Champion v. Ames*, also known as the Lottery Case, altered the delineation between interstate and intrastate commerce under article I, section 8, clause 3 of the U.S. Constitution, the so-called "commerce clause."

The circumstances brought before the Court originated in 1895 with an act of Congress. This act made it illegal to transport or conspire to transport lottery tickets from state to state. On February 1, 1899, C. F. Champion sent two Pan-American Lottery Company lottery tickets from Dallas, Texas, to Fresno, California. The tickets were transported by a vehicle owned by the Wells-Fargo Express Company. Champion was arrested in Chicago under a warrant based on his alleged violation of the act.

In 1903, the case was appealed to the U.S. Supreme Court for final review. The Court rendered its opinion in a five-to-four decision to uphold the conviction. Justice John Marshall Harlan delivered the majority opinion of the Court, while Chief Justice Melville W. Fuller gave the dissenting opinion.

When the Lottery Case appeared before the Court, the power to regulate interstate commerce was a concurrent power shared by the states and the federal government. Prior to the Lottery Case, several decisions had begun the process of liberalizing the connotation of "interstate," favoring federal control. One such case is *Gibbons v. Ogden* (1824). This decision played a major role in the Court's final disposition of the Lottery Case by initiating a method for analyzing commerce issues. A review of the facts in *Gibbons* shows that the state of New York granted a monopoly to Robert Livingston and Robert Fulton in the operation of steamboats in the waterways of New York. Aaron Ogden managed, under the monopoly, two licensed steamboats ferrying between New York and New Jersey. Thomas Gibbons obtained a coasting license under a 1793 act of Congress and began competing with Ogden.

Gibbons' steamboat was not licensed to operate under the New York monopoly. The pressure of additional competition encouraged Ogden to bring action in a New York Court to prohibit Gibbons from operating. Writing for the majority, Chief Justice John Marshall delivered the opinion of the Supreme Court, which held the New York monopoly law to be unconstitutional. In *Gibbons*, the Court aspired to denote interstate commerce. Gibbons' attorneys argued that it is traffic, to buy and sell, or the interchange of commodities. The Court agreed that interstate commerce includes traffic but added the notion of intercourse.

Generally, intercourse portrays exchange between persons or groups. With this notion, the Court reasoned that interstate commerce does not end at external boundary lines between states but may be introduced into the interior. They determined that commerce may pass the jurisdictional line of New York and act upon the waters to which the monopoly law applied, thus concluding that the transportation of passengers between New York and New Jersey constituted interstate commerce.

In the *Champion v. Ames* decision, the Court went on to reference other decisions that sanction federal authority. These cases continued to expand the essence of interstate commerce. Consequently, the Court resolved that commerce embraces navigation, intercourse, communication, traffic, the transit of persons, and the transmission of messages by telegraph.

In the Lottery Case, the use of a vehicle from Wells-Fargo Express traveling from state to state was relevant. The Court held that this travel provided sufficient intercourse with interstate commerce to allow federal domination. Further, the Court viewed the congressional justification for the creation of the act as being rational. It determined that the federal government is the proper means for protecting U.S. citizens from the widespread pestilence of lotteries. The Court deemed that such an evil act of appalling character, carried through interstate commerce, deserves federal intervention.

Chief Justice Fuller's dissenting opinion stated that the Court had imposed a burden on the state's powers to regulate for the public health, good order, and prosperity of its citizens. To hold that Congress has general police power would be to defeat the operation of the Tenth Amendment. This argument would constitute the foundation of many later dissenting opinions. This particular conviction never became the majority view.

At the time of the Lottery Case, there was an escalating struggle between a desire for a strong federal government, called federalism or nationalism, and the states' right to regulate themselves. This conflict roots itself as far back in U.S. history as the Constitution itself. After the war for independence with England, the states regarded themselves as independent sovereigns. The Articles of Confederation allowed only minimal intrusion into states' internal affairs by the Continental Congress.

Faced with the inability of the confederation to function properly, provincial patriotism had to concede. The delegates at the Constitutional Convention, in an effort to fabricate a more concentrated federal government, made many compromises. They maintained within the Constitution, however, certain seemingly inescapable limits on the federal government. As a consequence, the judiciary generally discerns the Constitution as being a limitation on federal power. Without an expressed or implied grant of authority from within the Constitution, the federal government cannot regulate.

This policy is not easily implemented in cases concerning commerce. Under the commerce clause, Congress has the authority to regulate commerce with foreign nations and among the several states and with Native Americans. The commerce clause seems to conflict with the Tenth Amendment. This amendment assigns all rights to the states, unless such control is prohibited or delegated to the U.S. government by the Constitution. The

Tenth Amendment is said to contain the states' police powers. Further, the Constitution does not expressly exclude states from regulating interstate commerce. It simply limits the federal government's jurisdiction over interstate trade and precludes interference with purely local activities.

To add another complication, consider the supremacy clause, article VI, paragraph 2. This states that if legitimate state and federal powers are in conflict, then the national interest will prevail. This power is enhanced by the Court's broad interpretation of the "necessary and proper clause" (article I, section 8) in *McCulloch v. Maryland* (1819). This ruling gave Congress a discretionary choice of means for implementing implied powers.

From a political perspective of the Court, it is notable that *McCulloch* and *Gibbons* were before the Court while John Marshall was chief justice. Marshall served under President John Adams as the secretary of state and was a devout federalist. During Marshall's tenure as chief justice, the Court vested within its jurisdiction an unusual allotment of power. It assigned to itself final interpretation rights over the constitutionality of all federal and state laws brought before the Court.

Impact of Event

The ruling given in the Lottery Case had an immediate influence on society. Social reformers quickly seized upon the rationale provided by the Court and began prompting Congress to regulate. In 1906, Senator Albert J. Beveridge successfully proposed a meat inspection amendment to an appropriations bill. The amendment prohibited the interstate shipment of meats that had not been federally inspected.

The amendment received an influential recommendation from President Theodore Roosevelt. Additionally, Upton Sinclair's novel *The Jungle* (1906) greatly intensified popular support for Beveridge's cause. Sinclair was an active socialist. His publication characterized the life of a worker in the Chicago stockyards and induced President Roosevelt to investigate the meatpacking industry. During the same term, Congress also approved the Pure Food and Drug Act.

Later, Beveridge would propose another bill based on the commerce clause. This legislation attempted to exclude from commerce goods produced by child labor. Beveridge was certain that the Lottery Case settled the constitutionality of his proposal. Convincing his colleagues of this would prove to be arduous and unsuccessful. When Congress finally passed the Child Labor Act of 1916, the Court would declare it unconstitutional in *Hammer v. Dagenhart* (1918). It would take another decade before such a law would be held valid under constitutional scrutiny by the Court.

Despite this setback, the precedent established in the Lottery Case was adequate to sustain a wide variety of laws. These statutes limit the movement of harmful goods. During the early twentieth century, the Court upheld the exclusion from interstate commerce of impure foods, white slaves, obscene literature, and articles designed for indecent and immoral use.

With only some antithesis, the Court continued to reform the meaning of interstate commerce to enhance federal control. A greatly extended application of the clause can be found in *Heart of Atlanta Motel v. United States* (1964). This case implicated the constitutionality of Title II of the Civil Rights Act of 1964. The act strives to eliminate racial discrimination in hotels, motels, restaurants, and similar places. The owners of the Heart of Atlanta Motel disputed the constitutionality of the act. It was the motel's policy to refuse lodging to people of color. It advertised in several surrounding states, and approximately 75 percent of its guests were from other states.

The Court upheld the constitutionality of the act. The tests employed by the Court were whether the activity is commerce that concerns more than one state and whether the act showed a substantial relation to a national interest. The Court postulated that the operation of a motel might appear local in nature, but it did affect interstate commerce. The Court resolved that a motel accommodating interstate travelers is engaged in commerce that concerns more than one state.

Again, as in the Lottery Case, the Court determined that the evil averted by the act was a legitimate national concern. The rationale offered by the Court in *Heart of Atlanta Motel* exhibits the accumulation of many years of precedents. The Court asserted that the same interest that led Congress to deal with segregation prompted it to control gambling, criminal enterprises, deceptive practices in the sale of products, fraudulent security transactions, improper branding of drugs, wages and hours, members of labor unions, crop control, discrimination against shippers, the protection of small business from injurious price cutting, and resale price maintenance at terminal restaurants. The Court affirmed that Congress, in many of these examples, was regulating against moral wrongs. It concluded that segregation is a valid moral issue that would support the enactment of the Civil Rights Act.

The Court has applied various constitutional tests to interstate commerce throughout its history. Initially, the Court viewed interstate commerce as physical movement between states. Soon it began examining federal jurisdiction based on the direct versus indirect influences the law in question has on interstate commerce. By the middle of the twentieth century, the Court began examining if the purely local activity had an appreciable effect on interstate commerce.

Another offspring of the commerce clause is the Interstate Commerce Commission (ICC). The ICC consists of experts who aspire to protect and represent the public in matters of transportation in interstate commerce. This agency has immense powers and is not without its opponents.

The need to unite the country necessitated a strong centralized government, but debates persist over the effects ensuing from the expanding role of the federal bureaucracy. Some critics perceive the federal government as an inadequate regulator of business, particularly in the area of environmental protection. Other commentators reason that businesses have become dependent on, and continue to use the government as, a form of protection from competition. Still others sense that business enterprises cannot mature and flourish because of excessive government control.

The judiciary appears to recognize one conspicuous restriction on the federal government's authority. Regardless of how significant the legal arguments are, most courts hesitate to make decrees that will prohibit major industries from operating. In addition, certain potential negative economic effects, such as the loss of many jobs, particularly in the automotive, steel, and oil industries, act as subtle legal shields from overly zealous government intrusion.

Bibliography

Cox, Archibald. *The Court and the Constitution*. Boston: Houghton Mifflin, 1987. A well-organized approach to major Court decisions. The author was a former solicitor general and the first Watergate special prosecutor. He details how the Court has kept the Constitution an important instrument.

Fellmeth, Robert C. *The Interstate Commerce Omission*. New York: Grossman, 1970. Presents an encompassing view of the problems haunting the Interstate Commerce Commission. The Center for Study of Responsive Law produced the report, and Ralph Nader wrote the introduction.

Gunther, Gerald. *Cases and Materials on Constitutional Law*. 10th ed. Mineola, N.Y.: Foundation Press, 1980. A well-written textbook that discusses the immense area of constitutional law. The text has remarkable depth but has a tendency to ask more questions than it answers. It provides a superior foundation in beginning constitutional research.

Hilsman, Roger. *To Govern America*. New York: Harper and Row, 1979. An admirable compilation of data describing all features of government, including many peripheral aspects, such as philosophy and the future of American democracy.

Mason, Alpheus T., and Donald Grier Stephenson, Jr. *American Constitutional Law: Introductory Essays and Selected Cases*. 12th ed. Englewood Cliffs, N.J.: Prentice-Hall, 1998. A commendable review and analysis of constitutional law. The authors take this complex subject and present it in a discernible manner.

Tindall, George B. *America: A Narrative History.* 5th ed. New York: Norton, 1999. A constricted narrative that shapes U.S. history into an eventful story. The account presents history in themes such as judicial nationalism.

Brian J. Carroll

Cross-References

The U.S. Government Creates the Department of Commerce and Labor (1903); The Supreme Court Strikes Down a Maximum Hours Law (1905); The Supreme Court Rules Against Minimum Wage Laws (1923); Roosevelt Signs the Fair Labor Standards Act (1938); The Civil Rights Act Prohibits Discrimination in Employment (1964); The Supreme Court Orders the End of Discrimination in Hiring (1971).

THE U.S. GOVERNMENT CREATES THE DEPARTMENT OF COMMERCE AND LABOR

CATEGORY OF EVENT: Government and business
TIME: February 14, 1903
LOCALE: Washington, D.C.

With the establishment of the Department of Commerce and Labor in 1903, the federal government became actively involved in matters of business, labor, and the national economy

Principal personages:
THEODORE ROOSEVELT (1858-1919), the president of the United States, 1901-1909
CARROLL D. WRIGHT (1840-1909), the labor commissioner before the cabinet position was created
GEORGE B. CORTELYOU (1862-1940), the first secretary of the Department of Commerce and Labor
JAMES R. GARFIELD (1865-1950), a member of the U.S. Civil Service Commission who became commissioner of the Bureau of Corporations

Summary of Event

The Department of Commerce and Labor Act of 1903 created the Department of Commerce and Labor, a cabinet department within the executive branch of the U.S. federal government. The department included the Bureau of Corporations and the Bureau of Labor. The staffs of these bureaus were to investigate and provide information on corporations, indus-

20

trial working conditions, and labor-management disputes. The creation of this department and its attendant federal agencies presaged an increasingly activist federal government in the twentieth century, one that would investigate, publicize, and intervene in the dealings of industry, labor-management disputes, and other matters deemed to be of importance to the national economy.

In June, 1884, Congress established a Bureau of Labor as part of the Department of the Interior. In 1888, Congress gave the bureau independent status as the Department of Labor, but its commissioner did not have a position with the president's cabinet. The commissioner reported directly to the president.

Theodore Roosevelt became president in 1901, when public opinion was increasingly concerned with the growing power that large corporations, monopolies, and trusts had in American economic, social, and political life. The anthracite coal miners' strike of 1902 (in Pennsylvania, Illinois, and Ohio), which lasted six months and threatened the nation's coal supply, exacerbated public and political concern over industrial labor-management relations and was itself a major spur to the creation of the Department of Commerce and Labor.

Political pressure from the public and from other elected officials encouraged Roosevelt to try to arbitrate the coal miners' dispute by inviting representatives from labor and management to the White House. Although the meeting did not resolve the crisis—the owners refused to accede to the union's demands—it was significant in that the president had brought labor representatives to the negotiating table. Previous presidents had tended to take the side of business in labor-management disputes. Representatives from the railroads that owned the coal mines attended the meeting, as did Roosevelt's commissioner of labor, Carroll D. Wright, and John H. Mitchell, president of the United Mine Workers (UMW).

The crisis still unresolved, Roosevelt created an arbitration commission to investigate the strike. Although no official representatives of the UMW were part of this arbitration commission, as the operators refused such recognition, Labor Commissioner Wright as well as other unofficial labor representatives were part of the commission. With winter closing in, making coal supplies an increasing concern, pressure from public opinion, influential business leaders, and other elected officials encouraged the strikers to go back to work on October 23, 1902, while the commission arbitrated the dispute. The commission finally forced a resolution on March 22, 1903, giving the coal miners wage increases but no official recognition of their union from the operators. The incident convinced Roosevelt of the need for a permanent federal agency to prevent or help resolve, through arbitration, any such future national economic crises. He also was con-vinced of the need for an increased federal role in the economy.

It was in this context that in early January, 1903, Roosevelt called for the creation of a Department of Commerce and Labor, to include a Bureau of Labor and a Bureau of Corporations. The functions of those agencies would be to investigate the operations and conduct of corporations and to provide information about business structure, operations, and working conditions. The bill creating the department also provided for six other bureaus within the department, dealing with matters of immigration, the census, naviga-tion, fisheries, standards, and business statistics.

Roosevelt adroitly used the opposition of business leaders to enlist the support of the public and Congress for the bill. He used a letter from an attorney representing John D. Rockefeller's Standard Oil, written to Mat-thew Quay, a senator from Pennsylvania, protesting against such govern-mental interference. Roosevelt portrayed such opponents of the Depart-ment of Commerce and Labor bill as those very forces of economic and industrial injustice that public opinion was increasingly worried about. By winning public support to his side, Roosevelt obtained overwhelming congressional backing. The bill to create the new department was passed on February 14, 1903.

Roosevelt named George B. Cortelyou, his private secretary, as the first secretary of the Department of Commerce and Labor. Roosevelt and Cor-telyou did not view the Department of Commerce and Labor as an agency to attack business but as an empowerment of government to expand services to businesses, particularly in providing market information. Cortelyou advised the president on labor disputes as well as on antitrust prosecution. Cortelyou also advised Roosevelt on the issue of the union shop in the Government Printing Office.

James R. Garfield, as commissioner of the Bureau of Corporations, used the agency to investigate many corporations. He shared Roosevelt's view that federal government should regulate businesses, not randomly break them up. Garfield received some outside criticism that the bureau was too lenient in dealing with the "trusts," particularly regarding an investigation of the United States Steel Corporation, which he and the president thought was a "good" trust. He initiated stringent investigations of the beef and oil industries. The investigation of Standard Oil led to an antitrust suit, and ultimately the Su-preme Court ordered the dissolution of Standard Oil in 1911.

Impact of Event

The creation of the Department of Commerce and Labor set an impor-tant precedent for the growing role of the federal government in the national economy. It was a significant departure from the policies of the legislative and executive branches in the late nineteenth century, which said that public agencies should not intervene in the private business sphere. The increased federal role in the economy was at times antagonistic to corporations. Investigations by the Bureau of Corporations led to antitrust litigation and dissolution of the American Tobacco Company and Standard Oil.

For the most part, however, the Department of Commerce (which split from the Department of Labor in 1913) has by design functioned to help business and commerce in the United States. By distributing commercial and business statistics as well as agricultural and population censuses, the Department of Commerce makes available information that can help an industry or business learn about the market in a region or across the nation. This type of comprehensive information can be very important, particularly to individuals starting businesses, but would probably be prohibitively expensive to collect privately. The department's national standards for weights and measures facilitate interstate commerce by standardizing the basis for trade and ensuring honesty. The department also helps industry by protecting its assets through patent and trademark registration. The Department of Commerce also provides information useful to the maritime and aviation industries by publishing nautical and aeronautical charts. All these actions represented a desire by both politicians and businesspeople to stabilize industry while promoting economic growth.

In 1913, President Woodrow Wilson signed a bill that created the Department of Labor, separating it from the Department of Commerce. The presidential campaign of 1912 had reflected the growing public concern with industrial-labor relations and the rights and powers of labor unions. Presidential candidates Roosevelt and Wilson had differences on the issues of labor and corporation regulation, but both advocated continuing government activism on these issues. Wilson came into the presidency in 1913 with a series of progressive commitments, with an added focus on the rights of labor chief among them. Wilson worked with Congress to establish a separate Department of Labor, creating a new cabinet position for a secretary of labor. President Wilson's choice for this position, William B. Wilson, president of the UMW, reflected his concerns over the rights of labor organizations. William Wilson was the first labor union representative to be named to the cabinet. President Wilson wanted a representative from the ranks of labor to have the authority of a cabinet-level position in representing executive branch efforts to arbitrate labor-management disputes. Secretary of Labor Wilson strengthened the Labor Department's Division of Mediation and Conciliation and played a significant role in President Wilson's efforts to arbitrate the Ludlow, Colorado, coal mine strike of 1914.

President Wilson also pushed through Congress the Keating-Owen Act, barring from interstate commerce goods produced with child labor; the Adamson Act, which gave railroad workers an eight-hour day; and the Workmen's Compensation Act, providing workplace insurance to federal employees. The enforcement of these new laws became the responsibility of the Department of Labor.

The functions of the Department of Labor grew dramatically through the twentieth century. In the interests of workers, the Labor Department enforces laws regarding labor-management relations, child labor, equal pay, minimum wages, overtime, public contracts, workmen's compensation, health and safety in the workplace, and industrial accidents. The Department of Labor also aids businesses by providing market information. This includes collecting economic information; analyzing trends in prices, employment, and productivity; and analyzing costs and standards of living. The department also created a number of agencies designed to relieve unemployment, such as the Neighborhood Youth Corps, the Job Corps, and the Bureau of Apprenticeship and Training.

In 1914, President Wilson and Congress created the Federal Trade Commission to replace the Bureau of Corporations as the federal government's primary antitrust and corporate investigatory agency. The Federal Trade Commission was the agency established to enforce the Clayton Antitrust Act of 1914. That act also represented the continuing and growing concern over competition, economic opportunity, and antitrust that grew from the precedent of the creation of the Department of Commerce and Labor in 1903.

Bibliography

Babson, Steve. *The Unfinished Struggle: Turning Points in American Labor, 1877-Present.* Lanham, Md.: Rowman & Littlefield, 1999.

Blum, John Morton. "Theodore Roosevelt and the Definition of Office." In *The Progressive Presidents: Theodore Roosevelt, Woodrow Wilson, Franklin D. Roosevelt, Lyndon B. Johnson.* New York: W. W. Norton, 1980. Good for an introduction to the progressive politics and policies of Theodore Roosevelt and Woodrow Wilson; also good chapters on Franklin D. Roosevelt and Lyndon B. Johnson. Concise, yet detailed and analytical.

Brands, H. W. *T. R.: The Last Romantic.* New York: Basic Books, 1997. Iconoclastic biography of Theodore Roosevelt.

Gould, Lewis L. "Immediate and Vigorous Executive Action." In *The Presidency of Theodore Roosevelt.* Lawrence: University Press of Kansas, 1991. Excellent history of the foreign and domestic policies of both of Roosevelt's administrations. Also good for students beginning study of the Progressive Era.

Kolko, Gabriel. *The Triumph of Conservatism: A Reinterpretation of American History, 1900-1916*. New York: Free Press of Glencoe, 1963. Excellent for those seeking an in-depth and challenging analysis of business-government relationships in the Progressive Era. Kolko contends that new regulations were not a victory for the "people" over the "interests." Leaders of industry desired regulation, which they would help formulate and influence, to avoid competition and stabilize their industries.

Miller, Nathan. *Theodore Roosevelt: A Life*. New York: William Morrow, 1992. The treatment of the Northern Securities case is particularly concise and well done, characteristics that hold for the book as a whole. Good for those with some familiarity with Roosevelt and the Progressive Era.

Pringle, Henry F. "Trimming Sail." In *Theodore Roosevelt: A Biography*. New York: Harcourt, Brace, and Company, 1931. Perhaps the most in-depth biography of Roosevelt. Very detailed on the policies of his administration, especially on the establishment of the Department of Commerce and Labor.

Bruce Andre Beaubouef

Cross-References

The Supreme Court Decides to Break Up Standard Oil (1911); Congress Passes the Clayton Antitrust Act (1914); The Wagner Act Promotes Union Organization (1935); The Social Security Act Provides Benefits for Workers (1935).

THE SUPREME COURT STRIKES DOWN A MAXIMUM HOURS LAW

CATEGORY OF EVENT: Labor
TIME: April 17, 1905
LOCALE: Washington, D.C.

By ruling that maximum hours laws were unconstitutional, the Supreme Court upheld the freedom of contract and severely limited the ability of states to enact reform legislation

Principal personages:
RUFUS WHEELER PECKHAM (1838-1909), an associate justice of the Supreme Court, 1895-1909, who wrote the majority opinion in *Lochner v. New York*
OLIVER WENDELL HOLMES, JR. (1841-1935), an associate justice of the Supreme Court, 1902-1932
JOHN MARSHALL HARLAN (1833-1911), an associate justice of the Supreme Court, 1877-1911
HERBERT SPENCER (1820-1903), an influential scientist and philosopher who championed the theory of social Darwinism

Summary of Event

On April 17, 1905, the Supreme Court ruled five to four in the case of *Lochner v. New York* that maximum hours laws were an unreasonable interference with the liberty of contract. The Court ruled that the power of the state to regulate did not outweigh the freedom of contract. The ruling struck down an 1895 New York statute that had limited the number of work hours for any employee in any bakery or confectionery establishment to no more than ten hours in a day or sixty hours in a week. New York's labor law

26

was an example of the aggressive interventionist and experimental policies that several states had begun pursuing around the turn of the century. The Court held that New York's experiment had been a "meddlesome interference" and an undue infringement on the right of free contract and thus of the private rights of the employer. In a powerful and eloquent dissent, Associate Justice Oliver Wendell Holmes, Jr., held that the states had the authority to pursue their own social experiments and enact reform legislation.

New York's Bakeshop Act had been enacted in an effort to regulate and improve the often dreadful working and health conditions in the state's cramped bakeshops, establishments that often employed only a handful of workers and were often located in the basements of tenement buildings. Passed as an act to regulate the manufacture of flour and meal food products, the Bakeshop Act established maximum hours and required that bakeries be drained and plumbed; that products be stored in dry and airy rooms; that walls and floors be plastered, tiled, or otherwise finished; and that inspections be carried out.

The law was not the first attempt to set limits on hours worked. Among the earliest efforts to regulate hours of work was an executive order signed by Martin Van Buren in 1840 that limited the daily hours of labor in government Navy yards to ten. Most early efforts to set limits on hours of labor concerned the employment of women and children. Massachusetts and Connecticut each passed laws limiting the number of hours for children employed in manufacturing establishments as early as 1842. By the late

By striking down laws limiting the numbers of hours women could work, the Supreme Court made it more difficult for states to protect workers—particularly women—against sweatshop conditions such as these seamstresses had to endure. (Deborah Cooney Collection)

nineteenth century, laws limiting hours for women, children, or both had been passed in New Hampshire, Maine, Pennsylvania, New Jersey, Rhode Island, Ohio, Illinois, Missouri, and Wisconsin. The arguments in support of limiting the hours of work included enhancing the efficiency or productivity of labor and improving public health. Proponents of maximum hours legislation argued that limits on the length of daily labor would lead to qualitative as well as quantitative improvements. Clearly, any bakeshop laborer who toiled long hours in cramped sweatshop conditions stood to gain some benefit, but proponents argued that there were also potential benefits for the consumers of baked goods. The principal arguments against such legislation were simply that it was an overextension of the police powers of the state and that it infringed on the right of freedom of contract. Moreover, theories of social Darwinism and laissez-faire economics insisted that such government intervention was an unjustified and inefficient disruption of the free market.

Joseph Lochner owned and operated a small bread bakery in Utica, New York. After being twice found guilty of violating New York's Bakeshop Act, he was fined $50. He appealed his conviction to the New York Supreme Court and the New York Court of Appeals, losing each time. His case ultimately made its way to the Supreme Court. Why this case emerged as the test case for a host of reform legislation is unclear; Lochner's bakery was a small and relatively obscure establishment. An ongoing clash between Lochner and the Utica branch of the journeyman bakers' union may have led to his fine and kept this case alive on appeal.

The majority opinion in *Lochner* was written by Associate Justice Rufus Peckham. Peckham was known for his staunch support of laissez-faire policies and his contempt for government regulation, beliefs that would lead others to link Peckham with the writings of Herbert Spencer, one of the most outspoken and best-known champions of social Darwinism. In an 1897 ruling in *Allgeyer v. Louisiana*, Peckham had written the opinion that held a law unconstitutional for depriving a person of liberty of contract. Any contract suitable to the operation of a lawful business was thus afforded protection under the Fourteenth Amendment. The doctrine of liberty of contract, established in *Allgeyer*, was advanced in *Lochner*.

In *Lochner*, Peckham held that there was no reasonable ground for interfering with the liberty of a person or the right of free contract by determining the hours of labor in this particular case. Although he acknowledged the power of states to protect the health and morals of citizens in specific situations, he questioned the need for protection of bakers. Laboring long hours in a bakery, though perhaps unpleasant and posing some health risks, was neither as arduous nor as unsafe as working at many other occupations. By restricting the freedom of contract, New York's Bakeshop Act had violated the due process clause of the Fourteenth Amendment and as such was unconstitutional. Since the connection between bakeries and health remained shadowy, the states were not free to exercise police or regulatory powers under the guise of conserving morals, health, or safety.

In a dissenting opinion, Associate Justice John Marshall Harlan held that New York's Bakeshop Act was not in conflict with the Fourteenth Amendment and that the states had the "power to guard the health and safety of their citizens by such regulations as they in their wisdom deem best." Justice Harlan held that it was clearly within the discretionary power of the states to enact laws regarding health conditions and that such statutes should be enforced unless they could be demonstrated to have plainly violated the "fundamental law of the Constitution." In Harlan's opinion, the use of the Fourteenth Amendment to invalidate New York's statute would in effect cripple the abilities of the states to care for the well-being of their citizens.

In a forceful and eloquent dissent, Associate Justice Oliver Wendell Holmes, Jr., held that the majority decision in *Lochner* was based upon an economic theory rather than law and that a "constitution is not intended to embody a particular economic theory." In this well-known dissent, Justice Holmes criticized the majority extending the doctrine of liberty of contract and for defining too narrowly the states' police power. Holmes went on to write that a constitution is written for people of fundamentally differing views and that the "Fourteenth Amendment does not enact Mr. Herbert Spencer's Social Statistics."

Impact of Event

The immediate impact of the Court's decision in *Lochner* was to restrict, or at least postpone, the ability of states to regulate such economic issues as maximum hours and minimum wages. Exactly how the Supreme Court would define the regulatory role of the states was an issue of great interest to reform-minded legislatures as well as to employers and their employees. The use of legislative reform was becoming more common, but such legislation often faced hostile review by the generally conservative courts.

Within a matter of a few years, the movement for shorter hours appeared to have won, lost, and then won again in significant cases before the Supreme Court. In 1898, the Court upheld a limitation on hours for Utah miners and smelters in *Holden v. Hardy*. In 1905, it reversed Joseph Lochner's conviction as an illegal and unwarranted interference with the liberty of contract, but in 1908 it upheld an Oregon law limiting hours for women in factories and laundries in *Muller v. Oregon*.

The Court's majority apparently viewed *Lochner* differently from the other two cases because its members saw no good reason that bakers should be singled out; if bakers' hours were regulated, then regulations on others would follow. Exceptions could be made for inherently dangerous occupations or in the case of women and children, but a general limitation on hours was not yet to be accepted. A 1917 ruling, in *Bunting v. Oregon*, accepted a ten-hour day for men and women on the grounds of preserving the health and safety of workers but only because the legislation did not apply to all workers, only those workers in certain inherently dangerous industries.

The implications of the Court's ruling in *Lochner* obviously extend far beyond Joseph Lochner and the treatment of bakers in Utica bakeshops. The Court's decision signified an ardent acceptance by the Court majority of the doctrine of laissez-faire capitalism and a belief that reform legislation and the regulatory movement could be suspended by the courts. By ruling against the state of New York, the Court sent a clear message of hostility to any reform-minded legislative body. Liberty of contract, in this case the right of Joseph Lochner to make his own contracts and control his property, took precedence over the right of the state to exercise its police powers.

Up until the economic crisis of the Great Depression, the mostly conservative justices of the Supreme Court used the doctrine of liberty of contract to limit the ability of states to enact reform legislation. Specific contracts could always be struck down, but only in those cases with narrowly defined public purposes. A notable example of prevailing judicial temperament can be seen in the 1908 case that outlawed "yellow dog contracts," *Adair v. United States.* A law protecting union members by prohibiting yellow dog contracts, under which employees promised not to join a union, was judged by the Court to be an unreasonable invasion of personal liberty and property rights. This reliance upon liberty of contract and devotion to laissez-faire economic doctrines remained a marked feature of the Court for some years. Not all scholars agree that the Court was as hostile to regulatory legislation and as antilabor as a few of these decisions might imply.

The decision in *Lochner* ranks among the most famous of all Supreme Court rulings, but for dubious reasons. Many consider it now, as Justice Holmes considered it then, an insensible ruling that ignored the hardships of sweatshop labor and launched a misguided assault on reform legislation. The premise of the decision later came into question. Rather than remove labor relations from the domain of politics, most people came to accept the notion that public debate and legislative action on economic issues is an appropriate use of police powers.

Social change is often a difficult and lengthy process. The necessary adjustments of an emerging industrial and increasingly urban society, with its resulting conflicts in labor relations, raised perplexing issues. Progressive reformers, and later New Dealers, who sought change through legislative enactments found, as in *Lochner*, that the courts were often unsympathetic. The realities and the pressures of the Great Depression led to a pervasive revision of judicial, political, and economic philosophies. New and inventive attempts were made to revitalize the economy, and legislatures were generally given more freedom to exercise regulatory powers.

Bibliography

Hall, Kermit L., ed. *The Oxford Companion to the Supreme Court of the United States*. New York: Oxford University Press, 1992. Contains a detailed and useful outline of the history of the Court, major decisions and doctrines that have guided and influenced Court rulings dating back to 1789, and brief biographies of every justice who served on the Court and other historically significant characters. Concise but detailed entries help to make landmark cases and legal terms accessible to a variety of users.

_____, ed. *The Oxford Guide to United States Supreme Court Decisions*. New York: Oxford University Press, 1999. Multiauthored collection of essays on more than four hundred significant Court decisions, with supporting glossary and other aids.

Kens, Paul. *Judicial Power and Reform Politics: The Anatomy of "Lochner v. New York"*. Lawrence: University Press of Kansas, 1990. Presents a well-written and well-documented analysis of the issues surrounding the Lochner case, turn-of-the-century bakeries, the politics of reform legislation, and the ramifications of the Court's decision.

Nichols, Egbert Ray, and Joseph H. Baccus, eds. *Selected Articles on Minimum Wages and Maximum Hours*. New York: H. W. Wilson, 1936. Outlines and defines the debate over whether Congress has the power to fix minimum wages and maximum hours for workers. Reprints of editorials and comments offer a variety of legal, political, and economic interpretations.

Siegan, Bernard H. *Economic Liberties and the Constitution*. Chicago: University of Chicago Press, 1980. An examination of changing judicial policy and the Court's review of economic legislation. Offers an explanation of alternative views of substantive due process and the protection of economic liberties.

Ziegler, Benjamin M., ed. *The Supreme Court and American Economic Life*. Evanston, Ill.: Row, Peterson, 1962. One of many books outlining the decisions in important Supreme Court cases. Despite being dated, this collection has the advantage of listing only cases with compelling economic themes.

Timothy E. Sullivan

Cross-References

Champion v. Ames Upholds Federal Powers to Regulate Commerce (1903); The Supreme Court Rules Against Minimum Wage Laws (1923); Roosevelt Signs the Fair Labor Standards Act (1938).

CONGRESS PASSES THE PURE FOOD AND DRUG ACT

CATEGORY OF EVENT: Consumer affairs
TIME: June 30, 1906
LOCALE: Washington, D.C.

The Pure Food and Drug Act of 1906 established the first federal standards for food and drug regulation, reflecting a commitment to consumer protection advocated by social reformers as well as some bureaucrats, businesspeople, and scientists

Principal personages:
HARVEY W. WILEY (1844-1930), the chief chemist with the United States Department of Agriculture, author of the Pure Food and Drug Act of 1906
THEODORE ROOSEVELT (1858-1919), the president of the United States, 1901-1909
UPTON SINCLAIR (1878-1968), a socialist, journalist, and author of *The Jungle* (1906), an exposé of the Chicago meatpacking industry

Summary of Event

The passage of the Pure Food and Drug Act by Congress in 1906 marked the culmination of a long struggle by an assortment of groups to enact federal legislation controlling the quality of foods and drugs widely available to consumers. Although many local and state authorities had attempted to guard against the sale of contaminated, or even harmful, food and medicinal products for several years prior to 1906, a variety of critics had charged that those regulations were ineffectual at best. Particularly as a result of the rapid growth of rail systems that could transport products between regions and states, dangerous or adulterated products were becoming threats not only in local markets but also for consumers across the nation.

Scientific and medical experts offered crucial support for the passage of the 1906 act. Advocacy for federal pure food and drug regulation by physicians' groups, notably the American Medical Association, came rather late in the process of securing passage in comparison with state and local efforts by physicians, research scientists, and even agriculture commissioners interested in scientific farming. Those scientific proponents had been quite active in some states and localities, such as Massachusetts and New York City, beginning in the decades immediately following the Civil War. The careful investigations and calm presentations of researchers such as E. F. Ladd, food commissioner of North Dakota, began to receive notice beyond that of fellow specialists in the early years of the twentieth century. Ladd's findings were stated in such an accessible manner in a paper on food adulteration he read in St. Louis in 1904 that they were published in popular periodicals such as the *Ladies' Home Journal*. They caused a sensation among middle-class readers. In Ladd's testing of cider vinegars, for example, it had been impossible to detect apple juice, a supposed ingredient. Products labeled as "potted chicken" and "potted turkey" contained no chicken or turkey that he could isolate. Cocoa shell and other foreign matter accounted for 70 percent of the substances found in his samples from chocolate and cocoa mixtures.

Congress had heard such allegations much earlier, for example when the Committee on Epidemic Diseases of the Forty-Sixth Congress published a report recommending the establishment of a commission to study contamination in food and drugs. Congressional committee members listened in 1880 to the precise testimony of such experts as George T. Angell of Boston, who already had argued successfully for stricter local regulations on the food trade. In 1899 and 1900, a Senate investigation focused on the manufacture of contaminated food.

The most consistent advocate for federal food and drug regulation was Harvey W. Wiley, the chief chemist for the United States Department of Agriculture (USDA). Wiley had been working at the USDA since 1883, when he published his findings on the adulteration of cane and beet sugars, milk, and butter. Ironically, the purpose of Wiley's research had not been to uncover massive adulteration in the food industry. He had been trying to develop better analytical methods for the Bureau of Chemistry. He continued to write about his investigations in a methodical series of USDA bulletins in the 1880's and 1890's. When he realized the impact of his research, however, he began to advocate delving more thoroughly into food and drug adulteration. Wiley rapidly became convinced of the necessity of federal government action and went so far as to sanction unorthodox methods of demonstrating the dangers of substances. The "poison squads" of the USDA, for example, were a dramatic device. Chemists used themselves as guinea pigs to test the human effects of potentially adulterated or toxic substances.

In the early twentieth century, no consumer lobby at the national level existed that could press for a national law providing interstate regulation of food and drug manufacture, distribution, and advertisement. Definitive congressional action was blocked repeatedly in several ways: openly by legislators closely tied to food or drug interests, or more subtly on constitutional grounds that federal regulation would be an intrusion on states' rights. Between 1879 and 1906, at least

Upton Sinclair, the author of The Jungle, *is one of the rare novelists who wrote a book that changed history.* (Library of Congress)

190 bills concerning food and drug regulation were considered and defeated. Wiley's careful efforts gradually began to convince some members of Congress and the public that a federal agency could be effective in detection, yet until early 1906, federal pure food and drug legislation seemed stymied.

The spark for passage of an act that had been introduced in December, 1905, came as a result of the publication of Upton Sinclair's shocking exposé of life among meatpackers in Chicago. That book, *The Jungle* (1906), had been intended by Sinclair more as a socialist condemnation of America's treatment of immigrant workers than as an indictment of a particular noxious industry. Sinclair later commented that he had aimed for the heart of the public but had hit readers in the stomach.

Certain images left in the minds of readers of *The Jungle* were indelible. The makers of processed meats such as sausages found themselves years later still fighting Sinclair's allegations that the brutal machinery inside packinghouses sliced off workers' fingers, which then were ground into meats. However uncommon such incidents were, especially in contrast with more usual contaminations, such as the presence of rat droppings in processing rooms, they captured some American consumers' distrust of the large-scale meatpackers. Other muckraking books of the era, such as Joseph Lincoln Steffens' *The Shame of the Cities* (1904) and Jacob Riis's *How the Other Half Lives: Studies Among the Tenements of New York* (1890), could be written off by members of the public as condemnations of conditions in specific urban areas, conditions that could be overlooked if one simply stayed away from the areas of blight. Food contamination as described in *The Jungle* clearly was a problem too far-reaching to avoid.

Sinclair's vivid descriptions of the conditions under which meat was processed raised alarm not only among the public in general but also among key players in Washington, notably President Theodore Roosevelt, who ordered his secretary of agriculture, James Wilson, to investigate the validity of Sinclair's book. Roosevelt, spurred on by his personal outrage, played a key role in ensuring passage of the act and in preventing its being watered down in committee.

The Pure Food and Drug Act, along with a meat inspection bill passed in tandem with it, outlawed the shipment, interstate or abroad, of food that was judged to be "unsound" or "unwholesome." The legislation gave new vigor to the inspection powers already exercised by several federal authorities, especially the Department of Agriculture, along with the Departments of Commerce, Labor, and the Treasury. The new laws expanded inspections already required for exported meats to make similar inspections mandatory for foods destined for American tables. Products that passed inspection were to be marked with a USDA stamp; unsuitable foods were to be destroyed in the sight of an inspector. The laws provided for truth in labeling, prohibiting false or deceitful advertising of food and drug products, known at the time as "misbranding." The penalties for violation of pure food and drug laws included fines starting at $200, up to one year of imprisonment, and seizure of contaminated goods.

Impact of Event

With its complex provisions regulating the manufacture, sale, and advertisement of a vast range of food products and popular medicines, the Pure Food and Drug Act promised difficulties in enforcement and engendered hostility from several quarters when it went into effect on January 1, 1907. Many manufacturers had opposed its passage and continued to resent its requirements. Even members of Congress openly grumbled that the measure was an unwarranted intrusion on the right of individual states to regulate the health and welfare of their own citizens.

Theodore Roosevelt was one of many individuals and groups who celebrated the achievement of the passage of the Pure Food and Drug Act. The act was the product of a series of delicate compromises between

Roosevelt, Department of Agriculture investigators, and key members of Congress. In ironing out differences between a Senate and a House version of the act, a congressional conference committee produced a bill with somewhat more teeth than either house's version, although certain provisions for which its sponsors had fought doggedly were abandoned, such as the placing of the date of canning on canned meats.

For Roosevelt, passage of the legislation was evidence of his skill at political maneuvering and an example of a personal commitment to good health, both his own and the public's. In Roosevelt's mind, efforts to clean up packinghouses and to ensure high-quality consumer goods meshed well with his goals to expand his role as chief executive and to enhance the role of the national government. Biographers of Roosevelt have noted that Roosevelt's part in the passage of the Pure Food and Drug Act, along with his advocacy of the Hepburn Act (passed in June, 1906, boosting the power of the Interstate Commerce Commission to examine railroad operations), marked his determination to provide decisive leadership in the wake of his convincing 1904 presidential election victory.

Although Roosevelt's support of the Pure Food and Drug Act was important to its eventual passage as "progressive" legislation, and although he was accused by some conservative Republicans of moving too far toward the left, he resisted easy categorization as a liberal or a follower of fads. For example, he characteristically announced his distrust of scientists' warnings about saccharin as a food additive, declaring that he used saccharin daily with the approval of his own physician and obviously was in excellent health.

In the aftermath of the passage of the Pure Food and Drug Act, the writers of editorials as well as lawmakers themselves sensed that several watersheds had been achieved in terms of the authority of the federal government, the regulation of big business, and the protection of the public's health by Congress. Those achievements came at a political price. Roosevelt had created or intensified divisions within the Republican Party. Most criticism of those developments, however, remained beneath the surface for a few years. Roosevelt's prestige as an international figure seemed to increase the confidence of the public and Congress that his leadership in domestic affairs was worthy of trust.

The furor surrounding publication of *The Jungle*, as well as intense political scrutiny of food production, was felt by manufacturers of consumer goods. One estimate put the drop in meat sales in the wake of *The Jungle* at 50 percent. The controversy made food processors and drug makers aware of the need to assure the public as well as potential regulators of the quality of their output. A number of producers of foods and drugs actually supported the Pure Food and Drug Act, on the grounds that regulation of their industry would reassure the public and increase consumption, both domestically and on world markets.

The Pure Food and Drug Act did not stem the tide of product injury lawsuits. It may have created more such suits by raising expectations by consumers that products would be produced carefully and that if they were not, a governmental entity would catch the mistake. In a legal sense, therefore, federal food and drug legislation helped dispel any lingering notion that it was solely the buyer's responsibility to beware of dangerous food and drug products. The act of 1906 also reflected the ideas that the collective protection of consumers was an appropriate function of the federal government and that federal food and drug regulation could be a more effective and scientific approach than were individual caution, local circumspection, or industry self-policing.

Bibliography

Anderson, Oscar E. *The Health of a Nation: Harvey W. Wiley and the Fight for Pure Food.* Chicago: University of Chicago Press, 1958. Emphasizes the role of Wiley, the importance of scientific investigations, and the publication of those investigations in technical and specialists' journals, especially in the 1880's and 1890's, in bringing about medical and expert calls for national food and drug regulation. Supplemented by James Harvey Young's 1989 study of the passage of the 1906 act.

Brands, H. W. *T. R.: The Last Romantic.* New York: Basic Books, 1997. Iconoclastic biography of Theodore Roosevelt.

Burrow, James G. *Organized Medicine in the Progressive Era.* Baltimore: Johns Hopkins University Press, 1977. Stresses the medical community's efforts at professionalization, its success with public relations strategies, its alliances with state authorities, and its links with progressive reformers who wished to apply scientific findings to address social problems.

Goodwin, Lorine Swainston. *The Pure Food, Drink, and Drug Crusaders, 1879-1914.* Jefferson, N.C.: McFarland, 1999. Survey of the history of lobbyists and elected officials fighting for new legislation.

Gould, Lewis. *The Presidency of Theodore Roosevelt.* Lawrence: University Press of Kansas, 1991. A balanced treatment of Roosevelt as a politician, showing his practical methods of operation in conjunction with Congress. Draws judiciously upon earlier biographies by William H. Harbaugh and John Morton Blum, and on Gould's own examination of Roosevelt's political style contained in earlier publications. Contains a detailed bibliographic essay.

Wiebe, Robert. *Businessmen and Reform.* Cambridge, Mass.: Harvard University Press, 1962. Along with Wiebe's *The Search for Order* (Westport, Conn.: Greenwood Press, 1980), provides an influential explanation of various reasons why businessmen supported or opposed progressive reforms, with emphasis on the desire by entrepreneurs to promote efficiency and predictability through governmental action. Utilizes in great detail the records of national business groups such as the National Civic Foundation as well as chamber of commerce publications.

Young, James Harvey. *Pure Food: Securing the Federal Pure Food and Drug Act of 1906.* Princeton, N.J.: Princeton University Press, 1989. Examines passage of the act in detail, sorting out Roosevelt's and Senator Albert Beveridge's behind-the-scenes pressuring of the Senate against the lobbying of meatpacking interests. Illustrates the process of publicizing the findings of governmental and scientific investigators.

Elisabeth A. Cawthon

Cross-References

Congress Sets Standards for Chemical Additives in Food (1958); Nader's *Unsafe at Any Speed* Launches a Consumer Movement (1965); The U.S. Government Bans Cigarette Ads on Broadcast Media (1970).

HARVARD UNIVERSITY FOUNDS A BUSINESS SCHOOL

CATEGORY OF EVENT: Management
TIME: April 8, 1908
LOCALE: Cambridge, Massachusetts

The Harvard Business School's innovative instructional methods helped professionalize management and the way managers are educated

Principal personages:
EDWIN F. GAY (1867-1946), the founding dean of the Harvard Business School
ARCH W. SHAW (1876-1962), a noted publisher and lecturer on business policy at Harvard
MELVIN T. COPELAND (1884-1975), a distinguished professor of business administration and historian of the Harvard Business School
CHARLES WILLIAM ELIOT (1834-1926), the president of Harvard University who suggested the establishment of a school of diplomacy and government
A. LAWRENCE LOWELL (1856-1943), a distinguished Boston lawyer and lecturer on government at Harvard, later its president
FRANK W. TAUSSIG (1859-1940), a professor at Harvard who drafted a detailed plan for the Harvard Business School
GEORGE F. BAKER (1840-1931), a president of the First National Bank in New York and a major financial contributor to the Harvard Business School

Summary of Event

The emergence of the multiunit form, a vision that institutions of higher education could serve a utilitarian purpose, and a popular desire to professionalize most occupations encouraged the development of collegiate business education in the late nineteenth century. An early participant in this exciting experiment in higher learning was the Harvard Business School, founded in 1908. Although preceded by the Wharton School at the University of Pennsylvania and the Amos Tuck School at Dartmouth, the Harvard Business School inaugurated a change in the education of professional managers through its innovative instructional methods and the high priority it placed on business research.

An emphasis on framing business problems, class discussion, written case analysis, and a climate that encouraged confident decision making were seen from the outset as vital to the development of top managers. It soon became apparent, however, that a rather large breach existed between the school's educational aspirations and its ability to achieve them. There were few teachers trained in business administration, and scholarship in the form of published works was almost nonexistent. In fact, course offerings, materials, and textbooks were sparse until the 1920's.

Early professors of business administration both at Harvard and elsewhere were drawn from a wide variety of academic disciplines. Economists such as Simon N. Patten were influential teachers and scholars at the Wharton School. The economics department also dominated academic life at the Amos Tuck School at Dartmouth. Business educators in this nascent stage of development were also drawn from less closely allied fields. Of the two accounting courses offered at Wharton, for example, one was taught by a professor of journalism who also instructed in business practices and banking. The other course was taught by a political scientist.

The recruitment of faculty proved to be the most challenging aspect of running the fledgling Harvard Business School for its first dean, Edwin F. Gay. Determined that the education of professional managers required a unique approach, he eschewed teachers from undergraduate business programs and scholars from the traditional social science disciplines. This represented a departure from accepted practice. The business school, in fact, had been envisioned as a school of diplomacy and government by Harvard University president Charles William Eliot. Gay quickly set out to establish a core faculty and to recruit practicing managers from New York, Boston, and Philadelphia. William Morse Cole and Oliver Mitchell Sprague joined the regular faculty to teach accounting and banking, respectively. Paul Terry Cherington, who would make seminal contributions in the field of marketing education through his work *Advertising as a Business Force: A Compilation of Experience Records* (1913), joined the faculty from the Philadelphia Commercial Museum. Lincoln Frederick Schaub became the school's first full-time instructor of commercial law. These individuals,

Harvard University president Charles William Eliot. (Library of Congress)

along with two part-time instructors, eight part-time lecturers, and fifty-five outside (guest) lecturers, composed the school's first teaching staff. Over the next decade, the permanent faculty grew, and as the case method became more widely used, the need for outside lecturers waned.

Initial courses at Harvard were analogous to those provided at the older business schools. The required first-year courses in accounting, commercial contracts, and economic resources of the United States (later marketing) were augmented by electives in industrial organization, corporate insurance, and banking. These traditional courses were seen as essential prerequisites for a career with a multiunit firm. Second-year courses examined the intricacies of management in specialized industries such as railroading, foreign trade, banking, and insurance.

The school made a marked advance toward achieving its unique mission of educating professional managers through a "problems" or "case method" approach with the addition of Arch W. Shaw to its faculty. Shaw was the energetic publisher of *System*, a journal that crusaded for more efficient business practices. Upon his appointment to the faculty at Harvard, he turned his energies to developing a course in business policy using the case approach. His use of "real life" cases animated his classes, and in time his course became the capstone for the school. His book *An Approach to Business Problems* (1916), along with colleague Melvin T. Copeland's *Problems in Marketing* (1920), did much to advance their respective specialties and advance business education in the United States.

These textbooks, along with other seminal contributions to the business literature by Cherington, Charles Edward Russel, Bruce Wyman, and Walter Dill Scott, became required reading in every business school and program soon after publication. Despite these works, however, there was a dearth of business information and research material needed for the development of cases and advanced coursework. The development of the marketing discipline, perhaps more than any other in the business curriculum, was constrained as a result of meager "real life" data. Even the trade journals of the day gave scarce attention to selling or marketing problems.

The collection of business information and data for course materials, cases, and textbooks proceeded in an ad hoc fashion through individual professors and in a more organized manner through bureaus of business research. J. E. Hagerty, an early marketing professor at Ohio State University, for example, was frustrated by the paucity of textual material in his discipline and attempted to fill this breach by interviewing local businesspeople. He discovered that these individuals gave freely of their time and information because of their curiosity about his research effort. They wondered why anyone would want to learn about their organizations, methods, procedures, and business problems.

The Harvard Bureau of Business Research was begun at the urging of Arch W. Shaw shortly after the founding of the school. Although its principal mission was to gather data to aid instruction in the school, especially in marketing, it was hoped that research results would prove beneficial to students and teachers in other schools and to individuals in the wider business community. Its first study, of the shoe industry, received wide distribution in trade papers and other business publications and aroused interest in the activities of the school. Soon, studies of the operating expenses of grocers, department stores, and variety chains were produced. Later, scholarly investigations of labor unions, the distribution of textiles, cotton mill hedging practices, and interstate power transmission not only provided a wealth of teaching material but also encouraged further exploratory work in other business schools throughout the United States.

Impact of Event

The founding and the early success of the Harvard Business School had a significant effect on the professionalization of management, which in turn had consequences for the education of managers. The bold and innovative instructional methodologies and the scholarly climate at Harvard in the early twentieth century became a model for all other business schools to follow. It soon became common for business careers to begin after formal education in business administration. General education would precede professional coursework. Students would take a core of business subjects that gave coherence and content to their professional studies. This core included business law, statistics, marketing, accounting, money and banking, and corporate finance. The problem approach would supersede rote memorization of formulas and data. Written and oral communication were stressed for future business leaders. The discovery of new business knowledge through research and investigation of active organizations would be attempted and encouraged. Classroom instruction and theoretical knowledge would be augmented and tested with internship experiences in business. The formal education of managers would not necessarily terminate in the nascence of their careers, as professional education for practicing managers was introduced.

Each of these innovations was a bold step. Each served to convince prospective students as well as academic and business leaders that the business site and academe could be connected through a business school or program. Within two decades of the opening of the business school at Harvard, numerous major public and private universities established similar ventures. Business schools were established at Ohio State (1916); Alabama, Minnesota, and North Carolina (1919); Virginia (1920); Indiana (1921); and Kansas and Michigan (1924). Columbia (1916) and Stanford (1925) were private institutions that established business schools during this period. In addition, it would not be long before an even larger number of public and private institutions established business programs "in town" to educate future business leaders living and working in large metropolitan areas.

The revolutionary changes in the education of future managers were the result of a courageous decision to foster the development of an educational experience free of the intellectual control of other long-established academic disciplines. Gay believed that the aims of a graduate school of business should be instillation of a rational method of attacking business problems and development of intellectual respect for the management profession. This also entailed appreciation for the social, cultural, and ethical dimensions of the field. Harvard's early commitment to developing a business administration paradigm that could stand on its own energized stakeholders to find new ways and means of educating a new profession, that of management. The case method, with its attendant vigorous analysis and discussion of companywide problems together with scholarly investigation of living organizations, was an important part of this philosophy of education.

Case studies adopting the companywide problems approach benefited students, teachers, and practitioners alike. Students benefited by seeing that rational decision-making processes could be applied to problems encountered in a wide variety of business settings. Professors gained because cases gave flexibility as well as content and depth to their courses. Well-researched and well-written cases provided a wealth of information about industry practices and technical matters in the process of teaching problem-solving skills. Perhaps most important, practicing managers benefited from their training in the case method. As business school graduates, they enjoyed a common basis for communication and a better understanding of mutual problems. In short, managers trained in this analytical method could relate better to their peers.

Business research, like the case method, can trace its origins to the first years of the school. It reached its full instructional potential some years later. Harvard's pioneering Bureau of Business Research had substantial pedagogical value to the academic community in the school and elsewhere while also providing strategic information to managers in industry. The work of the bureau helped make class discussions and teaching materials more interesting and relevant for the first students in the school and, in time, became the foundation for instruction conducted there. The style and method of research carried out in the early days of the business school also had important consequences for the conduct of business research in general. The bureau, with its strategy of focusing its efforts on a small area of business and studying it thoroughly to achieve notable results in a brief period, its refusal to be commercialized, and its aspiration to be at a level equal to Harvard's other schools, became a model for other researchers and institutions to imitate.

Bibliography

Chandler, Alfred D. *The Visible Hand: The Managerial Revolution in American Business*. Cambridge, Mass.: The Belknap Press of Harvard University Press, 1977. This seminal work by a distinguished historian of business examines the rise of modern business enterprise and its managers during the formative years of modern capitalism, from the 1850's until the 1920's. A superb book for anyone interested in the profession of management.

Copeland, Melvin T. *And Mark an Era: The Story of the Harvard Business School*. Boston: Little, Brown, 1958. An important study of the founding and development of the Harvard Business School through its first half century. Written by a distinguished member of the school's faculty during the period studied. An essential work for understanding the development of collegiate business education in the United States.

Elderkin, Kenton W. *Mutiny on the Harvard Bounty: The Harvard Business School and the Decline of the Nation*. Mansfield, Ohio: Elderking Associates, 1996.

Heaton, Herbert. *A Scholar in Action: Edwin F. Gay*. New York: Greenwood Press, 1968. A biography of the bold, imaginative, and scholarly first dean of the Harvard Business School. Provides interesting background information about this educational administrator whose early advocacy for the problem approach and business research aided the development of the profession of management.

Pierson, Frank C., et al. *The Education of American Businessmen.* New York: McGraw-Hill, 1959. Chapter 3 provides in a concise manner excellent historical information about American business schools from their origins through the early 1950's. Valuable as an overview while also providing interesting insights into the origin and growth—and often decline—of early American collegiate business schools.

Veysey, Lawrence R. *The Emergence of the American University.* Chicago: University of Chicago Press, 1965. An authoritative study of the social and cultural forces that helped transform the American university into a modern institution at the beginning of the twentieth century. An important work for those interested in placing business education in a larger cultural and intellectual context. Can be enjoyed by both serious scholars and generalists.

S. A. Marino

Cross-References

The A. C. Nielsen Company Pioneers in Marketing and Media Research (1923); Roosevelt Signs the G.I. Bill (1944); Nader's *Unsafe at Any Speed* Launches a Consumer Movement (1965).

CONGRESS UPDATES COPYRIGHT LAW IN 1909

CATEGORY OF EVENT: Business practices
TIME: March 4, 1909
LOCALE: Washington, D.C.

The Copyright Act of 1909 was the end product of hundreds of years of common and statutory copyright law

Principal personages:
WILLIAM MURRAY MANSFIELD (1705-1793), a British jurist and member of the House of Lords who argued for copyright protection and monetary reward for authors
JOSEPH STORY (1779-1845), an American jurist whose decisions formed precedent for the fair use doctrine
OLIVER WENDELL HOLMES, JR. (1841-1935), an American jurist whose opinions influenced future opinions on the nature of originality of works
LEARNED HAND (1872-1961), an American jurist whose decisions shaped future definitions of copyright infringement

Summary of Event

Under copyright law in general, authors or creators of original works have the exclusive right to reproduce (or authorize others to reproduce) these works and are protected against unlawful copying, known as plagiarism or piracy. "Original" does not mean "unique." Original works are those created by the author's own intellectual or creative effort, as opposed to having been copied. Copying all or part of a work without permission of the author (or any agency the author has authorized for copying) constitutes copyright infringement. Willful unauthorized copying for the purpose of making a profit is a criminal offense punishable by fine or imprisonment. When authors suspect infringement but have no grounds for charging

47

criminal intent, they can bring civil action against the alleged offender. Under certain circumstances, parts of authors' works can be copied without permission according to what is known as the fair use doctrine.

Works are protected by copyright for a specific length of time. At the end of that time, a work is said to be in the public domain and can be copied without permission. Ever since the concept of the right to copy was established and codified, copyright has existed under both common and statutory law. Common law is unwritten law, based on tradition and precedent. Statutory law is written law passed by a legislative body, such as the British Parliament or the United States Congress.

In general, common law protects a work before it is published and statutory law protects it after it is published. In both common and statutory law, it is assumed that what is written or created is property. The creator of a work has sole ownership of the work and the right to dispose of it as one would any other type of property; that is, to sell it, lease it, transfer it, or leave it in a will. Upon publication of the work, the author gives up some of the ownership rights granted by common law but is given monetary rewards for doing so. The law is based on two sometimes conflicting principles: authors should be rewarded for their labors and knowledge should be made readily available to the pubic for the good of society as a whole. Much of the history of copyright law is concerned with attempts to reconcile these two principles.

The concept and fundamental issues of copyright date back at least as far as the fifteenth century. With the invention of printing, copies of both ancient and contemporary works began to proliferate and become readily available to the public. Early English copyright law began to address the questions of what should be printed, who ultimately owned the works

One of the most distinguished American jurists never to sit on the Supreme Court, U.S. district court judge Learned Hand passed down decisions that made a permanent imprint on U.S. copyright law. (Library of Congress)

and for how long, how the owners should be compensated for them, and who should be authorized to copy them.

Throughout Europe, by the sixteenth century printing had developed from an unregulated cottage industry of craftsmen to a full-fledged profession and a thriving large-scale industry. Usually, the printers of books were also the vendors of them. In England, the printing and selling of books was done by a monopoly called the Stationers' Company. Copyright at this time was a license given to the Stationers' Company by royal decree. The decree gave the company exclusive rights to print all works the government deemed proper to print. The law was for the benefit of publishers and booksellers more than for authors. Furthermore, since the license to publish was granted on the basis of what the government decided could or could not be published, it was actually a form of censorship. It bore little resemblance to the laws that followed but did recognize that what was written in a book was as much property as was the book itself. Authors, who had hitherto been supported by wealthy, interested patrons rather than by sale of their work, could now earn money (although hardly a living wage) apart from patronage by selling their manuscripts to printers, who paid them a lump sum. It was generally accepted that once the manuscript was sold, the work was no longer the property of the author. Copyright infringement, which frequently consisted of printing unauthorized works outside the Stationers' monopoly, was more an offense against the publisher, or those who licensed the publisher, than against the author.

By the late seventeenth century, the English press was generally liberated from the dictates of the authorities. There was much less censorship, and licenses to the Stationers' Company were no longer renewed. Freedom of the press destroyed the Stationers' monopoly, for now anyone could print virtually anything. An unfettered press also meant a lack of protection for authors from piracy and plagiarism. Literary piracy long had been considered an outrage, if not actually a criminal offense, and was supposed to be prevented by common law, but there were few means of enforcing common law. Both authors and booksellers pressured Parliament for legislation that would protect authors from piracy and provide booksellers with enough security to allow them to stay in business. In 1710, Parliament responded with the Statute of Anne, named for the reigning queen. The Statute of Anne established time limits, with renewals, on how long a published work would be protected before it went into the public domain and outlined penalties for copyright infringement. The law was not clear, however, on how long an unpublished work was protected by common law or whether common law was superseded by statutory law after a work was published. It did not answer whether an author gave up all rights to a work after it was published.

There were many cases in which publishers freely copied works for which the statutory term of protection had expired. When the authors of the works complained that this free copying was a violation of their common law rights, the English courts decided that once a work had been published and the term of protection had expired, common law rights no longer applied. This conflict sparked long and heated debates over ownership and the balance between authors' rights and the public good. These debates continued through the twentieth century.

Limited and controversial as it was, the Statute of Anne became the pattern for all subsequent copyright legislation in both England and the United States. Twelve of the thirteen original states adopted copyright statutes before the federal Constitution was drawn up. These statutes were summarized in article 1, section 8 of the federal Constitution, which says: "Congress shall have power . . . to promote the progress of science and useful arts by securing for limited times to authors and inventors the exclusive right to their respective writings and discoveries." The first federal copyright law, enacted in 1790, was revised in 1831 and 1879. On March 4, 1909, Congress passed a copyright law that remained in effect until revisions were made in 1976.

The 1909 law states that the purpose of copyright is "not primarily for the benefit of the author, but primarily for the benefit of the public." Although unpublished works were still held to be covered by common law, publication was necessary in order for a work to be covered by statutory law, and an author's rights under statutory law were substantially different from what they were under common law. Under the 1909 law, there was no general protection of unpublished works. Omission of or serious error in a copyright notice or failure to deposit a copy in the Copyright Office resulted in loss or forfeit of copyright.

The Copyright Office, located in the Library of Congress in Washington, D.C., was established by the 1909 law to keep records and register works. The law outlined procedures for registration of copyright, detailed circumstances of and penalties for infringement, and listed fourteen categories of works that could be copyrighted. It codified the standard of copyrightability of a work as being original by the author and not copied from other work. It also lengthened the duration of copyright to twenty-eight years, renewable for twenty-eight more.

Impact of Event

Just as the Statute of Anne had responded to the implications of the new technology of the printing press, so the law of 1909 tried to respond to the new technology of the early twentieth century. The 1909 law grew out of centuries of political upheaval, factional controversy, technological development, and legislative compromise. As English government swung from monarchy to republic and back to monarchy again, up to the early eighteenth century, written work was first strictly censored and then liberated to the point of anarchy. Printing had made works of all kinds widely available, and once the press was liberated in England, the rights of publishers, authors, and the public came into sharp conflict. Some of the conflicts were resolved by the Statute of Anne, which served as a pattern for American copyright law.

In the spirit of the original state laws and the federal copyright law of 1790, the 1909 law stated its purpose as being "primarily for the public," thus favoring the rights of the public over the rights of authors but allowing for reward to authors in order to encourage them to continue producing. In this way, the conflicting principles of rewards to creators and the "promotion of progress in science and useful arts" for the common good seemed to be reconciled. By extending the term of copyright coverage, it gave more protection to authors than previous legislation had. It provided no protection, however, for unpublished work, and it tended to supersede common law, since publication was a necessary condition for copyright. Nor did it address the special issues of copyright involved for writers as employees or contractors, such as newspaper reporters and freelance writers, who do what is known as "work for hire."

The fair use doctrine had been applied even in early copyright law and was based on the constitutional principle of public benefit from authors' works. In 1961, while the 1909 law was still in effect, the Copyright Office listed what could be copied without permission and for what purpose. Research, instruction, and literary review, for example, were given fairly broad rights to copy. Fair use was not codified until the copyright law revision of 1976.

As technology improved and became more varied, the 1909 law lagged in its provisions. In describing the classes of works that were copyrightable, the language of the 1909 law indicated that it was still largely based on the technology of the printing press. It protected the "writings" of an author, whereas later law protects "original works of authorship," thus broadening the definition of "author" and lengthening the list of what can be considered to be authors' works. Although the 1909 law listed motion pictures and sound recordings among the classes of copyrightable works, it made inadequate provision for the protection of what was disseminated via these new technologies and no provision at all for infringement issues arising from the use of photocopy machines, television, videotapes, computers, or cable and satellite communications.

Beginning in 1955, there were several attempts to revise the law, but it was not extensively revised until 1976 (effective in 1978). The most significant impact of the 1909 copyright law on the writing and publishing world and on society in general, as beneficiary of authors' work, is that it was specific, whereas prior legislation had been general. By establishing a Copyright Office, listing the kinds of works that could be copyrighted, and outlining how they could be protected, it sought to resolve the ongoing conflict between rewarding creators and benefiting their audiences.

Bibliography

Bunnin, Brad. *The Writer's Legal Companion.* Reading, Mass.: Perseus Books, 1998. Practical handbook for authors.

Bunnin, Brad, and Peter Beren. "What Is Copyright?" In *The Writer's Legal Companion.* 3d ed. Reading, Mass.: Addison-Wesley, 1998. Contains practical and up-to-date legal advice for writers. Compares the constitutional foundation of copyright with current law and compares the 1909 and 1978 laws in outline form.

Dible, Donald M., ed. *What Everybody Should Know About Patents, Trademarks, and Copyrights.* Fairfield, Calif.: Entrepreneur Press, 1978. Provides a lengthy historical background to copyright and practical guidelines to what copyright is and how it is obtained. Contains the full text of the 1978 law.

Goldfarb, Ronald L., and Gail E. Ross. "What Every Writer Should Know About Copyright." In *The Writer's Lawyer.* New York: Times Books, 1989. Contains only brief historical background to copyright but provides important information on later developments in copyright law.

Johnston, Donald F. *Copyright Handbook.* 2d ed. New York: R. R. Bowker, 1982. Describes and interprets every element of copyright law in detail. Includes the full texts of both the 1909 and the 1978 laws.

Kaplan, Benjamin. *An Unhurried View of Copyright.* New York: Columbia University Press, 1967. Three lectures analyzing judicial decisions regarding copyright issues from the fifteenth century through the 1960's.

Moore, Waldo. "Ten Questions About the New Copyright Law." In *Law and the Writer,* edited by Kirk Polking and Leonard S. Meranus. Cincinnati, Ohio: Writer's Digest Books, 1978. Explains the 1976 revisions by comparing some of their elements to the 1909 law.

Wincor, Richard, and Irving Mandell. *"Historical Background—Copyright Law." In Copyright, Patents, and Trademarks.* Dobbs Ferry, N.Y.: Oceana Publications, 1980. Provides a concise, thorough, and extremely readable history of copyright from its origins to the status of the law in the 1970's.

Christina Ashton

Cross-References

Advertisers Adopt a Truth in Advertising Code (1913); The A. C. Nielsen Company Pioneers in Marketing and Media Research (1923); Congress Limits the Use of Billboards (1965).

THE TRIANGLE SHIRTWAIST FACTORY FIRE PROMPTS LABOR REFORMS

CATEGORY OF EVENT: Labor
TIME: March 25, 1911
LOCALE: New York, New York

Public outrage following the Triangle Shirtwaist Factory fire led to immediate fire safety legislation and reform demonstrations, but substantial labor reform did not come until years later

Principal personages:
ROSE SCHNEIDERMAN (1882-1972), an influential member and later president of the Women's Trade Union League
ALFRED E. SMITH (1873-1944), a New York state legislator who conducted investigations and made recommendations for fire safety legislation
ROBERT WAGNER (1877-1953), a New York state senator who conducted investigations
MAX BLANCK, a co-owner of the Triangle Shirtwaist Factory
ISSAC HARRIS, a co-owner of the Triangle Shirtwaist Factory

Summary of Event

Prior to the Triangle Shirtwaist Factory fire of 1911, garment workers had begun to organize and make known their desires for reform. In 1900, the International Ladies Garment Workers Union (ILGWU) was formed. In 1903, the Women's Trade Union League (WTUL) was established for the purpose of bringing more women into the trade unions. The Triangle

Shirtwaist Factory was the site of one of the first demonstrations, a 1909 event that grew into a general strike of garment workers known as the "Uprising of the 20,000." The Triangle workers were locked out during that strike but were encouraged by the ILGWU and the WTUL to picket. Factory owners Max Blanck and Issac Harris hired replacement workers and called in thugs to break the pickets. Throughout the year-long series of strikes that followed, other factories agreed to various reforms. Although not meeting all demands, most shirtwaist makers agreed to shorter hours, collective bargaining, and safety improvements. The Triangle Shirtwaist Factory, however, retained its fifty-nine-hour workweek and refused to make safety improvements.

Like many other plants of its kind during the first decades of the twentieth century, the Triangle Shirtwaist Factory was a loft factory, occupying the top three floors of an office building. Meeting the increased demand for tailored blouses for the growing number of female clerical workers during that era, Triangle was one of the most successful garment factories in New York City. It employed one thousand workers, mostly immigrant women who knew little or no English. They worked long hours in hazardous and unhealthful conditions for pennies a day.

Workers were jammed elbow to elbow and back to back at rows of tables. Scraps of the highly flammable fabric they worked with were scattered on the floor or stored tightly in bins. Cutting machines were fueled by gasoline. The few safety regulations were ignored. Smoking was prohibited, but workers commonly smoked while supervisors looked the other way. Water barrels with buckets for extinguishing fires were not always full. There was one rotting fire hose, attached to a rusted valve. In general, conditions were ideal for fire to break out and spread at any time.

Escape in case of fire was difficult or impossible. The only interior exit from the workroom was down a hall so narrow that people had to walk single file. There were four elevators, but usually only one was functional. The stairway was as narrow as the hall. Of the two doors leading from the building, one was permanently locked from the outside, and the other opened inward.

On March 25, 1911, the day of the fire, the offices below the factory were closed for the weekend. About half of the Triangle workforce was in the factory on that Saturday. The flames spread far too quickly to be extinguished by the meager water supply in the barrels, and the fire hose did not work. In the stampede to get down the narrow passages and stairways to the doors, peopled were trampled. Some tried to break through the locked door. Other surged to the other door and were crushed as they tried to pull it inward. As people crowded into the elevators, others tried to ride down on the tops of the cars, hanging onto the cables. Soon there were so many bodies in the shafts that the one functioning elevator could no longer be used. The women, girls, and few men trapped in the workroom threw themselves out of the windows and were dashed to death on the pavement. Others tried to use the fire escape. Already too flimsy to hold much weight, the fire escape soon melted in the heat and twisted into wreckage. Only twenty women managed to escape by it.

Firefighters arrived at the scene quickly but nevertheless too late. Once they arrived, several factors inhibited their efforts. Many of the women who jumped from the windows landed on the fire hoses. Their bodies had to be removed before the hoses could function. The nets and blankets that the firefighters spread to catch the jumping women tore, and the women crashed through to die on the pavement. The fire engine ladder reached no further than the seventh floor, one story short of the workroom. Those who escaped did so by being first out the door or down the elevator, or by climbing from the top floor onto the roofs of other buildings.

The death toll was 146, including 13 men. Several of the bodies were so badly charred that they could not be identified, even as to sex. The cause of the fire was never discovered. Given the number of fire hazards that were present, it was speculated that the cause might have been a match, a lighted cigarette, or a spark from a cutting machine igniting gasoline or the combustible fabric scattered on the floor and packed in bins.

On the evidence of the locked door, factory owners Blanck and Harris were indicted for first- and second-degree manslaughter. They claimed that they did not know the door was locked and were acquitted.

Impact of Event

The Triangle Shirtwaist Factory disaster was a terrible object lesson in the need for reforms in fire prevention in particular and labor reform in general. It also illustrated the need for solidarity among the organizations and labor groups working for reform.

Public outrage at the 146 deaths and the miserable conditions under which the victims had worked formed the basis for future legislation on factory safety. The New York state legislature appointed investigative commissions to examine factories statewide, and thirty ordinances in New York City were enacted to enforce fire prevention measures. One of the earliest was the Sullivan-Hoey Fire Prevention Law of October, 1911, which streamlined six separate agencies into one fire commission with a fire prevention division that required the installation of sprinkler systems in factories.

Significant labor reform for garment workers took longer to achieve.

Although they had gained only small victories compared to what they had demanded, the ILGWU and WTUL had demonstrated in the 1909 strike that workers could be organized and could be depended upon to fight with strength and determination. Immigrant women, who had to battle not only inhumane working conditions and language barriers but also a general hostility to their entering labor unions, had demonstrated a surprising show of force. The Triangle fire was a tragic example of how much more reform was still needed. At a memorial service held at New York's Metropolitan Opera House, Rose Schneiderman, an influential member of the WTUL and later its president, gave a scathing speech pointing out how the Triangle tragedy indicated that alleged reform was not taking place. She called the crowd of workers, public officials, and interested citizens of all classes to join a working-class movement for reform. This speech, along with tens of thousands of New Yorkers marching in tribute to those killed in the Triangle fire, strenghtened the resolve of reformers, inspired the labor unions to get legislative support for their demands, and stimulated reforms of social ills directly related to poor labor practices. Those ills included lack of education, which was encouraged by the employment of child labor.

State senator Robert Wagner and state legislator Alfred E. Smith began a series of investigations and recommendations to improve factory safety. Women connected with the unions and other reform organizations took to the streets to inform workers of the benefits to which they were entitled and encourage them to fight for those benefits when they were denied. Organizers conducted legislators on tours through factories, revealing the abuses that existed in them.

Progress continued to be slow. It was not until 1913 that the investigations, recommendations, and resolutions resulted in effective labor legislation. In that year, the fifty-four-hour workweek became law. That same year, Max Blanck, who owned a new Triangle Shirtwaist Factory, was fined for keeping his doors locked and received a court injunction against using a counterfeit ILGWU fair-practice label he had been using to sell more shirtwaists.

The Triangle fire acted as a catalyst to consolidate reforms in different sectors of society. Suffragists joined forces with the unions in their efforts to gain equal rights for women. Education reformers worked with the WTUL to teach immigrants English and to inform them about social issues and trade union practices. Women of the middle and upper classes held fund-raisers for the nearly empty coffers of the labor organizations. This sort of work was done nationwide, and its organizers had international counterparts.

The ILGWU tightened its organization and gained the power to negotiate contracts better than those of other unions. It was particularly effective in negotiating the right to strike. During the years of World War I, a period of full employment and high production, the ILGWU managed to maintain union contract standards under the pressures of increased production demands. At the same time, the union began a new drive for a shorter workweek and established a thriving union health center, the first of its kind in the United States, to provide preventive medical service.

Progress in labor reform continued to be slow and uneven, however, as it would be for decades to come. By 1915, management had increased efforts to reassert control over labor. This provoked a series of wildcat strikes, which provoked conflicts between conservative and more militant unions. Later, rank-and-file conflict with union leadership weakened union power further.

On the other hand, the ILGWU continued to increase its power. By 1916, five years after the Triangle Shirtwaist Factory fire, the union had enough power both to withstand a lockout in New York City that affected twenty thousand workers and to win in a fourteen-week general strike by two thousand shops employing sixty thousand members.

The immediate impact of the Triangle Shirtwaist Factory disaster on labor reform was that it provoked enough public outrage to establish stricter fire codes and inspire new and inexperienced labor organizations to press for supportive legislation. Response to the tragedy was part of the beginning of a long struggle for fair labor practices for all workers, equal treatment of women, and safe plants in which to work.

Bibliography

Babson, Steve. *The Unfinished Struggle: Turning Points in American Labor, 1877-Present.* Lanham, Md.: Rowman & Littlefield, 1999.

Butler, Hal. "New York's Triangle Tragedy." In *Inferno! Fourteen Fiery Tragedies of Our Time.* Chicago: Henry Regnery, 1975. Citing eyewitness reports, the author describes the Triangle fire in vivid detail. The article is part of a collection on disastrous fires in the United States.

Garrison, Webb. "Triangle Shirt Waist Fire." In *Disasters That Made History.* Nashville, Tenn.: Abingdon Press, 1973. The author gives detailed reports on the significance of twenty-three disasters. The report on the Triangle fire includes specific details on the sociopolitical and economic conditions surrounding the fire and its aftermath as well as on the incident itself.

Green, James R. "The Struggle for Control in the Progressive Era." In *The World of the Worker: Labor in Twentieth-Century America.* New York: Hill & Wang, 1980. The author places the Triangle fire as a significant incident in the American labor movement as well as in the social and cultural history of the nation as a whole.

Schneiderman, Rose. *All for One.* New York: Paul S. Eriksson, 1967. Written with editor Lucy Goldthwaite, this is the author's own story of her fifty years in the labor movement. Chapter 10 details the Triangle fire and its aftermath.

Wertheimer, Barbara Mayer. "Working Women in the National Women's Trade Union League: 1903-1914" and "The Rise of the Woman Garment Worker: 1909-1910." In *We Were There: The Story of Working Women in America.* New York: Pantheon Books, 1977. The volume is a narrative history of American working women from precolonial times to the mid-twentieth century. Contains valuable material on the significant developments in the labor movement and the influential women connected with it. Many illustrations, extensive notes, and an annotated bibliography.

Christina Ashton

Cross-References

The Supreme Court Strikes Down a Maximum Hours Law (1905); The Supreme Court Rules Against Minimum Wage Laws (1923); Congress Restricts Immigration with 1924 Legislation (1924); Congress Passes the Equal Pay Act (1963); The Civil Rights Act Prohibits Discrimination in Employment (1964); Nixon Signs the Occupational Safety and Health Act (1970); The Immigration Reform and Control Act Is Signed into Law (1986).

THE SUPREME COURT DECIDES TO BREAK UP STANDARD OIL

CATEGORY OF EVENT: Monopolies and cartels
TIME: May 15, 1911
LOCALE: Washington, D.C.

In its decision to break up the Standard Oil Company, the Supreme Court established the principle of the "rule of reason" in deciding whether companies were in violation of antitrust laws

Principal personages:
JOHN D. ROCKEFELLER (1839-1937), the president of Standard Oil Company, 1870-1911
JOHN SHERMAN (1823-1900), a senator from Ohio, 1885-1897, author of the Sherman Antitrust Act of 1890
EDWARD WHITE (1845-1921), the chief justice of the United States, 1910-1921

Summary of Event

Founded in 1870, Standard Oil Company became one of the largest companies in the United States by the end of the nineteenth century. In *Standard Oil v. United States* (221 U.S. 1), decided on May 15, 1911, the Supreme Court found the company guilty of violating the Sherman Antitrust Act of 1890 based on alleged "unreasonable" restraints of trade, including buying out small independent oil companies and cutting prices in selected areas to force out rivals. The case resulted in the separating of the parent Standard Oil from its thirty-three affiliates.

Eleven years after the historic oil discovery in Titusville, Pennsylvania, that marked the beginning of the modern oil refining industry, the Standard

Oil Company was incorporated by John D. Rockefeller in Cleveland, Ohio, on January 10, 1870. At the time of the company's formation, the oil refining industry was decentralized. Standard Oil's share of refined oil production in the United States was less than 4 percent, and Rockefeller had to compete with more than 250 other independent refineries.

During the last quarter of the nineteenth century, deflation and oversupply of oil brought down oil prices, causing fierce competition among oil refineries. The price for refined oil fell from more than 30 cents a gallon in 1870 to 10 cents a gallon in 1874 and to 8 cents in 1885. Compared with other oil refineries, Standard Oil was managed efficiently under Rockefeller and his associates, allowing it to survive while many competitors failed.

During the post-Civil War deflationary period, the railroad industry became very competitive. Rockefeller took advantage of Standard Oil's increasing size to secure secret rebates from shipping companies, thus reducing transportation costs and overall operating costs. Rockefeller further reduced Standard Oil's operating costs by vertically integrating the company, acquiring oil wells, railroads, pipelines, tank cars, and retail outlets. Vertical integration gave more control at all stages of production.

Meanwhile, because of declining market conditions, many small and nonintegrated oil companies that were unable to reduce their operating costs became unprofitable to operate. In addition, the method of destructive distillation introduced in 1875 increased the minimum efficient size of a refinery to more than one thousand barrels per day, making smaller companies even less competitive. Rockefeller began to take advantage of the situation, buying out many of the independent refineries in Pittsburgh, Philadelphia, New York, and New Jersey at low prices, often below their original cost. Standard Oil soon refined about 25 percent of the U.S. industry output. In 1882, Rockefeller and his associates formed the Standard Oil trust in New York, the first major "trust" form of business combination in U.S. history. The company held "in trust" all assets of the many regional Standard Oil subsidiary companies, one of which was Standard Oil of New Jersey, the third largest U.S. refinery in the 1880's. Despite the substantial drop in oil prices, Standard Oil was able to increase its profits by reducing costs from about 3 cents per gallon in 1870 to less than .5 cents in 1885. By 1900, the oil trust controlled more than 90 percent of the petroleum refining capacity in the United States.

The size and power of Standard Oil led to public hostility against it and against monopolies in general, prompting passage of the Sherman Antitrust Act in 1890. During the same year, immediately after New York State's action against the "sugar trust," the state of Ohio brought a lawsuit against Standard Oil for illegal monopolization of the oil industry. On March 2,

1892, the Ohio Supreme Court convicted Standard Oil of violating the Sherman Act by forming a holding company and forbade the company to operate Standard Oil of Ohio in that state.

The court decision led to dissolution of the Standard Oil trust back into its independent parts. The New Jersey unit took advantage of favorable state laws to become the Standard Oil Company of New Jersey, now known as Jersey Standard, as the trust's parent holding company. Rockefeller remained president, and management of the trust was consolidated through interlocking directorates of the more than thirty subsidiary companies. The supposedly separate companies thus were able to act as a single entity.

In 1901, the discovery of the Spindletop oil field created a boom in oil production on the Gulf Coast of Texas. The formation of new oil companies, such as Texaco and Gulf, increased the competition faced by Standard Oil. Standard Oil responded by continuing to buy out independent oil refineries. The Standard Oil trust's market share in the oil industry continued to expand.

Meanwhile, the commissioner of the Bureau of Corporations, James R. Garfield, investigated the oil company for violations of antitrust law. As a result of his studies, the government, led by Attorney General George Wickersham, brought charges in November, 1906, in the Federal Circuit Court of the Eastern District of Missouri against Standard Oil for monopoly and restraint of trade in violation of the Sherman Antitrust Act.

In 1909, the Missouri court found Jersey Standard guilty of violating section 1 of the Sherman Act by forming a holding company and of violating section 2 by restraining competition among merged firms by fixing transportation rates, supply costs, and output prices. Standard Oil appealed the decision to the U.S. Supreme Court. The Supreme Court upheld the Missouri decision on May 15, 1911, and later entered a dissolution decree to dismember the Standard Oil trust and divest the parent holding company, Jersey Standard, of its thirty-three major subsidiaries. Many of its offspring still bore the name Standard Oil. These new companies included the Standard Oil Company of Indiana (later American), the Standard Oil Company (Ohio), Standard Oil Company of California (later Chevron), Standard Oil of New Jersey (later Exxon), and Standard Oil of New York (later Mobil).

The Standard Oil case marked the beginning of a new direction in U.S. antitrust legislation and prosecution. Along with the decision in the American Tobacco case in 1911, the ruling of the Supreme Court, led by Chief Justice Edward White, departed from earlier cases. The new interpretation of section 2 of the Sherman Act was that only "unreasonable," instead of all, restraints of trade were illegal. The Standard Oil decision, followed closely by the American Tobacco case, gave birth to a new doctrine in U.S. antitrust policy called the rule of reason.

The allegedly "unreasonable" practices by Standard Oil that were ruled illegal under sections 1 and 2 of the Sherman Act included forcing smaller independent companies to be bought on unfavorable terms and selectively cutting prices in market areas where rivals operated, with the intent of bankrupting those rivals, while maintaining higher prices in other markets. Chief Justice White maintained that it was mainly Standard Oil's merger practices in an attempt to monopolize the oil refining industry that constituted illegal restraint of trade.

Impact of Event

The Standard Oil case of 1911 significantly altered the course of American business history as well as the development of U.S. antitrust laws. The victory of the government against a powerful trust provided an important lesson in the early history of antitrust. The dissolution of Standard Oil into many independent companies effectively increased competition in the oil industry. In addition, the case provides a classic study of the development of American big business at the beginning of the twentieth century.

The first major antitrust law was the Sherman Antitrust Act of 1890, which emerged largely from public dissatisfaction with the monopoly power gained by Standard Oil in the oil refining market. The Sherman Act prohibits conspiracies or combinations in restraint of trade (section 1), and any attempts to create them, known as monopolization (section 2). The limits of the law regarding what constitutes unlawful practices were not precisely defined, leading to different judicial interpretations of the act.

In the decade following passage of the Sherman Act, only sixteen cases were brought to court. Even though the courts began to establish that actions such as formal agreements to fix prices or limit output were definitely illegal, court judges were equivocal in their treatments of the existing large trusts in industries such as oil (Standard Oil), tobacco (American Tobacco), and steel (United States Steel).

The Supreme Court's decision against Standard Oil marked the beginning of a new era in antitrust legislation and prosecution. It established the "rule of reason" approach, by which Chief Justice White maintained that it was not the history or the relative size of a monopoly such as Standard Oil in its market that was an offense against the law, but rather its "unreasonable" business practices. This new doctrine set a precedent for cases involving antitrust laws that was not broken until the Alcoa case in 1945.

The Supreme Court decision in the Standard Oil case highlighted the need for additional legislation to define specific business practices that constituted "unreasonable," and thus illegal, conduct. That need led to passage of the Clayton Antitrust Act and the Federal Trade Commission Act in 1914. The Clayton Act declared illegal specific "unfair" business practices including price discrimination, exclusive dealing and tying contracts, acquisitions of competing firms, and interlocking directorates. The Federal Trade Commission Act gave birth to a new government authority, the Federal Trade Commission, to enforce compliance of the modified antitrust law.

The victory in the government's prosecution of Standard Oil, together with passage of the Clayton Act, led to more vigorous enforcement of the antitrust laws. The U.S. Justice Department filed suit in the 1910's and early 1920's against many trusts in other industries, including American Can Company (tin cans), United Shoe Machinery Company (shoe machinery), International Harvester (farm machinery), and United States Steel Corporation (steel). The Supreme Court decision against Standard Oil also signified the government's attitude toward mergers. Mergers and acquisitions subsided briefly, until the government's failure in prosecuting the merger practices of the United States Steel Corporation in 1920.

The dissolution of the oil monopoly, Standard Oil, effectively changed the structure of the oil industry. On one hand, its successor companies, particularly the New Jersey unit, maintained considerable market power in their regional territories. The retail price of gasoline increased sharply in 1915, leading to government investigation of the extent of competition in the oil industry. On the other hand, the government apparently succeeded in enforcing competition among the separated units. As a result of the dissolution, Standard Oil's successor companies were allowed to operate only in the oil refining business. They began to confront competition from other companies, such as Shell, Gulf, and Sun, which operated with the advantage of vertical integration.

In an attempt to battle the rising competition, two of Standard Oil's successor companies, Standard Oil of New York and the Vacuum Oil Company, proposed a merger in 1930. The government filed suit in federal district court against their merger, as violating the 1911 decree. The court's decision in favor of the merger began a new era of merger movement in the oil industry. Through mergers, the original thirty-four successor companies combined into nineteen companies during the 1930's.

In the 1920's, Standard Oil's successor companies began to expand their oil exploration overseas, particularly in the Middle East and Europe. That exploration continued as American resources were exhausted. Increased imports of oil, notably from the Organization of Petroleum Exporting Countries (OPEC) after its formation in 1960, intensified competition in the

U.S. oil market and reduced American companies' market shares. The oil refining industry developed into one with companies operating worldwide, many of them large relative to the industry as a whole but none with the power formerly held by Standard Oil.

Bibliography

Adams, Walter, ed. *The Structure of American Industry.* 7th ed. New York: Macmillan, 1986. Chapter 2 provides good coverage of the background and historical development of the petroleum industry as well as discussions of the industry's structure, price behavior, and performance. Valuable for undergraduate and graduate students in industrial organization.

Armentano, Dominick T. *Antitrust and Monopoly: Anatomy of a Policy Failure.* New York: John Wiley & Sons, 1982. Covers major antitrust lawsuits since the Sherman Act and the development of antitrust legislation. Covers the Standard Oil case in chapter 4. Includes an appendix of relevant sections of antitrust laws. Written for undergraduate business and economics students.

Bradley, Robert L. *Oil, Gas, and Government: The U.S. Experience.* Lanham, Md.: Rowman & Littlefield, 1996.

Destler, Chester McArthur. *Roger Sherman and the Independent Oil Men.* Ithaca, N.Y.: Cornell University Press, 1967. A biographical study of the person who fought for small independent oil refineries against the monopolization of the industry by Standard Oil in the northeastern region. Easy to read.

Gibb, George Sweet, and Evelyn H. Knowlton. *The Resurgent Years, 1911-1927.* Vol. 2 in *History of Standard Oil Company (New Jersey),* edited by Henrietta M. Larson. New York: Harper & Brothers, 1956. Deals with the evolutionary development of the New Jersey unit following the Standard Oil case in 1911, including operations overseas, increased competition with other Standard Oil successors, and labor relations.

Hall, Kermit L., ed. *The Oxford Guide to United States Supreme Court Decisions.* New York: Oxford University Press, 1999. Multiauthored collection of essays on more than four hundred significant Court decisions, with supporting glossary and other aids.

Hidy, Ralph W., and Muriel E. Hidy. *Pioneering in Big Business, 1882-1911.* Vol. 1 in *History of Standard Oil Company (New Jersey),* edited by Henrietta M. Larson. New York: Harper & Brothers, 1955. Comprehensive documentation of the company's early history, particularly its administration and vertically integrated operations in the oil business. Good discussion of the dynamic development of a big corporation from business administration and business history perspectives. Valuable for business students.

McGee, John. "Predatory Price Cutting: The Standard Oil (N.J.) Case." *Journal of Law and Economics 1* (October, 1958): 137-169. McGee's controversial article provides arguments and evidence against accusations of predatory pricing practices by Standard Oil. His critique led to debates about the profitability of predatory price cutting and its violation of antitrust law.

Whitney, Simon N. *Antitrust Policies: American Experience in Twenty Industries.* 2 vols. New York: Twentieth Century Fund, 1958. Chapter 3 of volume 2 provides a case study of the petroleum industry until 1950. Good economic analysis of the impacts of the antitrust suit on development of the industry. Other chapters are case studies of other major industries. The appendix contains critiques of the studies of economists and government officials.

Jim Lee

Cross-References

Discovery of Oil at Spindletop Transforms the Oil Industry (1901); The Federal Trade Commission Is Organized (1914); Congress Passes the Clayton Antitrust Act (1914); The Teapot Dome Scandal Prompts Reforms in the Oil Industry (1924); The United States Plans to Cut Dependence on Foreign Oil (1974).

ADVERTISERS ADOPT A TRUTH IN ADVERTISING CODE

CATEGORY OF EVENT: Advertising
TIME: August, 1913
LOCALE: Baltimore, Maryland

The Associated Advertising Clubs of America adopted "A Business Creed" in the hope that other organizations would adhere to similar high standards

Principal personages:
JOSEPH SWAGAR SHERLEY (1871-1941), a congressman from Kentucky who introduced a measure to amend the Pure Food and Drug Act
JAMES ROBERT MANN (1856-1922), a congressman from Illinois who made significant contributions to modifying Sherley's amendment
JOSEPH HAMPTON MOORE (1864-1950), a congressman active in development of the Sherley Amendment

Summary of Event

Adoption of a truth in advertising code by the Associated Advertising Clubs of America in 1913 was prompted by passage of the Sherley Amendment to the Pure Food and Drug Act of 1906. To better understand the significance of that 1912 amendment, it is necessary to review how the original act came into being. The purpose of the original act was to prevent the manufacture, sale, or transportation of adulterated, misbranded, or deleterious foods, drugs, medicines, and liquors. The act also intended to regulate traffic in foods, drugs, and medicine.

In section 8 of the 1906 Pure Food and Drug Act, the term "misbranded" applied to all drugs, articles of food, or individual contents as well as

TAKEN INTERNALLY,
CURES
Sudden Colds, Coughs, Fever
and Ague, Dyspepsia, Asthma
and Phthisic, Liver Complaint,
Acid Stomach, Headache, Indigestion, Heartburn, Canker in
the Mouth and Stomach, Canker Rash, Kidney Complaints,
Piles, Sea Sickness, Sick Headache, Cramp and Pain in the
Stomach, Painters' Colic, Diarrhœa, Dysentery, Summer Complaint, Cholera Morbus, Cholera
Infantum, and Cholera.

APPLIED EXTERNALLY,
CURES
Scalds, Burns, Frost Bites, Chilblains, Sprains, Bruises, Whitlows, Felons, Boils, Old Sores,
Ringworms, Rheumatic Affections, Headache, Neuralgia in
in the Face, Toothache, Pain
in the Side, Pain in the Back
and Loins, Neuralgic or Rheumatic Pains in the Joints or
Limbs, Stings of Insects, Scorpions, Centipedes, and the Bites
of Poisonous Insects and Venomous Reptiles.

A fresh supply of the
PAIN KILLER
*just received and for
sale by*

Public distrust in exaggerated advertising claims such as these for an alleged pain killer contributed to the decision of commercial advertisers to adopt a code. (Library of Congress)

packages or labels that bore any statement, design, or device regarding the ingredients or contents. The term "misbranded" also referred to any imitation or substitution. An item would be identified as "misbranded" if its label failed to state the quantity or proportion of any alcohol, morphine, opium, cocaine, heroin, alpha or beta eucaine, chloroform, cannabis indica, chloral hydrate, or acetanilide, or any derivative or preparation of such substances. In addition, if a package did not list the proper weight and measure of the contents, it was considered to be misbranded. A package could not be false or misleading in any way. Section 8 of this act further stated that ingredients could not be imitations or substitutes for the stated contents.

Debate over House Resolution 11877 to amend the 1906 Pure Food and Drug Act took place on August 19, 1912. Congressman Joseph Hampton Moore of Pennsylvania suggested that one more addition be made to Congressman Joseph Swagar Sherley's amendment regarding statements of contents in packages. He noted that in cases of nostrums and patent medicines, the statement in regard to the ingredients or therapeutic properties usually appeared on the inside of the cover of the package or bottle. Congressman James Robert Mann from Illinois stated that the effect of

Sherley's proposed amendment was not to keep drugs off the market but to keep sellers from making false claims about the curative powers of those drugs. The Sherley Amendment to section 8 of the Pure Food and Drug Act was approved on August 23, 1912. The amendment contained a clause stating that no package should make false or fraudulent claims pertaining to curative or therapeutic effects. A further amendment was approved on March 3, 1913, to state that reasonable variations would be allowed in regard to weight, measure, and numerical count.

In August, 1913, "A Business Creed" was published by the Associated Advertising Clubs of America (AACA). The creed stated belief in the continued and persistent education of the press and public in regard to fraudulent advertising. Members of the AACA further stated a belief that each and every member owed a duty to the association of enforcing the code of morals based on truth in advertising as well as truth and integrity in all functions pertaining to the creed. The AACA creed also endorsed the work of the National Vigilance Committee, a group similar to a commission of the Associated Advertising Clubs, in its belief in the continued education of the press and public in regard to fraudulent advertising. The AACA also encouraged every advertising interest to submit problems concerning questionable advertising and to uphold the code of morals based on truth in advertising. At the date of publication of this creed, few businesses or associations had formal codes of conduct of the same sort, but many people endeavored to make business more profitable while exerting pressure to keep business activity on a higher plane than it had been.

The adoption of a truth in advertising creed following on the heels of the Sherley Amendment was timely in its intent to promote the credibility of the AACA. At the time, magazines and other advertising media contained much material of dubious truth. Business suffered from mistrust by the buying public. Buyers often were taken in by false claims, some of which carried the potential for harm, as claims of cures or other benefits were made. The public was tired of throwing money away on false hopes, and this attitude was bad for business, as the members of the AACA well knew.

Impact of Event

Recognition of advertising as a viable means of widespread communication came around the beginning of the nineteenth century. The Industrial Revolution gave rise to the need to promote the abundant manufactured goods then being produced. Advertising as a profession developed in response to this need. As the profession grew into an industry, advertising practitioners became concerned with maintenance of high business standards. Advertising professionals saw the need to join together to protect and promote their trade. Across the United States, local organizations were formed to uphold industry standards. The aims of these associations were primarily education and self-regulation.

In 1911, the Advertising Federation of America formed a national vigilance committee and launched the truth in advertising movement, a forerunner to the Better Business Bureaus. The Advertising Association of the West entered the movement a year later. These groups worked in cooperation with each other over the years. In 1962, they held a joint convention to discuss a merger that became a reality in 1967. The new group was named the American Advertising Federation (AAF), headquartered in Washington, D.C. The AAF is dedicated to serving its members by promoting, protecting, and advancing advertising interests, including the freedom to truthfully advertise legal products. Its actions and goals rely heavily on the AACA creed as a basis.

The goals of the AAF include professional development, public education to promote awareness and understanding of how advertising contributes to the economy and society, fostering high standards of ethical conduct including truth in advertising, encouraging use of the advertising process for the public good, and recognizing and honoring excellence in advertising. The AAF upholds the high standards of the industry, including truth in advertising. It also opposes bans or restrictions on truthful, nondeceptive advertisements for legal products and services. It therefore opposed bans and restrictions on advertisements for tobacco products and alcoholic beverages.

Some consumer goods fall under the scrutiny of the Food and Drug Administration (FDA). Vitamin supplements and herbal remedies, for example, are types of products at which the Pure Food and Drug Act was aimed. Most of these products comply with truth in advertising to the extent that no claims are made on the labels, other than warnings. Some products, for example, warn that use can contribute to a rise in blood pressure. Labeling thus made no false claims and few claims of any sort. Information about benefits of the products must come from other sources.

A more subtle example of questionable advertising lies in the visual portrayal or image of a product. The Marlboro Man, for example, portrayed to impressionable audiences the idea that smoking is an activity undertaken by tough, masculine men. Another example is the slogan for Pepsi, "Be young, be happy, drink Pepsi." The slogan does not directly state that drinking Pepsi will make one young and happy, but the suggestion is there. A final example comes from the young models typically used in advertisements for wrinkle cream. Such models may use the product for prevention of wrinkles; the implication of the ads, however, is that use of the product will make anyone look as young as the models. The premise of truth in advertising does not cover such subtleties. Consumer advocates also criticize packaging claims that are truthful but leave out important facts. Some food packages, for example, contain claims of having fewer calories; the fact is that the calorie reduction comes from the simple fact that there is less food in the container.

Grocery shoppers are well advised to be wary because, although there is definitely truth in advertising as far as listings of ingredients, those listings often contain chemicals that are unfamiliar to all but the most informed shoppers. The FDA has banned certain food colorings as harmful. Other ingredients, however, can cause reactions in some people but not in others. Common reactions include rashes, digestive upset, and even heart palpitations. Many people have discovered a sensitivity to monosodium glutamate (MSG), but many packaged foods as well as certain sausage preparations still contain MSG. Consumers therefore must know their own situations. Labels will identify ingredients, but full truth does not extend as far as providing a warning that "this product may induce digestive upset." It is up to the consumer to know.

Truth in advertising codes and laws have extended to other sectors. A law firm in California was found guilty of false advertising, and an exterminating company honored a government order to produce scientific evidence for health and safety claims. One vacuum cleaner manufacturer filed suit against another to stop a campaign promoting its new cleaning effectiveness rating, which may have been misleading. It is evident that federal agencies, consumers, and the advertising profession are keeping watch to ensure that truth in advertising comes as close as possible to becoming a reality.

Bibliography

"A Business Creed." *The World's Work*, August, 1913, 384. The Business Creed was adopted by the Associated Advertising Clubs of America in an effort to keep business and advertising on a higher plane than previously. This is the text of the creed.

Goodwin, Lorine Swainston. *The Pure Food, Drink, and Drug Crusaders, 1879-1914.* Jefferson, N.C.: McFarland, 1999. Survey of the history of lobbyists and elected officials fighting for new legislation.

Pridgen, Dee. *Consumer Protection and the Law*. New York: Clark Boardman, 1986-1990. A comprehensive account of the history of consumer protection laws. Covers relevant court decisions. Topics include seller misrepresentation and the doctrine of *caveat emptor*.

Reid, Margaret G. *Consumers and the Market*. New York: F. S. Crofts, 1938. A summary of the problems then facing consumers in such areas as labeling, product quality, advertising, and price setting. Includes specific examples and historical references.

Sullivan, Mark. "The Crusade for Pure Food." In *America Finding Herself.* Vol. 2 in *Our Times: The United States, 1900-1925.* New York: Charles Scribner's Sons, 1927-1935. An account of the personalities and controversies that led to the 1906 Pure Food and Drug Act. Sullivan consulted with many of the people involved in passage of the law.

U.S. Department of Agriculture. Office of the General Counsel. *Food and Drugs Act June 30, 1906, and Amendments of August 23, 1912 and March 3, 1913 with the Rules and Regulations for the Enforcement of the Act, Food Inspection Decisions, Selected Court Decisions, Digest of Decisions, Opinions of the Attorney General and Appendix.* Washington, D.C.: Government Printing Office, 1914. A government report detailing the passage of the Pure Food and Drug Act and its amendments.

Young, James Harvey. *Pure Food: Securing the Federal Food and Drugs Act of 1906.* Princeton, N.J.: Princeton University Press, 1989. An authority on the history of medical misconduct presents a study of the evolution of the Food and Drug Administration and development of the Pure Food and Drug Act.

Corinne Elliott

Cross-References

The Federal Trade Commission Is Organized (1914); The A. C. Nielsen Company Pioneers in Marketing and Media Research (1923); Health Consciousness Creates Huge New Markets (1970's); *Time* magazine Makes an E-commerce Pioneer Its Person of the Year (1999).

FORD IMPLEMENTS ASSEMBLY LINE PRODUCTION

CATEGORY OF EVENT: Manufacturing
TIME: October, 1913
LOCALE: Highland Park, Michigan

The Ford Motor Company began use of mass-production techniques to reduce costs and prices, thereby becoming the industry leader in automobile sales for a decade

Principal personages:
HENRY FORD (1863-1947), the owner of Ford Motor Company
WILLIAM S. KNUDSEN (1879-1948), the factory manager for Ford Motor Company and General Motors
CHARLES E. SORENSEN (1881-1965), the production manager for Ford Motor Company
CLARENCE AVERY (1893-1943), the time study expert for Ford Motor Company
JAMES COUZENS (1872-1947), the business manager of Ford Motor Company

Summary of Event

Introduction of the sturdy, high-wheeled Model T Ford in 1908 was followed by immediate success. Six thousand of the cars were sold in its first year. In 1910, 32,000 were sold; in 1911, 70,000; and in 1912, 170,000. Henry Ford had made a pledge to reduce the price of the car as the success of his company was realized, and he reduced the 1908 price of $850 to $600 in 1912. This made the machine competitive with the low-cost Buicks, which were priced at $850 in 1908.

In 1908, Ford's business manager James Couzens performed a market study that indicated that a price of $600 would ensure a strong competitive situation for Ford's new Model T. At the same time, his best estimate of the price that could be offered with the current production methods was $850. In order to make the new car profitable, Ford had to find ways to cut costs. Couzens enlisted the aid of Clarence Avery, a time study expert, and Charles Sorensen, the production manager at Ford, in making a study of the practices then in use, with the intention of converting to mass-production methods.

Assembly lines reduced automobile production costs by having workers at stationary positions perform the same tasks more quickly as the cars rolled by. (Library of Congress)

Avery made exhaustive time studies to determine the labor costs of the various subassembly steps as well as the final assembly. At the same time, Sorensen conducted mock-up tests, simulating final assembly of the Model N car, another in the Ford line, as the chassis was pushed along on skids past the points at which components were fed in.

Several things were needed to realize mass production. First, parts and subassemblies had to be reliably supplied and interchangeable. In 1908, Cadillac had demonstrated that car parts could be made with such precision that three cars could be disassembled, have their parts mixed, and then be reassembled into working vehicles that made a successful five-hundred mile test run.

Mass production had been long practiced in firearms manufacture and in clock manufacture, as well as for other small assembled goods. Although automobiles had many more individual parts, most were not as complex nor as highly stressed as those in firearms, and they were not as dependent upon precision as those in timepieces. Ford believed that through better control of his sources for parts, including bringing many subassemblies into his works, he could satisfy requirements for precision and timely delivery.

As early as 1800, pulley blocks for the Royal Navy were produced and assembled with specialized machinery designed by Henry Maudslay. The work that specialized machinery could accomplish grew ever more complex. In 1881, cigarettes were made at the rate of 120,000 per day on a machine invented by James Bonsack. Diamond Match in 1881 had machines capable of making and packing matches automatically. In 1884, George Eastman invented a continuous-process system for coating photographic materials. By 1880, flour mills were built to move the grist from incoming bins to shipping containers in continuous-flow processes that required no human handling of the materials. In some cases, the grain processing became so inexpensive that breakfast cereals were invented to sell the surplus.

The next steps in reducing the cost of automobile manufacturing was much more difficult. Although standardized parts were available and the specialized machines to produce them had been invented, there was a need for a machine to aid in final assembly. Buick had experimented with the assembly line approach to automobile chassis assembly, moving cars along rude wooden tracks by hand. This innovation increased the production of Buicks from forty-five to two hundred per day, but it was not integrated with subassembly manufacture, nor was there any mechanical assistance to transport materials.

In the spring of 1913, William C. Klann, who was in charge of engine assembly, introduced moving belt assembly, first to assembly of the flywheel-mounted magneto, then to engine and transmission production. The moving belt system proved to be workable, but only in a one-dimensional system in which parts were fed to a single line that carried the assembled product to completion. A two-dimensional system would be needed to make mass assembly of an automobile possible; branches of subassembly lines would feed into a trunk line for the auto chassis.

To make this possible, Ford had to ensure that the "tree" would not wither for lack of parts along one "limb." He negotiated supply contracts with his subassembly suppliers based on a time-required basis. Those suppliers that he believed were unable to satisfy these requirements he purchased or replaced with subassembly shops of his own. By 1914, the company had bought more than fifteen thousand special-purpose machine tools to produce parts in Ford's own shops. In this way, Ford gradually acquired subassembly manufacturing capability for parts of his cars, beginning in some cases with raw material supply.

The first Ford automobile assembled on a moving line was built in October, 1913. The chassis was pulled along the line by a windlass and ropes. In January, 1914, the power was switched to an endless chain drive.

In 1936 Charlie Chaplin (right) satirized the dehumanizing effects of assembly lines in his film Modern Times. (Museum of Modern Art, Film Stills Archive)

On February 27, Ford integrated the system into a fully conveyorized assembly line, utilizing rails to guide and support the cars, which moved past workers at a convenient height at the rate of six feet per minute.

This new line demonstrated another innovation, the desirability of which was obvious once it had been tried. Raising the assembly line to about the level of a worker's waist eliminated the need for workers to bend or squat, greatly reducing worker fatigue. Each feeder line was located at a level enabling a worker to swing or slide a part into place. Nothing ever came to rest, and nothing was lifted or carried except by machinery.

Impact of Event

Introduction of the assembly line reduced the labor time required to build a Model T from twelve hours to one and one-half. As the cost of manufacture fell, so could the price. Although sales of the car were temporarily stifled as a result of a patent infringement suit filed by George Selden, who demanded royalties for use of his engine design, sales rose from the few thousands before 1910 to millions, and the price fell from $850 in 1908 to $290 in 1926. During this period, the profits of the company rose steadily. In 1909, the company earned slightly less than $2 million. By 1913, profits exceeded $11 million. As the effects of the moving assembly process were realized, profits rose more steeply.

Ford began to encourage his workers to be part of the market for his cars. On January 4, 1914, he and Sorensen met with other executives to discuss a general wage increase. At the time, workers received a starting wage of $2 a day, and the average wage was $2.20 per day. Ford made an executive decision that wages would start at $5 a day, about double the industry average. This decision had the desired effects on morale, labor turnover, and quality of work. In addition, it made it possible for a worker to buy a Ford car in 1914 for four month's wages, thus making a potent case for the Model T being "everyman's car."

Other automobile manufacturers were shocked that Ford would take such a huge step without consulting them. In order to compete for the semiskilled labor available in the Detroit area, they had to make similar wage adjustments, but from weaker financial positions. Ford remained the industry's wage leader.

Ford's progress in reducing costs followed a learning curve of surprising regularity considering the early date at which mass production was introduced. From 1909 through 1923, the curve of price versus cumulative units sold followed a smooth slope as production increased by a factor of more than a thousand. The fact that the curve continued smoothly through the later stages of development of the Model T shows that there was continual refinement of the mass-production process. Much of this resulted from Ford expanding his business to include the earliest stages of supply, such as mining of raw materials. These acquisitions ensured a reliable supply of materials to allow mass assembly to continue without interruption. It set the style for later development of mass-produced products such as home appliances.

An important effect of mass assembly was the change in the type of labor needed. When automobiles were assembled at a single staging area, a limited number of workers could work simultaneously at each site. Each performed several tasks and brought multiple skills to the job, including the ability to correct or mend defects in the parts being assembled. As production levels rose, the necessity of accepting laborers of lesser skill levels made greater supervision necessary. Even the one-dimensional system in which a car was moved from station to station still required clusters of semiskilled workers performing multiple tasks.

The two-dimensional system meant that tasks could be separated along the line. The division of labor was limited only by the number of workstations that would fit along a production line of practical length. As each worker had fewer tasks to perform and parts became more uniform, requiring no "fitting" tasks to mount them, necessary skill levels fell. Workers could be trained quickly to perform a limited number of tasks. With this came a concomitant drop in the technical skill of supervisors, until the task of the "gang boss" shrank to mere social and time-keeping functions, allowing supervisors to oversee larger groups. In 1913, 5 percent of Ford Motor Company's labor was salaried (management); by 1921 this had fallen to 2 percent.

The division of labor into simple tasks facilitated training, since new workers needed to be taught to perform only the single tasks for which they were needed. Retraining would be necessary as the mix of tasks changed, but this would then involve seasoned workers, making the training process simpler.

A large economic effect of the new production methods was a decrease in the "residence time," the time that an automobile was in the factory under construction. Before mass assembly methods were introduced, residence time was twenty-one days for the Ford Model T. This fell to four days as the gains in efficiency of the mass assembly system were realized. This meant that the firm had less money lying idle in the form of expensive, partially completed products. This freed the company's capital for factory expansion and other improvements.

The introduction of mass assembly methods forced a change in manufacturing culture in the auto industry. In the heyday of the Model T, many cars were "assembly cars," built under the name of the factory owner from parts, and even major subassemblies such as bodies, purchased from firms not related to the assembler. There were hundreds of brand names. Outside the town where a company's factory was located, an automobile owner was vulnerable unless he or she could repair the car or find a general mechanic to do so. Mass manufacture meant that precise and interchangeable Ford parts could be shipped anywhere. Repair often meant simple replacement.

With the availability of cheap, repairable, rugged automobiles came popular travel away from cities, with their mass transit systems. With that came pressures for better roads that was so intense that the federal govern-

ment was forced to take an active role in their construction and maintenance. To stimulate interest, a private organization, the Lincoln Highway
Association, was formed to plan for and provide an all-weather road from
coast to coast. In 1916, the Road Aid Act was passed by Congress to provide
federal funds to assist the state in improving rural roads. This was followed
in 1921 by a more comprehensive federal highway act.

Bibliography

Abernathy, William, Kim Clark, and Alan Kantrow. *Industrial Renais-
sance*. New York: Basic Books, 1983. A compact treatise on the rise of
industry in the United States, using the automobile industry as an illustration. It studies the economics of the industry from its birth and projects
economic progress based on continued technological improvements.

Bruchey, Stuart. *Enterprise: The Dynamic Economy of a Free People*.
Cambridge, Mass.: Harvard University Press, 1990. Bruchey presents a
history of industrial enterprise from colonial times until the present,
showing the effects on the American economy and culture of domestic
and foreign influences. Contains much demographic and economic data
in tabular form.

Chandler, Alfred. *The Visible Hand*. Cambridge, Mass.: Belknap Press,
1977. A study of the changing role of management in the burgeoning
American manufacturing industry. Contains a concise history of manufacturing methods and projections of future changes in various industries as a consequence of continued changes in technical and managerial
methods.

Crabb, Richard. *Birth of a Giant*. Philadelphia: Chilton, 1969. A history of
the American automobile as it was affected by the talents and personalities of the men who created it. There are anecdotes, some possibly
apocryphal, about the principals as well as illuminating vignettes showing their flaws and foibles. Of interest are many clear photos of early
auto manufacturing and testing.

Flink, James. *The Car Culture*. Cambridge, Mass.: MIT Press, 1975. Flink
presents a complete history of the manufacture of the American automobile, including design, management, financing, and marketing. Of particular interest is a thorough treatment of the effects of large-scale auto
manufacture and widespread ownership upon the American culture.

Hayes, Robert. *Restoring Our Competitive Edge*. New York: Wiley, 1984.
A comprehensive treatment of economic competition in manufacturing
as it arises from production planning, improved processes, and technological innovation. Contains case studies of mass-production facilities
and the effects of various hardware and managerial factors.

Piore, Michael. *The Second Industrial Divide.* New York: Basic Books, 1984. A study of the rise of productivity in America resulting from technological innovation. Selected corporations are studied to illustrate various elements of industrial growth. Mass production is treated separately as affecting large-scale manufacture.

Rae, John. *The American Automobile.* Chicago: University of Chicago Press, 1965. A brief, popularized history of the American automobile from its origins until the 1950's. It focuses strongly on the pioneers in the industry and their interactions.

Wolf, Winfried. *Car Mania: A Critical History of Transport.* Translated by Gus Fagan. Rev. English ed. Chicago: Pluto Press, 1996.

Loring Emery

Cross-References

Nader's *Unsafe at Any Speed* Launches a Consumer Movement (1965); The U.S. Government Reforms Child Product Safety Laws (1970's); American Firms Adopt Japanese Manufacturing Techniques (1980's); Bush Signs the Clean Air Act of 1990 (1990).

THE FEDERAL RESERVE ACT CREATES A U.S. CENTRAL BANK

CATEGORY OF EVENT: Finance
TIME: December 23, 1913
LOCALE: Washington, D.C.

By establishing the Federal Reserve System, the Federal Reserve Act of 1913 provided a central banking arrangement with the potential to improve the functioning of the American economy's financial sector

Principal personages:
CARTER GLASS (1858-1946), the chairman of the House Banking Subcommittee, which formulated the act
HENRY PARKER WILLIS (1874-1937), a banking expert who assisted Glass in drafting the law; secretary of the Federal Reserve Board, 1914-1918
ROBERT LATHAM OWEN (1856-1947), the chairman of the Senate Banking Committee; coauthor of the Federal Reserve Act
PAUL MORITZ WARBURG (1868-1932), a partner in the investment bank of Kuhn, Loeb & Company; a member of the Federal Reserve Board, 1914-1918

Summary of Event
In the wake of the severe financial panic of 1907, the Aldrich-Vreeland Act of May 30, 1908, authorized emergency currency issues and established a National Monetary Commission to study the issue of permanent reform. The commission supported the Aldrich bill of 1911, calling for a banker-controlled single central bank with branches, but public opinion weighed against it. Although the Aldrich bill was not passed, it outlined the

81

basis for the Federal Reserve Act, enacted into law on December 13, 1913. The act represented the culmination of two decades of debate on how to remedy deficiencies in the American banking system.

The preamble to the 1913 law enumerates its goals: to provide for the establishment of Federal Reserve Banks, to supply currency in amounts appropriate to the needs of the economy, to afford means of rediscounting commercial paper, and to establish more effective supervision of banking in the United States. The preamble did not mention discretionary central bank intervention intended to stabilize the economy countercyclically, but this type of intervention became commonplace. The twelve branches of the central bank were expected to operate fairly automatically. Changes in gold reserves would lead to corresponding movements in currency and credit under the rules of the international gold standard then in effect. Federal Reserve bank note and deposit liabilities would automatically expand and contract according to the volume of U.S. business activity.

Under the law, banks that were members of the Federal Reserve System would own the Federal Reserve Banks, as they would be required to purchase shares. The member banks would elect six of the nine directors of the system. The Federal Reserve Board, appointed by the president of the United States, would exercise general supervision of the system and implement policy. President Woodrow Wilson would not agree to putting full control of the system in the hands of bankers. Instead, the Federal Advisory Council would make recommendations regarding the operations of the Federal Reserve Board and the Federal Reserve Banks. The council was to be composed of twelve members, with the board of directors of each Federal Reserve Bank electing one member. All national banks, numbering about seventy-five hundred at the time, were required to join the system. Some national banks converted to state charters to avoid joining the system. State-chartered banks were permitted to join, but were not required to do so. At first, very few chose to join, but amendments to the Federal Reserve Act in 1916 made membership more attractive. In response to the amendments and to President Wilson's appeal to join the system out of patriotism, about nine hundred of the nineteen thousand state-chartered banks joined by the end of 1918.4

Carter Glass, chairman of the House Banking Subcommittee and a key sponsor of the act, never tired of insisting that the Federal Reserve System was not a central bank. The decentralized nature of the system, with twelve separate banks, came as a response to a deep-rooted suspicion of concentrated financial power and hostility to Wall Street financial interests. Central banking had been tried twice before in the United States with mixed success. The Federal Reserve Banks were expected to loosely supervise, rather than strictly control, the monetary system of the United States.

The boundaries of the twelve Federal Reserve Bank districts reflected convenience and how business was conducted at the time. District boundaries split twelve states. Most of Pennsylvania, for example, was in the third district, headquartered in Philadelphia, but the western counties were in the Cleveland district. The Boston district comprised all six New England states, except for Fairfield County, Connecticut, which was part of the New York City district.

The system as a whole was under the supervision of the seven-member Federal Reserve Board, appointed by the president. It included the secretary of the treasury and the comptroller of the currency as *ex officio* members. Two of the five other members were to have experience in finance. That requirement was eliminated in 1922, when the number of freely appointed members was increased to six, so that an "agriculturalist" could be added to the board.

Charles S. Hamlin, a Boston lawyer, was the first governor, or head, of the Federal Reserve Board. Frederic Delano, a Chicago railway executive, was the first vice governor. The other appointed members were Paul Moritz Warburg, a partner in the investment banking firm of Kuhn, Loeb & Company; W. P. G. Harding, president of the First National Bank of Birmingham, Alabama; and Adolph C. Miller, professor of economics at the University of California. Miller and Hamlin remained on the board until it was reorganized in 1936.

The amount of national bank notes issued previously had depended on the profitability of national bank ownership of government securities. By 1865, a congressional resolution had recognized the need for a paper currency that could change in its amount circulated according to the requirements of legitimate business. The Federal Reserve Act represented a shift from a bond-based to an asset-based currency reflecting the volume of commercial transactions. The amount of currency would expand and contract automatically to meet the needs of trade. To satisfy the followers of William Jennings Bryan, who opposed a strict gold standard, Federal Reserve notes were made obligations of the U.S. Treasury, though they were not given the status of legal tender until 1933. To assure an appropriate volume of currency for each district, each Federal Reserve Bank was responsible for issuing its own notes.

Banks that were members of the Federal Reserve System had the right to "rediscount" loans that they had issued, using them in effect as collateral against loans from the Federal Reserve Bank in their district. To simplify this procedure, a 1916 amendment to the Federal Reserve Act permitted advances to member banks secured by this type of collateral or by U.S. government securities. The district reserve banks established the interest rate charged for discounts and advances "with a view of accommodating commerce and business," according to the words of the law. In the early years of the system, discount rates varied among the districts, with the rate structure adapting to local conditions. After 1917, the rates tended to uniformity.

Loans that were eligible to be discounted, or used as security for loans from the Federal Reserve Banks, were defined elaborately in the law. That definition relied heavily on the commercial loan theory, also known as the real bills doctrine. Loans eligible for discounting were to be self-liquidating; that is, they were not to be speculative but instead were to finance carrying, production, or marketing costs for products that already had been contracted for sale. In order to encourage development of a market in bankers' acceptances, a source of credit to finance international transactions, the Federal Reserve System stood ready to buy them at favorable rates.

Member banks were required to keep reserves against withdrawals by depositors as a safety measure. Mandatory reserves of member banks were lower than previously required of national banks and could be kept as vault cash or deposits at a Federal Reserve Bank. The reduction in required reserves was deemed appropriate in view of the centralization of reserves within the Federal Reserve System and the availability of rediscounting at the Federal Reserve Banks, through which member banks could get cash to meet withdrawals. The 1913 law also distinguished between demand deposits and time (including savings) deposits, requiring a much lower percentage of the latter to be set aside as reserves. Under a June, 1917, amendment, all required reserves had to be in the form of deposits at a Federal Reserve Bank. Vault cash no longer counted, but the percentages of deposits that had to be held as reserves declined dramatically. Later, vault cash would again be counted against the reserve requirement.

Impact of Event

With the opening in November, 1914, of check-clearing facilities of the twelve Federal Reserve Banks came significant improvements in the payments mechanism. Circuitous, time-consuming arrangements to collect payment on out-of-town checks were no longer needed. Member banks were required to pay the face value of checks drawn against them when those checks were presented for collection at a Federal Reserve Bank. The Federal Reserve System had a goal of making payment of checks at face value, or "par," universal. That goal was abandoned under pressure from Congress after the Supreme Court declared in 1923 that state laws protecting nonpar payments were constitutional. By the end of 1928, almost four thousand state banks that were not members of the Federal Reserve System chose to be "nonpar banks." Ineligible because of this choice to clear checks through the Federal Reserve System, these banks turned to large "correspondent" banks in financial centers to collect out-of-town checks and for other services. Many banks eligible for clearing services through the Federal Reserve System also found it more convenient to use correspondent banks. Member banks, in addition to keeping legal reserves with their local Federal Reserve Bank, continued to keep active balances with correspondent banks. Private banks thus did not abandon their prior relationships to take full advantage of what the Federal Reserve System had to offer.

The federal government itself made little use of the Federal Reserve Banks before World War I. The Treasury continued to use national banks as depositories, but beginning in 1916 it increasingly did business through the Federal Reserve Banks. The role of the Federal Reserve System as fiscal agent of the government was enhanced when subtreasuries, an arrangement in effect since 1846, were discontinued in 1921.

An amendment to the Federal Reserve Act in September, 1916, allowed advances by Federal Reserve Banks to member banks to be secured by the member banks' holdings of U.S. government securities. At the time, the federal debt was declining, and most of it served to secure national bank notes. That situation changed radically within a few months as the United States entered World War I. The U.S. Treasury used the Federal Reserve System to finance a swelling national debt on easy terms. Reserve Banks made loans at preferential rates to member banks that in turn made loans to purchasers of war bonds. The Federal Reserve did not regain its freedom to raise the rates it charged on loans to member banks (the discount rate) until November, 1919, after installment payments on the Victory Loan of April, 1919, had been completed.

In the face of a severe postwar recession in 1920-1921, the discount rate was not reduced until May, 1921, a year after the index of wholesale prices had peaked. The Federal Reserve Act allowed for open market operations (purchases and sales of government securities by the Federal Reserve System) as a device to make the discount rate effective and to control interest rates in the open market. In 1922, the Federal Reserve System bought $400 million in securities, partly as a means of obtaining earnings so that it could pay the dividends to member banks that were required by law. In 1923, open market operations began to be used as a major instrument to control credit conditions.

During the economic downturn between May, 1923, and July, 1924, the Federal Reserve System cut the discount rate and the Open Market Committee authorized purchases of government securities as a means of providing banks with reserves that they could then lend out. Similar measures were taken in response to the more mild recession between October, 1926, and November, 1927.

The Federal Reserve Banks were expected to act as a "lender of last resort" to member banks, providing loans to financially sound member banks that could not get loans elsewhere. This provision was expected to prevent financial panics, as depositors did not have to worry about banks running short of cash to meet withdrawals as long as those banks were financially sound. The banks could simply discount some of their loans at the local Federal Reserve Bank if they temporarily came up short of cash.

The stock market boom of the late 1920's led Federal Reserve System officials to worry about speculation in the market absorbing excessive amounts of credit. They therefore increased the discount rate in January, 1928, in an attempt to slow speculative lending. They reversed direction and eased credit slightly when stock prices collapsed in the fall of 1929. The system largely stood by, however, as the means of payment (currency plus demand deposits) declined by about one-fourth between 1929 and 1933 and as the American banking system collapsed in the early 1930's. When banks failed, many depositors lost most or all of their money.

Bank runs and losses inflicted on small depositors by bank failures prompted passage of the Banking Act of 1933, which established the Federal Deposit Insurance Corporation (FDIC). Through the FDIC, deposits were insured against bank failure. In 1935, Congress reorganized and significantly strengthened the Federal Reserve System, giving it more centralized control over the American banking system in the hope that greater control could be used to avoid a recurrence of the disaster of the early 1930's.

Bibliography

Beckhart, Benjamin Haggott. *Federal Reserve System.* New York: American Institute of Banking, 1972. A clearly written survey of the structure, functions, and history of domestic and international policies of the Federal Reserve System since its founding.

Board of Governors of the Federal Reserve System. *The Federal Reserve System: Purposes and Functions.* 7th ed. Author, 1984. An official exposition for the general public. Periodically updated.

Burgess, Warren Randolph. *The Reserve Banks and the Money Market.* Rev. ed. New York: Harper & Brothers, 1936. Overview featuring the impact of monetary policy actions on financial markets, written by an expert who was with the Federal Reserve Bank of New York from 1920 to 1938.

Goldenweiser, Emanuel Alexander. *American Monetary Policy*. New York: McGraw-Hill, 1951. A presentation in straightforward prose by an economist who was director of research and statistics for the Federal Reserve Board from 1926 to 1945.

Kemmerer, Edwin Walter. *The ABC of the Federal Reserve System*. 12th ed. New York: Harper, 1950. A posthumous edition. The core of this lucid, brief exposition was first published in 1918.

Laughlin, James Laurence. *The Federal Reserve Act: Its Origins and Problems*. New York: Macmillan, 1933. A comprehensive investigation presenting a distinctive position in the scholarly controversies surrounding the subject.

Moore, Carl H. *The Federal Reserve System: A History of the First Seventy-five Years*. Jefferson, N. C.: McFarland, 1990. Concise, clear, and interestingly written by an economist associated for thirty-two years with the Federal Reserve Bank of Dallas.

Toma, Mark. *Competition and Monopoly in the Federal Reserve System, 1914-1951: A Microeconomics Approach to Monetary History*. New York: Cambridge University Press, 1997.

Warburg, Paul Moritz. *The Federal Reserve System: Its Origin and Growth*. 2 vols. New York: Macmillan, 1930. A collection of writings by the German-born banker who labored indefatigably for central bank reform and sound practice.

West, Robert Craig. *Banking Reform and the Federal Reserve, 1863-1923*. Ithaca, N.Y.: Cornell University Press, 1977. A scholarly monograph on the intellectual background to the Federal Reserve Act.

Willis, Henry Parker. *The Federal Reserve System*. New York: Ronald Press, 1923. An insider's in-depth view. Willis helped draft the Federal Reserve Act.

Benjamin J. Klebaner

Cross-References

The U.S. Stock Market Crashes on Black Tuesday (1929); The Banking Act of 1933 Reorganizes the American Banking System (1933); The Banking Act of 1935 Centralizes U.S. Monetary Control (1935); Congress Deregulates Banks and Savings and Loans (1980-1982); Bush Responds to the Savings and Loan Crisis (1989).

THE PANAMA CANAL OPENS

CATEGORY OF EVENT: Transportation
TIME: August 15, 1914
LOCALE: Panama

*The completion and opening of the Panama Canal significantly low-
ered shipping costs and improved transit time*

Principal personages:
ULYSSES S. GRANT (1822-1885), the president of the United States,
    1869-1877; initiated exploration in Panama
GEORGE WASHINGTON GOETHALS (1858-1928), the director of the Pan-
    ama Canal project
FERDINAND DE LESSEPS (1805-1894), a French pioneer of the canal
    project
THEODORE ROOSEVELT (1858-1919), the president of the United States,
    1901-1909

Summary of Event

Early maps were based as much on belief as on facts. When Christopher
Columbus searched for a new route to the Orient, he happened to land first
in the West Indies. The people there told him stories about a strait through
which one might sail westward into waters that led directly to the land he
sought. He believed in these stories and sought that strait, in the process
coming closer and closer to the North American continent. His belief in the
secret strait is reflected in a map inspired by him, though not published until
two years after his death. The map has no isthmus of Panama, showing in
its place a strait permitting direct passage from Europe to India.

Vasco Nunez de Balboa followed Columbus with exploration of the
isthmus, ultimately discovering the Pacific Ocean. Even at that time, the
legend of the strait persisted. Native people told Balboa that a newly
discovered isthmus provided a connection between the oceans. Balboa also
believed the story. Many explorers and geographers accepted the existence

of this unseen strait, leading to exploration up and down the coast. Explorers never found the mysterious strait, but their work spawned the idea of digging a waterway to connect the two oceans. The Panama Canal therefore is not entirely a project of the nineteenth and twentieth centuries. Its conception falls back to a much earlier time, in particular to a proposal given to Charles V of Spain in 1523. It was, in fact, Hernán Cortés, the Spanish conqueror of Mexico, who first proposed constructing this great waterway. When Cortés failed to find the legendary strait, he proposed constructing an artificial waterway.

The creation of the Panama Canal thus represents a historical legacy as well as an unprecedented feat of engineering and design. It became a major transportation link, facilitating direct trade and changing the face of the political and economic world. It has critical historic dimensions, as it represented the largest, most costly single effort attempted in modern times. The canal's construction held much of the world's attention over a span of forty years, affecting the lives of tens of thousands of people at almost every level of society and of many races and nationalities. The nations involved were much affected by the process. The Republic of Panama was born; Colombia lost its prize possession, the Isthmus of Panama; and Nicaragua was left to wait for some future chance to participate in such a venture.

The Panama Canal marked significant advances in engineering, in government planning, and in labor relations. Planning focused on the construction of an enduring wonder, a canal of unprecedented length and breadth. Its construction and operation would require considerable government planning and direction as well as an unheralded organization of large numbers of laborers. The canal was born of the conviction that sea power would become the political and economic base for the future. It was judged to be the greatest enterprise of the Victorian era and the first significant demonstration of American power at the dawn of the new century. Its completion in 1914 marked the conclusion of a dream as old as the voyages of Columbus.

The cost of the canal was enormous. Dollar expenditures totaled $352 million, including $10 million paid to Panama for land rights and $40 million paid to the French company involved in the original canal project. The cost was more than four times that of the Suez Canal and much higher than the cost of anything previously built by the United States government. Except for wars, the only remotely comparable federal expenditures up to the year 1914 had been for acquisition of new territories. The price for all acquisitions as of that date—the Louisiana Territory, Florida, California, New Mexico, and other western lands acquired from Mexico, Alaska, and the Philippines—was $75 million, or only about one-fifth of the amount

President Theodore Roosevelt (center) during an inspection tour of canal work in 1906.
(Library of Congress)

spent on the canal. French companies earlier had been involved in the canal project, beginning in 1880. Taken together, French and American expenditures came to almost $639 million.

The canal also involved nonmonetary costs. According to hospital records, more than 5,600 lives were lost to disease and accidents during the canal's construction. Approximately 4,000 deaths were those of black workers, with only 350 white Americans dying in the process. If one includes earlier French efforts, the total loss of human lives may have been as high as 25,000.

Unlike most government projects, the canal cost less in dollars than was projected. The final price was $25 million below what had been estimated in 1907, despite a change in the width of the canal and the building of fortifications. Had these additional expenses been calculated into original budgets, Congress might not have approved the project. The Spooner Act of 1902 approved a $40 million payment to the French company involved in the original canal project, but Colombia, which controlled Panama, stood in the way of further construction. Panama declared its independence from Colombia on November 3, 1903. Construction of the canal by the U.S. team began in 1904.

Even though it was completed at a cost below that estimated at mid-project, the canal was opened six months ahead of schedule. The final product came amazingly close to precise engineering targets as to location, structure, and operation. There were no signs of graft, kickbacks, payroll padding, or other corruption in the process. Successful completion of such a vast project is noteworthy, since most previous and subsequent projects had shortcomings in the dimensions mentioned above. Much of the project's success resulted from the management and expertise of the director of the project. George Washington Goethals exhibited considerable insight in the design of the project, considerable influence in coordinating the various constituencies affected by and involved in the project, and unusual management control techniques used to monitor expenditures and progress. No excessive profits were registered by the thousands of firms involved with a project under the auspices of the Interstate Commerce Commission.

Impact of Event

Much of the history of the world is based on the quest for improved transportation, particularly the discovery of and building of all-water routes connecting bodies of water. With the completion of the canal came direct and lower-cost transportation from the Atlantic Ocean to the Pacific Ocean. Savings came in terms of both dollar outlays and time. The cost savings that resulted from the canal encouraged businesspeople to explore new markets that now appeared to be profitable.

World War I kept the traffic flow through the canal low, with only four or five ships passing through per day, on average. It was not until July, 1919, that the vision of President Theodore Roosevelt came true by virtue of the transit of an American armada of thirty-three ships through the canal. The first thirty made it through in only two days. This was an astounding feat given the rigors of the previous route around the tip of South America.

About ten years after it opened, the canal was handling more than five thousand ships a year, traffic approximately equal to that of the Suez Canal. Even then, large British and U.S. carriers squeezed through the locks with only feet to spare. By the late 1930's, annual traffic exceeded seven thousand ships. Following World War II, that figure more than doubled. Channel lighting was installed in 1966, allowing nighttime transit, and ships were going through the canal at the rate of more than one an hour, twenty-four hours a day, every day of the year. Many of them were giant container and bulk carriers of a size never imagined when the canal was designed and built. The 950-foot *Tokyo Bay* was the largest container ship in the world at the time it made its first Panama Canal transit in 1972. By the 1970's, traffic reached fifteen thousand ships a year, with annual tonnage well beyond 100 million tons, twenty times that of 1915. Clearly, shippers were taking advantage of the improvement in transport speed made possible by the canal. The canal made feasible the opening of Far Eastern markets to the East Coast of the United States. It can be argued that the facilitation of trade allowed by the canal markedly altered the configuration of world industrial patterns.

The *Queen Mary*, launched in 1934, was the first ship too large for the locks. Many others followed, even though the builders realized at the time of construction that ships of more than 1,000 feet in length and beams of 150 feet could not pass through the canal. Proposals to find an alternate route or to build a larger canal were considered. Attention was once again given to Nicaragua and a route through that nation. Earlier proposals for an isthmus canal had considered Nicaragua.

Tolls collected in 1915 reached only $4 million. In 1970, they exceeded $100 million, even though rates remained unchanged. In 1973, the Panama Canal Company recorded its first loss, largely as a result of mounting costs of operation. In 1974, tolls were raised for the first time, from $0.90 per cargo ton to $1.08. The Queen Elizabeth II locked through the canal in 1975 and paid a record toll of $42,077.88. The average toll per ship was approximately $10,000, approximately one-tenth of the cost of sailing around Cape Horn as an alternate direct all-water route. The lowest toll on record was paid by Richard Halliburton, a world traveler who in the 1920's swam the length of the canal in installments. Although he was not the first to swim the canal, he was the first to persuade authorities to allow him through the locks.

In design matters, some changes were made in the canal over time. Parts were widened by up to 500 feet; a storage dam was built across the Chagres; and the original towing locomotive was retired and replaced by more powerful models. The fundamental characteristics of the canal remained unchanged. Only two issues of design received significant criticisms. It has been argued that the two sets of locks should have been replaced by a single unit at Miraflores, and Goethals seemed to have underestimated the impact of slides. The canal has been influenced by slides on many occasions. In 1914, a slide at East Culebra caused blockage of the entire channel. Slides have posed a continuing problem.

As ships grew in size, the canal handled a lower proportion of the world's sea traffic. By provisions of the 1977 Panama Canal Treaty, the canal itself was scheduled to be turned over to the Panamanian government. The Canal Zone was abolished, and all U.S. troops were to be removed before December 31, 1999, when the Panamanian government took over the canal.

The all-water passage across Panama is a supreme achievement. It completed a dream held through hundreds of years. Its impact has been enhanced East-West trade, shorter times in transit, a dedication to technological improvement in transportation, and a unification of political and economic interests in the Eastern and Western worlds.

Bibliography

Brands, H. W. *T. R.: The Last Romantic.* New York: Basic Books, 1997. Iconoclastic biography of Theodore Roosevelt.

Gause, Frank Ales, and Charles Carl Carr. *The Story of Panama.* 1912 Reprint. New York: Arno Press, 1970. A comprehensive analysis of the development of the Panama Canal, drawn from materials prepared at the time.

Harmon, George M., ed. *Transportation: The Nation's Lifelines.* Rev. ed. Washington, D.C.: Industrial College of the Armed Forces, 1968. Some general comments about the developing role of the transportation infrastructure, including the Panama Canal.

Kemble, John H. *The Panama Route: 1848-1869.* Berkeley: University of California Press, 1943. Covers the entirety of the construction and operation process.

McCullough, David. *The Path Between the Seas.* New York: Simon & Schuster, 1977. A readable and comprehensive coverage of the building of the canal, including many interesting statistics and helpful perspectives.

Marlowe, John. *The World Ditch.* New York: Macmillan, 1964. A readable coverage of the canal and its impacts.

Mellander, Gustavo A., and Nelly Maldonado Mellander. *Charles Edward Magoon: The Panama Years.* Río Piedras, P.R.: Editorial Plaza Mayor, 1999. Biography of an early governor of the Panama Canal Zone.

Theodore O. Wallin

Cross-References

The General Agreement on Tariffs and Trade Is Signed (1947); The United States Suffers Its First Trade Deficit Since 1888 (1971); The Alaskan Oil Pipeline Opens (1977); The North American Free Trade Agreement Goes into Effect (1994).

THE FEDERAL TRADE COMMISSION IS ORGANIZED

CATEGORY OF EVENT: Government and business
TIME: September 26, 1914
LOCALE: Washington, D.C.

Creation of the Federal Trade Commission (FTC) empowered an agency of the federal government to protect competition and proactively deter potential monopolies

Principal personages:
THEODORE ROOSEVELT (1858-1919), the president of the United States, 1901-1909
WOODROW WILSON (1856-1924), the president of the United States, 1913-1921
LOUIS D. BRANDEIS (1856-1941), an economic adviser to President Wilson
GEORGE RUBLEE (1868-1957), an attorney who assisted in drafting the FTC bill

Summary of Event

The establishment of the Federal Trade Commission (FTC) in 1914 signaled a dramatic change in the relationship between government and business. No longer would the courts and the executive branch be the only interpreters of antitrust legislation; instead, the independent regulatory commission was empowered to define "unfair competition" and was also granted the requisite discretionary authority to apply the standard of unfairness.

Although enacted in 1914, the Federal Trade Commission Act can trace

94

its roots to the late nineteenth century. It was the exercise of corporate economic power in that period by men such as John D. Rockefeller, J. P. Morgan, and Cornelius Vanderbilt that seemed to galvanize an antibusiness sentiment among small business owners, labor unions, and the middle class. These groups would become the core of the Progressive movement.

The turn of the century witnessed the beginning of the Progressive Era, characterized by the use of social, economic, and political reform movements aimed at creating a society organized for collective action in the public interest. In 1901, Theodore Roosevelt advocated the supremacy of the "public interest" over business when he assumed the presidency. In 1903, the newly created Department of Commerce contained a Bureau of Corporations with a function of investigating corporate practices and publicizing unethical competitive methods of businesses. A series of informal agreements evolved between big business and the bureau, under which firms granted the government access to their records and the bureau approved mergers when it found them to be in the public interest.

During the Progressive Era, there developed a clear sense of obligations of business to society. The role of the state started to evolve from laissez-faire to the belief that it had a moral obligation to provide for the general welfare. It was during the first administration of Woodrow Wilson that the Bureau of Corporations was transformed into the FTC.

Wilson and the Democrats swept the country on election day in November of 1912. A key component of the winning party platform was a program Wilson called the New Freedom, aimed at the destruction and prevention of industrial and financial monopoly. Wilson proposed to accomplish this goal by reducing tariffs, reforming the banking and currency systems, and strengthening the Sherman Antitrust Act. A tariff reduction bill was quickly passed, and the Federal Reserve System was created in 1913. The last major item on the New Freedom agenda was the creation of legislation to strengthen the Sherman Act.

The Sherman Act of 1890 to this point was the sole federal antitrust legislation. It did not enumerate specific monopolistic behaviors, instead declaring as illegal any contracts, combinations, and conspiracies in restraint of trade. The act's vagueness ultimately left determination of the meaning of its prohibitions to the courts. The attorneys general of the 1890's were reluctant to exercise their discretionary authority to initiate prosecutions under the act's provisions. The act was further weakened by the Supreme Court's promulgation of the "rule of reason" in the Standard Oil and American Tobacco cases of 1911. The Court held that only "unreasonable" restraints of trade were illegal.

The first response in an attempt to strengthen the Sherman Act was the

Clayton bill. Drafted by Representative Henry Clayton, it attempted to overcome the vagueness of the Sherman Act and the rule of reason by enumerating specific illegal business practices. Prohibited acts included discriminatory pricing, tie-in selling, exclusive dealing, and interlocking directorates. These acts were deemed illegal per se, regardless of their reasonableness. The political compromises necessary to obtain passage of the bill led to an act with provisions that were easily circumvented. The act was signed into law three weeks after the Federal Trade Commission Act, on October 15, 1914. President Wilson described the Clayton Act as "so weak you cannot tell it from water." A major cause of concern was that the primary responsibility for enforcement remained with the Department of Justice and the judicial system.

Originally, neither Wilson nor his primary economic adviser, Louis D. Brandeis, supported the concept of a strong trade commission. Wilson at first proposed the creation of an agency that would moderate but not unduly restrict business. In keeping with this philosophy, the administration supported a bill introduced by Representative James Covington that envisioned a commission that would secure and publish information, conduct investigations as requested by Congress, and support methods of improving business practices and antitrust enforcement.

This proposal submitted to Congress, to create an advisory commission, was transformed into an act creating a powerful commission with broad regulatory powers. This metamorphosis can be attributed to the inability to pass a strong version of the Clayton Act and the pragmatic difficulty of specifying all unlawful trade practices. Faced with these difficulties, Wilson, in consultation with congressional leaders, decided on a new strategy that would abandon a legislative solution for an administrative one. The new strategy was greatly influenced by George Rublee, a former member of the Progressive Party called in by Wilson to assist in the drafting of antitrust legislation when Brandeis was occupied by an Interstate Commerce Commission rate case. Rublee's intervention and the deadlock over the Clayton bill were primary factors in the creation of a regulatory agency as the primary method of restraining the activities of business. The FTC Act was signed into law on September 26, 1914.

The newly created commission had two major duties: to see that unfair methods of completion were prevented and to keep the public and Congress informed as to developments within an industry that threatened competition. This mission would be carried out by the utilization of the agency's three major powers: the cease and desist order, the stipulation, and the trade practice conference. The FTC was structured as an independent regulatory commission with five members (no more than three from the same political party) serving staggered seven-year terms, appointed by the president and confirmed by the Senate. Creating a bipartisan, independent commission with broad discretionary authority was viewed as a radical step in the government's attempts to control and regulate business. The FTC was to become perhaps the most controversial of the independent regulatory commissions, and its broad discretionary powers the primary source of the controversy.

Impact of Event

In assessing the impact of the FTC, it is necessary to analyze both the political and pragmatic consequences associated with its creation. Politically, the FTC represented the institutionalization of the widespread public opinion that competition was beneficial and an integral part of the American economy. It further inexorably altered the relationship between the federal government and the private sector. The commission represented a continuing repudiation of the laissez-faire doctrine, which commenced with the creation of the Interstate Commerce Commission in 1887.

The FTC was a permanent administrative apparatus, granted broad statutory powers, discretionary authority, and a jurisdiction not limited to a specific industry. These delegations of authority created an agency that could attack economic and societal problems without reliance on the judicial or executive branches of government to initiate antitrust actions. As an independent regulatory commission, the FTC combined the functions of policy-making, administration, and adjudication. The agency set precedents for the evolution of the administrative state in America. Starting in the late nineteenth century and continuing into the 1970's, the federal government became increasingly involved in regulating industries and activities.

The creation of the FTC was surrounded by great controversy, and the commission is one of the most studied of federal agencies. The major source of the controversy is the FTC's broad legislative delegation of authority. Section 5 of the FTC Act defines the commission's primary reponsibilities as identifying and preventing "unfair methods of competition" by issuing enforceable cease-and-desist orders. Section 6 outlines eight additional powers: to investigate corporations, to request reports from corporations, to investigate compliance with antitrust decrees, to conduct investigations for the president or Congress, to recommend business adjustments to comply with law, to make public the information obtained, to classify corporations, and to investigate conditions in foreign countries that affect trade. The Wheeler-Lea Act (1938) amended the FTC Act to empower the agency to protect the consumer as well as to promote competition. A 1974 amendment expanded the commission's jurisdiction from "methods, acts, practices in commerce" to " methods, acts, practices affecting commerce."

The discretionary authority granted the FTC proved to be a double-edged sword. Discretion theoretically allowed action in numerous areas with various tools, but it also allowed the agency to choose to take no action. It is the perceived failure of the FTC to exercise its discretion in the form of action that has been the source of much criticism.

The commission has been accused of misallocating its resources toward minor issues and failing to take action on substantial matters. Critics argue that the cases investigated involved minor matters with only minimal impact on the economy or the public interest. The agency's broad mandate has contributed to its inability to articulate definite goals, objectives, and standards of performance. The absence of direction left the commission rudderless in a complex environment.

The FTC has also been accused of failing to detect violations, since its primary means of detecting deceptive practices is to wait for a business-person to inform on practices of competitors. The failure to establish priorities led to the commission handling too many cases, the vast majority having little impact on the public interest. The FTC has been accused of failing to exercise enforcement powers, all too often relying on voluntary correction of behavior. The agency was also accused of allowing its power to dissipate by allowing unreasonable time lapses from investigation to final decision. During the period of investigation, the FTC has no punitive power to discourage illegal behavior, and many firms continued their behavior until actual sanctions were imminent. Delay also undermines a major goal of the FTC, that of preventing unfair practices. The delay in starting agency proceedings is primarily a function of poor staff work, raising the issue of the efficacy of FTC personnel. Critics question the ability of staff and cite the high turnover rate among FTC personnel.

The FTC was born of political compromise, with no consensus as to the agency's mission, and as such it has been exposed to shifting political winds. The FTC was created as an independent, bipartisan regulatory commission, but too often the FTC employs or promotes the politically well connected and allocates resources to marginal issues solely because of requests by members of Congress.

The FTC is not without its advocates, who are as vigorous as its critics. Criticisms of personnel and actions, they argue, should have produced significant reform if valid. Defenders of the FTC counter that incompetence is asserted but not proven. Allegations that the absence of precise standards has led the commission to concentrate on smaller firms is rebutted by citing incidents in which the commission has been both innovative and courageous. Proponents of the FTC further state that its activities are severely hampered by the lack of financial resources in comparison to the vast array of tasks allocated to the FTC. The speed at which the commission resolves cases is defended by reminding critics that the FTC is bound by procedures of due process.

In the final analysis, the evaluation of the impact of the FTC on the American economy, society, and public interest is probably a function of one's expectations of the commission and perceptions of the optimal level of governmental involvement in the private sector. FTC advocates demand greater involvement in reaction to evils of business, while critics view any action as tampering with the market system.

Bibliography

Blackford, Mansel G., and Austin K. Kerr. *Business Enterprise in American History*. 2d ed. Boston: Houghton Mifflin, 1990. Provides a concise coverage of the history of the American business firm and the evolution of government-business relations, from colonial times to the present.

Clements, Kendrick A. *The Presidency of Woodrow Wilson*. Lawrence: University Press of Kansas, 1992. Provides a brief coverage of the Wilson presidency. Valuable for highlighting major issues in a direct and concise manner. The coverage of major domestic issues (chapter 3) is especially pertinent.

Cox, Edward, Robert C. Fellmeth, and John E. Schulz. *The Nader Report on the Federal Trade Commission*. New York: Richard W. Baron, 1969. Represents a scathing criticism of the Federal Trade Commission's operations, highlighting its failures, politicization, and attempts to mask inefficiency.

Green, Mark J. *The Closed Enterprise System*. New York: Grossman Press, 1972. Analyzes the impact of the FTC on American antitrust policy.

Link, Arthur. *Woodrow Wilson and the Progressive Era, 1910-1917*. New York: Harper, 1954. Addresses the political and diplomatic history of the United States from the disruption of the Republican Party in 1910 to the entrance of the United States into World War I. Provides excellent coverage of America's transitionary reform period and the increasing role of government in society.

Stid, Daniel D. *The President as Statesman: Woodrow Wilson and the Constitution*. Lawrence: University of Kansas Press, 1998.

Stone, Alan. *Economic Regulation and the Public Interest*. Ithaca, N.Y.: Cornell University Press, 1977. Presents an analysis of the Federal Trade Commission in theory and practice, and provides an objective analysis of the agency's strengths and weaknesses.

Wilson, James Q., ed. *The Politics of Regulation*. New York: Basic Books, 1980. Wilson and other contributors analyze the politics of the major regulatory agencies. Of special interest is Robert A. Katzmann's chapter on the FTC, which presents an unconventional explanation of the agency's political behavior.

Eugene Garaventa

Cross-References

Champion v. Ames Upholds Federal Powers to Regulate Commerce (1903); Congress Passes the Clayton Antitrust Act (1914); The Celler-Kefauver Act Amends Antitrust Legislation (1950); Carter Signs the Airline Deregulation Act (1978); Congress Deregulates Banks and Savings and Loans (1980-82); AT&T Agrees to Be Broken Up as Part of an Antitrust Settlement (1982).

CONGRESS PASSES THE CLAYTON ANTITRUST ACT

CATEGORIES OF EVENT: Monopolies and cartels; government and business
TIME: October 15, 1914
LOCALE: Washington, D.C.

With the passage of the Clayton Antitrust Act in 1914, the federal government further codified the prohibitions against unlawful restraints of trade and monopolies

Principal personages:
WOODROW WILSON (1856-1924), the president of the United States, 1913-1921
LOUIS D. BRANDEIS (1856-1941), a well-known public advocate who influenced Wilson's antitrust policy
HENRY D. CLAYTON (1857-1929), the U.S. representative from Alabama who proposed the Clayton antitrust bill
THEODORE ROOSEVELT (1858-1919), the president of the United States, 1901-1909, and presidential candidate in 1912
ARSÈNE PUJO (1861-1939), a U.S. representative from Louisiana who chaired the House subcommittee on the "Money Trust"

Summary of Event

On October 15, 1914, Congress passed and President Woodrow Wilson signed the Clayton Antitrust Act (H.R. 15657). This law was designed to strengthen the Sherman Antitrust Act of 1890 by fully codifying specific illegal antitrust activities. The Clayton Act forbade a corporation from purchasing stock in a competitive firm, outlawed contracts based on the condition that the purchaser would do no business with the seller's competitors, and made interlocking stockholdings and directorates illegal. It also contained provisions designed to make corporate officers personally responsible for antitrust violations. The Clayton Act also declared that labor unions were not conspiracies in restraint of trade, thus exempting them from provisions of the bill. To carry out and enforce the Clayton Act and the Sherman Act, Congress created the Federal Trade Commission in a related measure.

For more than a decade after its passage, the Sherman Antitrust Act of 1890 had very little effect upon corporations in the United States. President Theodore Roosevelt, however, pushed enforcement of the Sherman Act. In 1902, the Roosevelt Administration brought suit against the giants of the railroad industry and the "Beef Trust." The Supreme Court ordered dissolution of the Morgan-Hill-Harriman railroad holding company in the Northern Securities case (1904); in the case of *Swift & Company v. United States* (1905), the Supreme Court enjoined the "Beef Trust" from engaging in collusive price-fixing activities. In 1906 and 1907, Roosevelt had the Justice Department bring suit against the American Tobacco Company, the E.I. Du Pont Chemical Corporation, the New Haven Railroad, and the Standard Oil Company. The Supreme Court ordered the dissolution of the American Tobacco (1910) and Standard Oil (1911) companies. Between 1890 and 1905, the Department of Justice brought twenty-four antitrust suits; the Roosevelt Administration brought suit against fifty-four companies. The single administration of William Howard Taft later prosecuted ninety antitrust cases.

Despite this increase in federal antitrust regulation and prosection, the trend toward large corporations grew. The economic concentration that had increased dramatically in the late nineteenth century continued to increase in the early twentieth century. The greatest period of business mergers in the United States occurred during the William McKinley Administration, from 1897 to 1901. Between 1896 and 1900, there were approximately two thousand mergers, with nearly twelve hundred mergers occurring in 1899. Business consolidations took place in phases after that. Between 1904 and 1906, there were roughly four hundred mergers; between 1909 and 1913, there were more than five hundred mergers.

During this time of increasing economic concentration, interlocking directorates increased. An interlocking set of directorates involves individuals serving on the boards of directors of several corporations, particularly within the same industry. By 1909, 1 percent of the industrial firms in the United States produced nearly half of its manufactured goods. By 1913, two financial groups, the investment banking firm of J. P. Morgan and the interests of John D. Rockefeller, held 341 directorships in 112 corporations with an aggregate capitalization of more than $22 billion. These facts and many others were made public by the House of Representatives subcom-

Part of President Woodrow Wilson's appeal to voters was his reputation as a trust buster. (Library of Congress)

mittee on the "Money Trust" in the summer of 1912. Led by Representative Arsène Pujo (D-Louisiana), the hearings heightened existing public fears about economic concentration and intensified the political debate over the trust issue during the presidential campaign of 1912.

Louis Brandeis, a Boston attorney who had developed a reputation for being the "people's lawyer," greatly influenced Democratic presidential candidate Woodrow Wilson's policies on business trusts and government regulation. Brandeis often represented small- and medium-sized manufacturers, retailers, and wholesalers and had developed a philosophy he believed would protect them against the actions of their larger competitors. Brandeis met Wilson in the summer of 1912, and later advised Wilson on matters of banking reform, monopoly and antitrust policy, and a trade commission to enforce existing antitrust laws.

Brandeis also publicized his regulatory philosophy in a series of articles appearing in *Harper's Weekly* entitled "Other People's Money and How the Bankers Use It." Coming in the wake of the Pujo Committee hearings, these articles further directed public attention to the issues of banking reform, antitrust, and economic concentration. Brandeis denounced combinations and trusts of all kinds, including interlocking directorates.

In the 1912 presidential campaign, Theodore Roosevelt, in his attempt to regain the presidency, proposed an increase in governmental agencies to regulate large corporations. Agencies would police certain corporate actions rather than focusing on corporate size. Roosevelt believed that large corporations could be more efficient than smaller businesses and that unlimited competition could be devastating to corporations and ultimately to the economy. His Progressive/Bull Moose Party platform advocated a trade commission to begin a cooperative regulatory approach. Wilson, influenced by Brandeis and to some extent by former Populist/Democratic presidential candidate William Jennings Bryan, opposed bigness in general, both in business and in government. Wilson favored dissolutions such as those of Standard Oil and American Tobacco. He believed that such large corporate monopolies squeezed economic opportunity away from smaller or medium-sized businesses. For much of the 1912 campaign, Wilson failed to propose an antitrust agency or trade commission, as Roosevelt did. Toward the end of the campaign, and certainly once in office, Wilson came to support positions on the issues of antitrust and a trade commission that were closer to those of Roosevelt.

The general public wanted increased regulation of large corporations, but businesses of all sizes wanted a clarification and further codification of the Sherman Antitrust Act. Both small and large businesses wanted a clear line between legality and illegality to be embodied in legislation and enforced by a trade commission that would work with the private sector. What the business community opposed was being subject to the unpredictable policies of the Justice Department and the shifting jurisprudence of the Supreme Court. That court had clouded the already vague standards and definitions of antitrust with its decisions in the Standard Oil and American Tobacco cases. In those cases, the Supreme Court ruled that not every restraint of trade was illegal in terms of the Sherman Act. The Supreme Court had ruled in the Standard Oil case that it would determine whether combinations restrained trade rather than using size alone as a criterion of noncompetitive behavior. Firms would be within the law, through the "rule of reason," no matter how large they were, if they did not engage in "unreasonable" behavior. The main objectives of additional antitrust legislation were thus clear: to obtain statutory specifics on antitrust prohibitions, to make monopolistic price-fixing agreements and price discrimination illegal, and to eliminate interlocking directorates.

After obtaining legislation on tariff and banking reform in 1913, Wilson turned his attention to antitrust in 1914. In his message to Congress of January 20, 1914, Wilson stated that although further antitrust legislation would make a number of activities illegal, the main purpose was to help businesses remain within the bounds of legality. "Nothing hampers business like uncertainty," said Wilson. "The best informed men of the business world condemn the methods and processes and consequences of monopoly as we condemn them." With this presidential support, two days later Representative Henry D. Clayton (D-Alabama) introduced four bills in the House to amend the Sherman Act. Proposed antitrust bills and trade commission bills developed from February through June as the House Judiciary Committee and the Senate Interstate Commerce Committee held hearings.

Although businesses wanted antitrust clarification, some provisions of the developing Clayton bill alarmed smaller and "peripheral" businesses, which often engaged in trade or associational activities and price agreements initially prohibited by the bill. Businesses such as merchants, grocers, small manufacturers, and retailers desired prosection of "unfair price competition" engaged in by larger firms. Conversely, these peripheral businesses feared government prosecution of trade association activities that included "fair-price agreements" designed to ensure profitability.

Smaller businesses had been hit especially hard by federal antitrust policies in the past. From 1905 to 1915, seventy-two antitrust cases had been against these peripheral businesses; fewer than thirty had involved the largest firms. Under pressure from business groups such as the U.S. Chamber of Commerce, the Chicago Chamber of Commerce, and the National Association of Manufacturers, Congress amended the bill. The Clayton Act illegalized price discrimination but attached amendments that gave businesses considerable allowances and exemptions.

Other amendments undermined the strength of the bill. The prohibition against corporate mergers in the Clayton Act was modified to apply only in those cases in which merger tended to decrease competition, a vague standard open to judicial interpretation. The exemption of labor unions under the Clayton Act was equivocal and subject to judicial review. It was in fact the intention of Congress and the Wilson Administration to allow the courts to settle the ambiguity of the new antitrust law. As a consequence, federal courts often ruled that the Clayton Act was inapplicable to business mergers, and labor unions found that they had no more protection under the Clayton Act than they had before.

In its final form, the Clayton Act prohibited a corporation from discriminating in price between purchasers, engaging in exclusive sales, and tying purchases of one good to purchases of another if the effect of any of these actions was "to substantially lessen competition or tend to create a monopoly," a standard open to broad judicial interpretation. Executives, directors, and officers of a corporation were made personally liable for corporate antitrust violations. The Clayton Act also prohibited one corporation acquiring the stock of a competitor or a holding company acquiring the stock of two competitors if such acquisition would substantially lessen competition, restrain commerce, or tend to create a monopoly; these were again standards open to judicial review. The Federal Trade Commission Act, also passed in 1914, transferred the functions of the United States Bureau of Corporations to the Federal Trade Commission (FTC) and authorized the FTC, among other duties, to issue cease-and-desist orders enjoining "unfair methods of competition and commerce."

Impact of Event

The Clayton Act proved to be an enduring piece of legislation, and it has been strengthened a number of times since its passage. Just after its passage, however, the antitrust movement began to fade away. The great period of antitrust activity in the United States began in the McKinley Administration and peaked under President Taft. The Wilson Administration brought fewer antitrust suits than did either the Roosevelt or the Taft administrations. Late in 1914, Wilson stated that he believed federal regulation had gone far enough. The president viewed the Clayton Act as the concluding act in the antitrust movement. "The reconstructive legislation which for the last two decades the opinion of the country has demanded," stated Wilson, "has now been enacted."

At least as important, however, was the fact that foreign policy and World War I increasingly demanded Wilson's attention. Many historians have contended that although the antitrust movement had reached a natural decline, World War I further undermined it. War mobilization required the coordinated efforts of leaders of each industry. Economic concentration and collusive efforts were necessary and accepted for the war effort. For example, in early 1918 the Fuel Administration, a wartime agency, suppressed an attempt by the Federal Trade Commission to begin litigation against Standard Oil of Indiana for violation of the Clayton Antitrust Act.

Some economic historians contend that the Clayton Act actually promoted economic concentration. The Clayton Act clarified illegal actions, thereby helping to eliminate some monopolistic activities, but in so doing it allowed business combinations and trusts to engage in collusive activities not specifically prohibited. By codifying illegal behavior, Congress tacitly sanctioned other collusive activities designed to reduce chaotic competition and ensure stability. Large corporations such as General Motors and the Du Pont Chemical Company grew much larger just immediately after the Clayton Act and especially during the war effort.

Desire for further antitrust reform was rekindled, briefly, by the federal New Deal response to the Great Depression of the 1930's. The Public Utilities Holding Company Act of 1935 prohibited public utility systems with more than three tiers of companies and designated the Securities and Exchange Commission to regulate their size and finances. The Robinson-

Patman Act of 1936 and the Miller-Tydings Act of 1937 both supplemented the Clayton Act by attempting to protect small business from wholesalers that practiced price discrimination and by establishing "fair trade" price floors on numerous items. In 1938, Congress created the Temporary National Economic Committee to hold hearings on the issue of antitrust. Attorney General Thurman Arnold reinvigorated federal antitrust prosecution. Arnold brought a number of antitrust suits, notably against General Electric and the Aluminum Company of America. Like the earlier antitrust effort of the Progressive Era, this campaign lost its strength and direction as a result of foreign policy concerns and economic mobilization for a war effort.

There have been some important antitrust cases since World War II. In 1945, the Aluminum Company of America was found to be in violation of the Sherman Antitrust Act. In 1948, the federal government forced a number of major U.S. film studios to divest themselves of studio-owned theaters. In 1961, the Supreme Court ordered the Du Pont Company to divest itself of its holdings in General Motors Company. In 1967, the Federal Communications Commission ordered the American Telephone and Telegraph Company (AT&T) to lower its rates. In 1982, after eight years of battling a private antitrust suit in federal court, AT&T agreed to be broken up, and a number of rival long-distance communication companies came in to challenge AT&T's control over the market.

In 1950, the Celler-Kefauver Act extended the Clayton Act by tightening prohibitions on business mergers that lessen competition and lead to monopoly. In 1976, Congress passed the Hart-Scott-Rodino Act, or Concentrated Industries Act. This was a mild reform law that attempted to strengthen provisions of existing antitrust laws. Clearly, monopolistic behavior remained a fact of American economic life, but federal prosecution of anticompetitive mergers and acquisitions had become rare.

Bibliography
Blum, John Morton. "Woodrow Wilson and the Ambiguities of Reform." In *The Progressive Presidents: Theodore Roosevelt, Woodrow Wilson, Franklin D. Roosevelt, Lyndon Johnson*. New York: W. W. Norton, 1980. Good for an introduction to progressive policies and politics, as well as foreign policies, of Roosevelt and Wilson. Has a concise section on the development of Wilson's legislative reform efforts, especially the Clayton Act and the Federal Trade Commission.
Clark, John D. *The Federal Anti-Trust Policy*. Baltimore: Johns Hopkins University Press, 1931. This work is analytical, detailed, and still brief enough to be of use both to those seeking an introduction to the topic of

antitrust at the federal level and to those with some familiarity with the topic. Contains the varying economic analyses of the time and a chapter on the Clayton and Federal Trade Commission acts.

Kolko, Gabriel. *The Triumph of Conservatism: A Re-interpretation of American History, 1900-1916.* New York: Free Press of Glencoe, 1963. Presents an interpretation challenging the standard view of progressive regulation and business-government relationships in the early twentieth century by showing the ways in which businesses desired and influenced regulatory legislation as a means to achieving their own goal of ending cutthroat competition and stabilizing industries. Contains a lengthy section on the development of the Federal Trade Commission and the Clayton Act in this vein.

Link, Arthur S. *Wilson: The New Freedom.* Princeton, N.J.: Princeton University Press, 1956. Part of a series on Wilson, this work is the best on Wilson's "New Freedom" progressive reforms. Detailed section on the development of the Clayton and Federal Trade Commission bills in Congress, along with Wilson's role with them.

McCraw, Thomas. *Prophets of Regulation: Charles Francis Adams, Louis D. Brandeis, James M. Landis, Alfred E. Kahn.* Cambridge, Mass.: Harvard University Press, 1984. An excellent study of business-government relations in U.S. history. Uses the efforts of these prominent individuals to assess the success and failure of regulation. Focuses more upon Brandeis and the development of the FTC than on the Clayton Antitrust Act, although it contains a good analysis of the problems of the Clayton Act. Very readable.

Peritz, Rudolph J., Jr. *Competition Policy in America, 1888-1992: History, Rhetoric, Law.* New York: Oxford University Press, 1996. History of federal government policies relating to antitrust issues. Includes a substantial bibliography and index.

Thorelli, Hans B. *The Federal Antitrust Policy: Origination of an American Tradition.* Baltimore: Johns Hopkins University Press, 1955. A comprehensive and in-depth treatment of antitrust policy in U.S. history. Covers economic, social, and political formation of the antitrust movement in the legislative, executive, and judicial branches of government in the late nineteenth and early twentieth centuries. For those seeking a highly sophisticated and detailed treatment of U.S. antitrust policy.

Bruce Andre Beaubouef

Cross-References

Champion v. Ames Upholds Federal Powers to Regulate Commerce (1903); The Supreme Court Decides to Break Up Standard Oil (1911); The

Celler-Kefauver Act Amends Antitrust Legislation (1950); Carter Signs the Airline Deregulation Act (1978); Congress Deregulates Banks and Savings and Loans (1980-82); AT&T Agrees to Be Broken Up as Part of an Antitrust Settlement (1982); Federal Court Rules That Microsoft Should Be Split into Two Companies (2000).

LABOR UNIONS WIN EXEMPTION FROM ANTITRUST LAWS

CATEGORY OF EVENT: Labor
TIME: October 15, 1914
LOCALE: Washington, D.C.

Provisions of the Clayton Antitrust Act sought to exempt unions from prosecutions under the Sherman Antitrust Act of 1890 and under the Clayton Act itself

Principal personages:
WOODROW WILSON (1856-1924), a Democratic reform president who supported the Clayton Act
LOUIS D. BRANDEIS (1856-1941), a controversial reform lawyer and Supreme Court justice
HARRY DAUGHERTY (1860-1941), a conservative U.S. attorney general who favored antilabor injunctions
SAMUEL GOMPERS (1850-1924), the leader of the American Federation of Labor

Summary of Event

Labor reforms embodied in provisions of the Clayton Act of 1914 had been decades in coming to realization. American labor legislation in the mid-nineteenth century had been as advanced in some regards as any in the world. The famed decision of the Massachusetts Supreme Court in *Commonwealth v. Hunt* in 1842 exemplified wide public acknowledgment that efforts by labor combinations to raise wages did not constitute a "conspiracy" and that laborers were justified in striking to win a closed, or all-union, shop. Half a century later, however, this tolerance of labor's right to

110

organize in its own self-interest had altered drastically in the public mind and therefore had changed the character and interpretations of labor legislation.

The unprecedented industrialization of the United States and the attendant political ascendancy of the business classes were reflected in judicial decisions relevant to labor organizations and their methods. By the 1880's, the nation's courts were stipulating that labor's right to combine and to strike were subject to serious legal restrictions.

The judiciary's antilabor bias was attributable in part to the violence that had marked labor protests, notably in an 1877 national railroad strike and in the Haymarket Square bombing in 1886. The judiciary's hostility to many of the tactics associated with the growing labor movement was explained only in part as a reaction to labor violence. More basically, judges' antilabor decisions mirrored fresh interpretations about the nature of property and the presumptive rights of business. That is, during the last quarter of the nineteenth century, the right to do business became a "property." However troublesome they were, strikes against employers' physical properties usually could he dealt with by police, by troops, or through criminal law. Labor's picketing and boycotts, however, disrupted employers' claimed right to have access to their markets. Beginning in the 1880's, this perspective brought court injunctions into play as a preferred weapon of business against labor. Injunctions first won general public attention in 1894, when they were issued under provisions of the Sherman Antitrust Act of 1890 against labor organizer Eugene Debs.

Injunctions were one cause of labor's cries for national legislative reform. What turned such cries into screams were injunctions with provisions that led to the assessment of damages against unions resulting from boycotts that prevented employers from doing business. The U.S. Supreme Court's decision in the Danbury Hatters' case in 1908 (*Loewe v. Lawlor*) not only gave specificity to this menace to labor but also, by subjecting labor organizations and their members to damages under antitrust law, threatened trade unions with extinction.

Labor's salvation, if there were to be any, appeared in 1913 with the inauguration of President Woodrow Wilson. Wilson, taking a positive view of his office under the banner of his New Freedom, sponsored or supported a whirlwind of reform legislation. These measures affected tariffs, banking, the hours and conditions of labor, the protection of seamen, income taxation, popular election of U.S. senators, aid to agriculture, and, by way of strengthening the Sherman Act, the regulation of business trusts. It was from this latter step toward improved trust regulation that the Clayton Act emerged.

Three bills that had been drafted by the chairman of the House Judiciary Committee, Henry D. Clayton (D-Alabama), were subsequently combined into one. In its original form, the bill left the proclaimed needs of labor unaddressed. Primarily, the bill sought to abolish the trusts' characteristic unfair trade practices, including price discrimination, tying contracts, and interlocking directorates and stockholdings.

Eugene Debs, seen here speaking at a labor convention, was imprisoned in 1894 for his activities during a railway workers strike. (Library of Congress)

The bill was assailed immediately by representatives of big business, but the most vociferous of its critics were representatives of organized labor, led by a founder and the president of the American Federation of Labor (AFL), Samuel Gompers. Anticipating Wilsonian reform, Gompers had broken AFL tradition by throwing the group's political support behind Wilson's election campaign. Nothing in the initial Clayton bill removed labor from the purview of Sherman Act antitrust injunctions and prosecutions. Vowing that he would lead the AFL into Republican arms against Wilson's antitrust reforms, Gompers declared publicly that "without further delay the citizens of the United States must decide whether they wish to outlaw organized labor."

President Wilson remained adamant, but pressure from Gompers produced a congressional compromise. It was engineered by North Carolina's

Representative E. Y. Webb, who believed, as did many others, that the Sherman Act was never intended to apply to labor unions. The compromise therefore incorporated labor provisions in a bill otherwise aimed at eliminating restraint-of-trade strategies employed by trusts. Affirmed by an overwhelmingly favorable vote, the Clayton bill cleared the House of Representatives on June 5, 1914. After its Senate passage, it was signed into law on October 15, 1914.

Because of the Clayton Act's sections 6 and 20, Gompers instantly hailed it as providing basic but important rights. On its face, the act appeared to confirm this appraisal. Section 6 asserted that human labor was neither a commodity nor an article of commerce and further declared that nothing in federal antitrust laws forbade the existence of labor and agricultural unions or their lawful activities. Section 20 prohibited federal courts from issuing injunctions in labor disputes, except when irreparable damage to property might result and when there was no legal remedy for the dispute. More specifically, section 20 forbade federal injunctions prohibiting the encouragement of strikes, primary boycotts, peaceful assembly, and any other labor activities that were lawful otherwise under federal statutes.

Impact of Event

With passage of the Clayton Act, organized labor had its day in Congress, but it had not had its day in the nation's judicial system. Outside labor circles, many experts agreed that the act in no sense gave labor organizations immunity from antitrust prosecution. Evidence indicates that Wilson himself opposed such exemption. Sharp critics of the act's provisions further noted that the original bill had been so diluted in debate that its final version was an anemic sop to labor.

As swift and brilliant as President Wilson's reform legislation had been, its momentum was halted by America's preparation for and participation in World War I. At war's end, the public soon wearied of ideological and partisan battles over Wilson's foreign policy and became disillusioned with reformist exuberance. The 1920's witnessed a revival and strengthening of traditional conservative probusiness politics.

Taking advantage of the nation's postwar lassitude, fears generated by violence attending postwar strikes, and antipathy toward Communists, who were said to be leaders of the labor movement, employers again went on the offensive against labor. They created thousands of company-sponsored unions and again resorted to hiring armed company guards and strikebreakers. Capitalizing on antilabor sentiments, employers drew upon local and state authorities to deploy police and troops to harass and arrest union organizers. Yellow dog contracts (threatening workers with dismissal should they join a union) became commonplace and, chiefly under the auspices of the National Association of Manufacturers, antilabor propaganda was circulated widely and systematically in favor of open shops, which allow nonunion workers to be employed even though a union may have organized the workplace.

The fabric of protective legislation that Gompers and his fellow labor leaders presumed to be embodied in the Clayton Act's labor provisions was shredded by a U.S. Supreme Court decision in 1921. This seminal case was *Duplex Printing Press Company v. Deering*. It represented the Court's interpretation of the Sherman and Clayton acts as protecting employers from labor violence, from secondary boycotts, and from the use of other labor tactics that could be construed as unlawful interference with interstate commerce. The *Duplex* case involved attempts by a Michigan union in 1919 to organize the Duplex Company, one of only four such companies manufacturing printing presses and the only one remaining unorganized. To this end, the Michigan union persuaded workers and their employers in New York to boycott Duplex products; that is, to impose a secondary boycott.

Speaking for a conservative Court, Justice Mahlon Pitney held that certain union tactics constituted unlawful interference with interstate commerce and therefore were subject to antitrust laws. Secondary boycotts fell under antitrust laws as restraints of interstate trade and conspiracies. Section 6 of the Clayton Act, Pitney asserted, protected unions solely in regard to their lawful pursuit of legitimate objectives. Since in the Court's view secondary boycotts were unlawful, unions that instituted them were deprived of protection by the Clayton Act. The act's provisions in section 20 shielded unions from the issuance of injunctions against them, but injunctions were prohibited, Pitney noted, only in regard to the employees of an offending employer, the immediate parties to a labor dispute. The act thus did not prohibit an injunction against the New York workers and employers secondarily involved in the dispute.

By holding unions accountable under antitrust laws for anything the Court deemed to be other than normal and legitimate union activity, the Court effectively nullified the Clayton Act's labor provisions. As experts observed, the only remaining union actions that fell under protection of the Clayton Act were those considered lawful before passage of the act. This narrow judicial interpretation of sections 6 and 20 effectively negated the intent of a reform Congress and made it almost impossible for unions to organize workers in nonunion companies.

It scarcely mattered in the short run that Supreme Court Justice Louis D. Brandeis, one of the architects of Wilson's New Freedom, defended labor's right to push its struggle to the limits of its self-interest through encouraging sympathetic strikes. Employers benefited from judicial protection, a fact seemingly confirmed in a 1922 decision that confirmed the possibility of prosecution of unions as trusts. That same year, U.S. Attorney General Harry Daugherty invoked a wholesale issuance of court injunctions, nearly three hundred of them, against striking railway workers. Final hearings on these injunctions were repeatedly postponed until union battles against employers had failed. The wide latitude allowed to courts by the *Duplex* decision meant not only a denial of jury trials but the use of injunctions against payment of strike benefits and even against the public's feeding of strikers' families.

Relief from what labor and most liberals regarded as the blatant injustices of a probusiness and ultraconservative decade seemed possible by the end of the 1920's. In 1928, the planks of both major political parties featured anti-injunction proposals. The public pressures that resulted in enactment of the prolabor Norris-LaGuardia Act in 1932 and passage of the seminal National Labor Relations Act (Wagner Act) three years later were mounting. The New Deal administrations of Franklin D. Roosevelt ushered in an era rich in labor reform.

Bibliography

Babson, Steve. *The Unfinished Struggle: Turning Points in American Labor, 1877-Present.* Lanham, Md.: Rowman & Littlefield, 1999.

Brooks, Thomas R. *Toil and Trouble: A History of American Labor.* 2d ed. New York: Delacorte Press, 1971. A colorful and not uncritical prolabor account. Solid and informative. Chapters 11 and 12 are especially relevant.

Greene, Julie. *Pure and Simple Politics: The American Federation of Labor and Political Activism, 1881-1917.* New York: Cambridge University Press, 1998.

Gregory, Charles O. *Labor and the Law.* New York: W. W. Norton & Company, 1946. A law professor's pithy and straightforward account. Excellent on labor, injunctions, and antitrust problems in chapters 7 and 8. Includes a list of cases.

Link, Arthur S. *Woodrow Wilson and the Progressive Era, 1910-1917.* New York: Harper & Brothers, 1954. Authoritative survey by the leading Wilson scholar. Reads easily. Chapter 3 is excellent on Wilson, Congress, labor, and the Clayton Act. A fine introduction to the topic.

Northrup, Herbert R., and Gordon F. Bloom. *Government and Labor.* Homewood, Ill.: Richard D. Irwin, 1963. Authoritative, detailed, and clear reading. Balanced and outstanding. Includes a table of cases.

Taft, Philip. *The A. F. of L. in the Time of Gompers.* New York: Harper &

Brothers, 1957. Dry, dense narrative, but an authoritative study. Invaluable for Gompers' views on and politics involving the Sherman and Clayton acts and injunctions.

Wilcox, Clair. *Public Policies Toward Business.* 3d ed. Homewood, Ill.: Richard D. Irwin, 1966. Splendid analysis of the subject. Balances the interests and motives of government, business, and labor in regard to antitrust regulations. Chapters 1 through 5 are pertinent. Table of cases.

Clifton K. Yearley

Cross-References

The Federal Trade Commission Is Organized (1914); Congress Passes the Clayton Antitrust Act (1914); The Norris-LaGuardia Act Adds Strength to Labor Organizations (1932); The Wagner Act Promotes Union Organization (1935); Roosevelt Signs the Fair Labor Standards Act (1938); The Celler-Kefauver Act Amends Antitrust Legislation (1950).

THE UNITED STATES ESTABLISHES A PERMANENT TARIFF COMMISSION

CATEGORY OF EVENT: International business and commerce
TIME: September 8, 1916
LOCALE: Washington, D.C.

Seeking to restructure and reform America's tariffs along "scientific" lines, the administration of President Woodrow Wilson created the Federal Tariff Commission

Principal personages:
WOODROW WILSON (1856-1924), the president of the United States, 1913-1921
FRANK WILLIAM TAUSSIG (1859-1940), an economist, tariff expert, and proponent of moderate tariffs
OSCAR WILDER UNDERWOOD (1862-1929), a tariff reformer and congressional leader
THEODORE ROOSEVELT (1858-1919), the president who originally proposed a permanent tariff commission
ROBERT JOHN WALKER (1801-1869), a treasury secretary who laid the basis for tariffs as a source of revenue

Summary of Event

Establishment of the independent Federal Tariff Commission in 1916 represented a turning point in reformers' half-century struggle against the politics of protectionism. Tariffs are schedules of duties levied by government fiat upon imports, and sometimes on exports. Since 1789 and the

117

levying of the first such American duties, tariffs had been the subject of debate and often of passionate controversy. Debates concerned the levels of tariffs and their uses, such as promoting free trade; protecting and subsidizing "infant industries" (those in the process of development and therefore unable to compete in international markets), sectional interests, and politically powerful farmers and manufacturers; providing a source of federal revenues; and acting as weapons of trade policy and foreign policy. Such questions have surrounded the tariff issue in many local elections and in nearly every presidential campaign from the founding of the United States into the 1990's. In pre-Civil War years, while Southern and Western agricultural interests held sway in Washington, the tendency of the Democratic administrations representing them to maintain low tariffs became an article of faith. With the ascendance of Northern and Western Republicanism from the 1860's to the early 1900's, and again in the 1920's, the political allegiance of the dominant party shifted to protectionism and high tariffs.

Reform impulses of the Progressive Era emerged during a fifty-year period of high, at times exclusionary, Republican-made tariffs. Rarely did political pronouncements of the dominant Republicans discuss the virtues of liberalizing foreign trade. The momentum of reform, which cut across party lines, did encompass tariff rates. Convictions about tariff issues thus became a simplistic touchstone of whether individuals were identified as conservative champions of economic privilege or were marked as liberals eager to relieve consumers of tariff-raised prices and to restore a competitive marketplace.

Without publicly abandoning their support of high tariffs, Republican administrations beginning early in the 1880's nevertheless negotiated a series of short-term reciprocal trade treaties that in principle modified their protectionism. Even a paragon of Republican conservatism such as President William McKinley had concluded privately by 1897 that, as the world's major industrial power, the United States had outgrown the need to isolate and safeguard its economy behind high tariff walls. America's productivity and attendant surpluses of goods, its new international interests, its growing imperial commitments, and its increasingly restive anti-tariff forces all indicated that prosperity was no longer tied exclusively to the domestic market. Consequently, under McKinley's presidential successor, Theodore Roosevelt, there were signs of tariff moderation and of lowered rates, including passage of the Payne-Aldrich Tariff of 1909.

President Woodrow Wilson, an eloquent advocate of reforms and a learned exponent of "positive government," engineered or supported the largest packet of American reform legislation in history, most of it during his first term in office. Tariff reform was ranked foremost on his legislative agenda and proved in 1913 to be the earliest of his political tests before Congress.

Wilson chose the Underwood bill, vetoed by his predecessor, William Howard Taft, as the vehicle to affirm his commitment to making American business and agriculture genuinely competitive through a restructuring of tariffs. After his inauguration, Wilson consulted with the bill's author, Oscar Wilder Underwood, an Alabama Democrat who chaired the House of Representatives' powerful Ways and Means Committee. The bill stung hordes of lobbyists into action and was debated hotly. Wilson's personal appearance before Congress to urge its passage was almost unprecedented and constituted a daring gamble with his party stature and his executive authority.

Successfully enacted in 1913, the Underwood Tariff was described appropriately as the most revolutionary tariff reduction and revision in more than half a century, matched only by Treasury Secretary Robert John Walker's classic enunciation in 1846 of principles of low tariffs, to be used only for revenue and not for protectionism. The Underwood Tariff specifically invested wide discretionary authority in the secretary of the treasury to examine the books of importers suspected of dishonesty, to strengthen the power of collectors, and to improve the assemblage of accurate trade and tariff statistics. These were all subtle extensions of federal authority. Of more lasting significance, the Underwood Tariff carried provisions for an income tax to compensate for the $100 million in revenues expected to be lost from tariff reduction, a tax soon institutionalized by the Sixteenth Amendment to the Constitution.

The Federal Tariff Commission, created in 1916 as one of the first independent federal agencies, was designed as a keystone to this lengthy and often tortuous process of tariff reform. The immediate aims of the commission were to winnow the morass of often-unreliable information on which previous tariffs had been based and to collect accurate data that would inform the structuring of "scientific" tariffs. The Wilson Administration hoped to depoliticize the tariff-setting process, removing it from insidious lobbying and favoritism that generally had marred it in the past. It was hoped that future Congresses and presidents could be informed by the unbiased advice of experts. The six members of the commission, among them the distinguished Harvard economist and tariff historian Frank William Taussig, were presidential appointees. Members were three from each party, serving six-year terms upon their Senate confirmations.

Neither political party was enthused about establishing the commission. Wilson's demonstration of his presidential authority alone carried it into being. Wilson was clear about wanting to depoliticize the process of setting tariffs, about eliminating the special privileges masked behind earlier tariffs, and about listening to the complaints of small businesses and reformers. Wilson was not an unbridled advocate of free trade. He described himself as a "rational protectionist" and had insisted in campaign speeches on "a competitive tariff," a position close in practice to the Republican call for tariffs designed to equalize domestic costs of production with the costs of imported goods. The fate of the commission and the services it might be called upon to perform depended on presidential perceptions about the objectives to be sought in the formulation of national policies.

Impact of Event

Tariff experts and economists such as Taussig were aware of the inherent limitations imposed upon the Federal Tariff Commission at its inception. They saw as illusory the hope among reformers that the commission could help the enactment of scientific tariffs. As Taussig wrote dismissively in this connection, "there are no scientific laws applicable to economic problems." Later, Nobel Prize-winning economist Paul Samuelson described pleas for a scientific tariff as "the most vicious" argument for a tariff, one that for generations had ignorantly informed federal policy and reflected adversely upon the "economic literacy" of the American people.

Many of the justifications advanced by Wilson and other Progressives in the battle to establish a tariff commission were fallacious. Reformers hoped to make the tariff scientific by making it "competitive," and Republican conservatives insisted on a tariff that "equalized the costs of production at home and abroad." In practice, these were nearly identical positions. The unsoundness of them rests on the fact that trade is based on differences in costs and advantages among individuals and nations. Contrary to this, a so-called "scientific tariff" gave sanction to the prejudices that all industries were equally worth having; that when cost differences between nations grew, duties accordingly should rise; and that every industry, regardless of the quality of its products and its adaptation to America's natural resources, should enjoy the equalizing protection of the tariff.

The fallacious reasoning was part of politics and not of economics, but its prevalence highlighted the political limitations that weighed on the Federal Tariff Commission. The commission was an administrative agency and as such was incapable of significantly influencing national policy-making. Moreover, as friendly observers of the commission noted during its first years of operation, even if it were to be charged with preparing a tariff or elaborating a tariff bill, it was ill-equipped to do so. The experience of the Tariff Commission of 1882 and the Tariff Board of 1910 (both temporary organizations) indicated that the time required for requisite investigations of costs and conditions at home and abroad, as well as for reviews and the actual formulation of tariff schedules, would prove much too lengthy for such work to be of service to Congress.

Exactly how contingent the work of the Federal Tariff Commission was upon the varying degrees of enlightenment that characterized national politics was manifested by a renascence from 1921 to 1934 of high protectionism. Wilson's Emergency Tariff (1921) raised import levies on most agricultural products and reversed the pronounced downward trend of the Underwood Tariff. This reversal was followed swiftly by the Fordney-McCumber Tariff in 1922, which elevated levies imposed on manufactured imports and farm products substantially above the Payne-Aldrich levels of 1909. Presidential selection of tariff commission members, moreover, ran to the mediocre. Then, in the midst of economic crisis at the onset of the Great Depression and against the advice of more than a thousand economists, the administration of President Herbert Hoover enacted the Smoot-Hawley Tariff in 1930, imposing the highest protective tariffs in the nation's history. Tariff commissioners could draw some comfort from changes in the law that allowed presidents, after receiving the commission's recommendations, to alter individual tariff rates by half of those set by Congress.

When President Franklin D. Roosevelt's first New Deal administration shifted from economic isolationism to the initiation of long-term tariff reductions by means of reciprocal trade agreements in 1934, vitality was infused into the commission's functions by the perceived mandates of a new trade era. After 1934, and continuing almost unabated into the 1990's, protectionism was repudiated as national policy. That change was reflected in the Federal Tariff Commission's redesignation in 1974 as the U.S. International Trade Commission (ITC). The ITC, in conjunction with advising presidents, Congress, and other governmental agencies on a wide array of trade and tariff questions, has exercised important investigatory and reporting functions in regard to the fiscal and industrial effects of American customs laws. These encompass relationships between duties on raw materials and finished products, the impact of customs laws on national revenues as well as upon industry and labor, the trade and tariff relations between the United States and other countries, economic alliances, commercial treaties, multilateral trade negotiations, and the effects of foreign competition with American industries. Its data analysts monitor the impacts of hundreds of categories of imports on the domestic economy. As always, the utility and effectiveness of such agencies remained determined by the nation's political course.

Bibliography

Leech, Margaret. *In the Days of McKinley*. New York: Harper & Brothers, 1959. McKinley's career was closely identified with protectionism.

Insightful on changes in his views. Fine background to an understanding of why reformers wanted a permanent commission. Chapters 2 and 6 are especially relevant.

Link, Arthur S. *Woodrow Wilson and the Progressive Era, 1910-1917.* New York: Harper & Brothers, 1954. Authoritative synthesis by the leading Wilson scholar. Excellent on tariff issues and the commission. Photos, ample footnotes, essay on sources, excellent index. Invaluable for context and specifics.

Lyon, Leverett S., and Victor Abramson. *Government and Economic Life.* Vol. 2. Washington, D.C.: The Brookings Institution, 1940. Authoritative and easy to read. Chapter 20 is a superb summary of tariff history and the tariff commission. Updates and condenses Taussig's works.

Taussig, Frank W. *Free Trade, the Tariff, and Reciprocity.* New York: Macmillan, 1920. Taussig remains the chief authority on tariff history through 1930. His work is clear, is easy to read, and reflects his interactions with working government as well as his academic specialization. Chapters 5, 6, 9, and 10 are especially relevant.

_____. *The Tariff History of the United States.* 1892. Reprint. New York: A. M. Kelley, 1967. Still an essential, authoritative, easy-to-read survey. Chapters 8 through 11 are relevant on the commission's evolution and functions. Few notes and no bibliography, but a useful index.

Clifton K. Yearley

Cross-References

The Panama Canal Opens (1914); The General Agreement on Tariffs and Trade Is Signed (1947); Eisenhower Begins the Food for Peace Program (1954); The North American Free Trade Agreement Goes into Effect (1994).

STATION KDKA INTRODUCES COMMERCIAL RADIO BROADCASTING

CATEGORIES OF EVENT: New products and advertising
TIME: November 2, 1920
LOCALE: Pittsburgh, Pennsylvania

The first commercial radio broadcast demonstrated radio broadcasting's potential both as a source of communication and as a source of advertising revenue

Principal personages:
DAVID SARNOFF (1891-1971), a young wireless operator for American Marconi, later president of RCA
WILLIAM S. PALEY (1901-1990), the owner of CBS
FRANK CONRAD (1874-1941), an amateur radio station operator and engineer with Westinghouse
GUGLIELMO MARCONI (1874-1937), the inventor who first popularized wireless communication
REGINALD FESSENDEN (1866-1932), an inventor who presented the first known voice broadcast
OWEN D. YOUNG (1874-1962), the board chair of GE and RCA

Summary of Event

On November 2, 1920, station KDKA of Pittsburgh, Pennsylvania, broadcast the results of the Warren G. Harding-James Cox presidential election. This presentation is generally considered to be the first commercial radio broadcast. Although the event is more a milestone than an indication of innovation, it was the demonstration that finally pushed the wireless industry into the realm of big business.

The KDKA broadcast was the culmination of efforts begun in the late nineteenth century. The idea of wireless communication began to take shape in 1873, when physicist James Clerk Maxwell theorized the existence of electromagnetic waves. Maxwell's theory was proven by Heinrich Hertz, and a young Italian inventor, Guglielmo Marconi, experimented with and improved upon the ideas of Hertz. Others would make contributions, including Reginald Fessenden, who arranged what many refer to as the first public broadcast. On Christmas Eve, 1906, Fessenden successfully broadcast music and voice messages to ships at sea. This was the first time that wireless communication had been used for anything other than Morse code or coded messages.

In its early development, wireless communication was a fairly specialized endeavor. Initially it was used only when existing telephone and telegraph applications were impossible, as in ship-to-shore communications. It was of particular interest to private shippers and to the military.

Controversies over patent rights and alleged infringements threatened to strangle the development of wireless communication. World War I pushed the development forward. When the United States entered the war, the Navy took control of wireless operations, suspending amateur licenses and controlling key facilities. It also called for a moratorium on patent suits, asking all manufacturers to pool their resources for the war effort. The resulting cooperation not only sped up the development of wireless communication but also served as a precedent for cooperation in the 1920's.

After the war, reprivatization meant that once again competing companies each held important pieces of the radio puzzle. After complex negotiations, General Electric (GE), the Radio Corporation of America (RCA), American Telephone and Telegraph Company (AT&T), and Westinghouse signed a patent-pooling agreement on July 1, 1920. This agreement seemed to make good economic sense to all the new partners. GE and Westinghouse would manufacture radio receivers, which would be sold by RCA. AT&T would manufacture transmitters and would also hold the rights to "radio telephony" operations. RCA, because it was jointly owned by GE, Westinghouse, and AT&T, became the common ground for the pooling of information and cooperation. The agreement was effective only for a short time, in large part because it had not taken into account a new use for radio telephony, that of radio broadcasting.

The evolution of station KDKA is a good example of the swift changes in the industry. KDKA began as an amateur experimental station (8XK) licensed to Frank Conrad, a Westinghouse engineer. Shortly after World

War I, Conrad resumed his private broadcasts. On October 17, 1919, he became an instant celebrity when he placed his microphone in front of a phonographic machine to broadcast prerecorded sound. Conrad's broadcasts proved so popular that a Pittsburgh department store began selling amateur receivers designed to pick up Conrad's signal. This activity caught the attention of Westinghouse vice president H. P. Davis, who suggested to Westinghouse executives that the company could both boost sales of its receivers and promote its own name by building its own station. In October of 1920, the company filed an application. Its station KDKA became the first governmentally licensed radio station. On November 2, the station inaugurated its broadcasting with the results of the presidential election.

Impact of Event

Although station KDKA broadcast a number of program types later to become standard radio fare, it did not run commercials or paid advertisements. Its owner, Westinghouse, financed the operation as a means of selling its own products. RCA and GE also began to fund broadcasting facilities, each with the purpose of encouraging the sale of radio receivers.

A different philosophy was expressed by AT&T, which started station WEAF in New York City in 1922. AT&T planned to lease its broadcasting facility, just as it leased its long-distance telephone wires, charging a "toll" for advertising. Although the WEAF experiment was not an immediate success, the concept would ultimately prove to be the answer to a question that had baffled broadcasters for years, that of how broadcasting could pay its own way. It would also be the catalyst for renewed conflict in the industry.

In 1926, a new set of agreements was reached that effectively redefined radio broadcasting. AT&T maintained a monopoly on providing connections between stations (forming "networks") and in return sold WEAF and agreed not to buy any other station for at least eight years. RCA, with newly purchased WEAF as its flagship station, formed a new subsidiary to oversee its network operations. This new enterprise, the National Broadcasting Company (NBC), became the first company organized solely to operate a network. Some two dozen stations, most of them independently owned, carried NBC's first network program on November 15, 1926. This set of stations became the basis of NBC's "Red Network." RCA's station WJZ in New York City served as the anchor for NBC's second group of stations, the "Blue Network." By operating two networks, NBC controlled two stations in most major markets, creating a formidable economic enterprise.

The Columbia Broadcasting System (CBS) emerged from the merger of the United Independent Broadcasters and the Columbia Phonograph Corporation. The Columbia Phonographic Broadcasting System began in 1927 but would struggle until controlling interest was purchased by William S. Paley, then an executive with the Congress Cigar Company. Under Paley's leadership, CBS expanded from seventeen affiliates in 1928 to ninety-one affiliates in 1933. Although all three networks were still heavily dependent on their owned and operated stations for income, by 1933 the basis for modern network practices was in place.

The first commercial radio broadcast by KDKA, followed in 1922 by the airing of the first paid radio advertisement on WEAF, demonstrated the potential of radio broadcasting both as a communication source and as a vehicle for economic gain. Once the "toll broadcasting" idea took root, a new mass medium was created.

An important element in the development of radio broadcasting, one that differentiated the United States from other countries, was that broadcasting was essentially privately owned and commercially supported. Initially, stations were built by manufacturers as a means of selling radio receivers. Other stations were started as publicity gimmicks, or even on a whim. In the early 1920's, most stations expected to reap indirect values such as future sales or good will rather than direct revenues. By the late 1920's, however, the need for increased power, better equipment, and more sophisticated programming (in order to attract and maintain an audience) meant that radio could no longer be supported as a "hobby." Station owners began to look for ways to make radio pay its own way. To this end, the "toll experiment" of WEAF was closely monitored.

In the late 1920's, radio stations still did not have the production and programming skills necessary to meet the increasing demand for entertainment. Filling this void, advertising agencies began to take over part of the programming role, expanding the notion of program sponsorship. During the "Golden Age" of network radio in the 1930's and early 1940's, most major entertainment programs were produced by advertising agencies for their clients. The agencies sometimes charged the usual 15 percent commission rate both to the station and to their clients.

Network radio would literally change the way advertising was bought and sold. For the first time, radio advertisers were able to send their messages to every part of the country via one purchase. By the end of World War II, networks accounted for the vast majority of the radio audience.

Radio was one of the few industries to survive, and even grow, during the Depression. Unlike other media, radio was free to its audience. The periodic interruption of programming for commercials was a small price to pay for a populace desperate for any sort of escape from daily reality.

Advertising revenues increased dramatically after the advent of networks. In 1926, the estimated total sale of commercial time was $200,000. This rose to $4,820,000 in 1927, the first complete year of network operations. Revenues almost tripled in 1928, then almost doubled again in 1929, to $26.8 million. By the end of the decade, radio had clearly proved itself as an effective advertising medium.

The KDKA broadcast demonstrated that commercial broadcasting was possible, and the WEAF experiment in "toll" broadcasting identified a means of economic survival. The formation of radio networks created the first real opportunity for national advertising, an opportunity that would forever change the way goods and services were marketed.

Bibliography

Barnouw, Erik. *A Tower in Babel: To 1933.* Vol. 1. In *A History of Broadcasting in the United States.* New York: Oxford University Press, 1966. A detailed chronology of the history of broadcasting. Emphasizes the important individuals and their contributions. Later volumes continue the research. An important work.

Douglas, George H. *The Early Days of Radio Broadcasting.* Jefferson, N.C.: McFarland, 1987. An informal history of the early years of radio broadcasting, paying particular attention to the 1920's. Focuses on political, financial, manufacturing, and entertainment developments.

Godfrey, Donald G., and Frederic A. Leigh, eds. *Historical Dictionary of American Radio.* Westport, Conn.: Greenwood Press, 1998. Encyclopedic reference work on broadcasting history, with extensive bibliography and index.

Head, Sydney W., and Christopher H. Sterling. *Broadcasting in America: A Survey of Electronic Media.* Boston: Houghton Mifflin, 1987. A detailed and analytical look at the electronic media. An excellent resource, one of the most popular textbooks in the field.

Keith, Michael C., and Joseph M. Krause. *The Radio Station.* Boston: Focal Press, 1986. Combines an overview of the history of radio broadcasting with detailed explanations of commercial station operations. Useful primarily as a means of understanding how a contemporary station works.

Sterling, Christopher H., and John M. Kittross. *Stay Tuned: A Concise History of American Broadcasting.* Belmont, Calif.: Wadsworth, 1978. A good overview of radio and television, organized both chronologically and by topic. Does an effective job of blending events with explanations of their significance. A popular textbook.

Summers, Robert E., and Harrison B. Summers. *Broadcasting and the*

Public. Belmont, Calif.: Wadsworth, 1966. Looks at the history of broadcasting both as a social force and as a business. A useful background source.

William J. Wallace

Cross-References

The A. C. Nielsen Company Pioneers in Marketing and Media Research (1923); Congress Establishes the Federal Communications Commission (1934); The 1939 World's Fair Introduces Regular U.S. Television Service (1939); The U.S. Government Bans Cigarette Ads on Broadcast Media (1970); Cable Television Rises to Challenge Network Television (mid-1990's).

THE A. C. NIELSEN COMPANY PIONEERS IN MARKETING AND MEDIA RESEARCH

CATEGORY OF EVENT: Marketing
TIME: 1923
LOCALE: The United States

Pioneering in market research, the A. C. Nielsen Company became a leader in the field, having significant technical and financial effects on commerce, advertising, and media research worldwide

Principal personages:
A. C. NIELSEN, SR. (1897-1980), the company founder
A. C. NIELSEN, JR. (1919-   ), the successor to A. C. Nielsen, Sr., and company president, 1957-1959
JOHN C. HOLT (1940-   ), the chairman and chief executive officer of the company beginning in 1987
SERGE ORKUN, the president of the company in 1993
JOHN DIMLING (1938-   ), the president and chief executive officer of Nielsen Media Research in 1993
ANNE ELLIOT (1953-   ), the director of communications for Nielsen Media Research in 1993

Summary of Event
The A. C. Nielsen Company was founded by A. C. Nielsen, Sr., in 1923 as a firm of engineering consultants who measured product movement and market size for industrial machinery and equipment. By 1933, this service had been abandoned and replaced by a marketing information service

known as the Nielsen Drug Index. This service used a standing panel of drug stores to measure sales of products distributed through retail drug stores and attempted to identify factors that influenced sales. Seven months later, Nielsen established a similar service for the food industry known as the Retail Index Services. With the establishment of these services, Nielsen grew to be the leading market research company in the world. In 1984, the company merged with the Dun and Bradstreet Corporation. As of 1993, the A. C. Nielsen Company was divided into two separate business units: Nielsen Marketing Research and Nielsen Media Research.

By the early 1960's, many United States companies had begun to expand their operations abroad. In 1959, A. C. Nielsen, Jr., then president of the company, explained the research approach to marketing and set down a number of guidelines to successful marketing, particularly overseas. He stressed adapting the product to the market, gauging the impact of customs and traditions of prospective consumers, studying differences in advertising, identifying the product with the local scene, knowing the trade channels, and understanding the consumers' views of price and quality.

The Nielsen name is best known to the general public for the television rating system established by Nielsen Media Research. Radio audience research began in 1936 as a service to advertisers, advertising agencies, and radio station business managers who looked to the medium as a means of selling products. The idea was to identify links between what people listened to and what products they were buying or were likely to buy. The company used a device known as the Audimeter, which was attached to a radio and connected to a moving roll of paper. The machine created a permanent record of the stations tuned in by a sample population of about one thousand consumers. This replaced the slower and less accurate method of telephone surveys of what people were listening to at a given time.

During the 1950's, Nielsen began measuring and indexing the audiences of network and local television stations and assigning ratings points according to how many people in a sample audience were watching a given program at a given time. To select a sample of four thousand households with television sets, Nielsen used the U.S. Census Bureau's decennial census counts of all housing units in the country and randomly selected about five thousand blocks in urban areas and correspondingly small geographical units in rural areas, then selected one household from each. Field researchers then collected data on the demographics of households and individual information on persons in each home. At first, Nielsen relied on telephone surveys and diary reports as audience indicators, but later the company developed mechanized means of data collection and reporting. Even this relatively small sample of households was statistically reliable.

Each Nielsen household represented thousands of American homes. Nielsen used the sample results to project ratings for the entire American television audience. If fifteen percent of the sample watched a particular show, Nielsen would award it fifteen ratings points.

By 1964, Nielsen had discontinued its radio audience measurement to concentrate entirely on television viewership. By the late 1980's, the techniques of measuring the audience, collecting and computing data, and reporting to marketers, advertisers, and programmers who used the information had been streamlined and computerized. Television ratings could be reported overnight.

Nielsen used the People Meter, a device developed by AGB Research in the United Kingdom. People in the sample households recorded which channel they were watching by pushing buttons on the machine. The meter recorded which channel was being watched, by whom, and for how long. The machine removed some of the unreliability of diary reports. By 1987, Nielsen was relying solely on the People Meter to produce national television program ratings. Supplementary information on individual viewership was provided by weekly diaries kept by individual household members.

Data collection, computation and reporting, and technological engineering took place in an operations facility in Dunedin, Florida. As of 1993, Nielsen provided five basic services to its customers: the Nielsen Television Index (NTI), tracking national network television audiences since 1950; the Nielsen Station Index (NSI), tracking local television audiences since 1954; the Nielsen Syndication Service (NSS), tracking audiences for syndicated programming since 1985; the Nielsen Home Video Index (NHI), tracking audiences for cable, videocassette recorders (VCRs), and other new television technologies using People Meters, set-tuning meters, and paper diaries since 1980; and Nielsen New Media Services, providing custom research and start-up service for measurement of nontraditional markets, such as Hispanic viewers, since 1992. In 1992, the company reached an agreement with Telemundo and Univision in order to launch a national Hispanic measuring service.

Impact of Event
Nielsen Marketing Research introduced and formalized the concept of products holding percentage shares of their market. This concept can be said to have brought the overlapping disciplines of advertising and marketing closer together. Nielsen tracked what stores were selling, and advertisers tracked what people were buying and how they made their purchase decisions. Nielsen's quantitative statistics on product movement, its categorization of products moved, and its demographic statistics on buyers pro-

vided valuable information to producers, marketers, and advertisers. In 1959, Nielsen Marketing Research was operating in eleven countries. By 1991, that figure had grown to twenty-seven, and the company reported worldwide revenues of $1.2 billion.

By the early 1990's, Nielsen Marketing Research had expanded its research on product sales and the demographics of consumers to Europe, Latin America, and the Pacific Rim. It counted among its customers not only advertising agencies but also local companies or foreign branches of United States companies producing and selling food, pharmaceuticals, cosmetics, and durable goods. Targeting the emerging free economies of Eastern Europe, Nielsen established offices in Hungary in 1991, with plans to expand to Poland and Czechoslovakia. For companies engaged in multinational trade and marketing, Nielsen provided an international database service, instructional software on market research methods, and statistics on product movement. Such well-known corporations as Cheeseborough-Ponds, Procter & Gamble, and Pillsbury relied heavily on Nielsen's services and technology for the success of their operations. Giant advertising agencies including Saatchi & Saatchi and J. Walter Thompson also used Nielsen data.

During the mid-1980's, Nielsen Media Research's rating system came under criticism by television programmers, writers, and producers as well as segments of the television audience. Audience choices for viewing and the percentage of the population owning television sets had multiplied since the 1950's, when Nielsen began its television audience measurement. Advertisers relied on Nielsen's statistics for their choices of which programs to sponsor, and programmers relied on the advertisers to finance the programs they decided to air. Critics of the rating system charged that reliance on ratings as the basis for programming choices had a negative impact on the quality of commercial television programs. New programs did not get a chance to prove themselves, and homogeneity became the rule. Nielsen answered these charges by pointing out that rating points are based on statistical estimates of how many people watch a show, not an opinion poll of what they think of it or an artistic criticism of its value. Nielsen emphasized that the quality of programming depended on how programmers and advertisers interpreted the statistics.

As network television viewership continued to decrease, network executives were ready to admit that the increase in program choices made available by cable television and VCRs was part of the cause for their declining ratings. Questions arose, however, regarding whether the Nielsen rating system was giving an accurate picture of network viewership. Ratings had become the currency of negotiation between advertiser and the networks. Air time had become extremely expensive, and the cost of it was determined by the number of Nielsen rating points expected for the program during which an advertisement was aired. Networks sometimes were forced to give refunds because ratings were lower than anticipated. In the late 1980's and early 1990's, the television networks joined forces to commission a committee on nationwide television audience measurement (CONTAM). CONTAM was asked to investigate and report on the practicality and reliability of the People Meter, the way the viewing panel was recruited, and the accuracy of data on audience size at a given time.

The People Meter had been indicating lower numbers of viewers for the networks and higher numbers for their competitors. CONTAM concluded from observations and field interviews that pressing the buttons of the People Meter became tedious and that members of the viewer panels did not always use the device. Therefore, there was no way of telling with certainty whether they were watching television at all, let alone watching a particular program at a certain time. Furthermore, telephone surveys of what people were watching at a certain time indicated that in many cases there were more people watching network television than had been indicated by the People Meter results because household members did not record themselves as watching or because household visitors were in front of the set.

In regard to how the viewer panel was selected, the committee discovered that Nielsen divided candidates for the panels into "basics" and "alternates." Basics, chosen because of the number of children in the household and the presence of cable television services, were the first people invited. If these people refused, alternates were chosen. CONTAM discovered a high rate of refusal by basics and a subsequent high recruitment of alternates. This implied that the people viewing were more committed to television watching but were not necessarily the cross section of the population that Nielsen promised.

As for the accuracy and reliability of the numbers, the committee pointed out that increasing numbers of channels available meant fewer people watching each channel. Smaller shares implied greater margins of error in estimating ratings. The laws of statistics show that smaller proportions are more difficult to measure with precision. Because the number of households watching a particular channel was smaller, each household's decision carried greater importance, and ratings were more subject to fluctuation.

Nielsen became synonymous with United States television audience measurement and expanded television audience research worldwide. By 1990, Nielsen's metered research covered twenty-eight particular U.S. markets that included half of the country's population. CONTAM reports notwithstanding, Nielsen ratings continued to be the currency of negotiation between buyers and sellers of air time, sales of which came to $30 billion in 1990. Programming decision makers in the television industry continued to rely on Nielsen Media Research statistics to determine which programs to air.

Bibliography

Clark, Eric. *The Want Makers.* New York: Viking, 1989. This book traces the advertising process from research and creation to the worldwide impact of electronic methods of marketing research and the advertising that results from it.

Nielsen, Arthur C., Jr. "Do's and Don'ts in Selling Abroad." In *International Handbook of Advertising,* edited by S. Watson Dunn. New York: McGraw-Hill, 1963. One in a compilation of articles written by experts in the fields of international marketing and advertising. Discusses how to advertise in specific foreign markets and how international advertising is organized.

Nielsen Media Research. *The Quality Behind the Numbers.* New York: Communications Department, Nielsen Media Research, 1992. Outlines the history of the A. C. Nielsen Company in general and its media research in particular, including detailed information on Nielsen's marketing philosophy, methods, services, and technology.

Norback, Craig T., and Peter G. Norback, eds. "Audience Research: A. C. Nielsen Company." In *TV Guide Almanac.* New York: Ballantine Books, 1980. This is an overview of all factors of television programming and production, detailing the history, purpose, and methods of audience research used by Nielsen and other research companies as of the 1970's.

Schwerin, Horace S., and Henry H. Newell. *Persuasion in Marketing.* New York: John Wiley and Sons, 1981. Gives extensive coverage of consumer research and how its results can help in formulating advertising campaigns. A. C. Nielsen's research techniques are mentioned throughout.

Tedlow, Richard S. *New and Improved: The Story of Mass Marketing in America.* Boston: Harvard Business School Press, 1996.

Christina Ashton

Cross-References

Station KDKA Introduces Commercial Radio Broadcasting (1920); Congress Establishes the Federal Communications Commission (1934); The 1939 World's Fair Introduces Regular U.S. Television Service (1939); The U.S. Government Bans Cigarette Ads on Broadcast Media (1970); Cable Television Rises to Challenge Network Television (mid-1990's).

THE SUPREME COURT RULES AGAINST MINIMUM WAGE LAWS

CATEGORIES OF EVENT: Government and business; labor
TIME: April 9, 1923
LOCALE: Washington, D.C.

By ruling that minimum wage legislation was unconstitutional, the Supreme Court declared its support of laissez-faire policy and upheld the doctrine of freedom of contract

Principal personages:
GEORGE SUTHERLAND (1862-1942), an associate justice of the Supreme Court who wrote the majority opinion in *Adkins v. Children's Hospital*
WILLIAM HOWARD TAFT (1857-1930), a former U.S. president, Chief Justice of the United States
OLIVER WENDELL HOLMES, JR. (1841-1935), an associate justice of the Supreme Court
FELIX FRANKFURTER (1882-1965), a counsel in support of the legislation in *Adkins* who later served as an associate justice of the Supreme Court

Summary of Event
On April 9, 1923, the Supreme Court ruled five to three in the case of *Adkins v. Children's Hospital* (261 U.S. 525) that minimum wage laws violated the freedom of contract between employers and workers as well as the due process clause of the Fifth Amendment and therefore were unconstitutional. The Court's decision, surprising to many, was consistent with established laissez-faire economic policies of the time as well as the Court's own doctrine of freedom of contract that it had been developing since the

135

Chief Justice William Howard Taft (seated, center) wrote the dissenting opinion in Adkins v. Children's Hospital. (Library of Congress)

late 1890's but would eventually repudiate in its 1937 decision in *West Coast Hotel v. Parrish* (300 U.S. 379). The freedom of contract doctrine held that private parties to a contract were to be free from state intervention except in those limited cases in which public health, welfare, or the morals of the community were involved.

A minimum wage law had been adopted by Massachusetts in 1912, quickly followed by similar laws in several other states. The Adkins case stemmed from a 1918 federal law that created a Minimum Wage Board within the District of Columbia. The board's function was to inspect working conditions and then establish a legal minimum wage after negotiating with representatives of employers and employees. Moreover, the board was given the power to enforce its standards of minimum wages in order to protect female and teenage workers within the District of Columbia from economic conditions detrimental to their "health and morals." Failure of an employer to abide by the act was classified as a misdemeanor and carried a possible fine and imprisonment.

In 1920, the board determined that the cost of the "necessaries of life" had risen to a minimum of $16.50 a week and that many of the women working in the district's hotels, restaurants, and hospitals were being paid less, often much less, than the estimated living wage. The Children's Hospital, which employed a large proportion of women, refused to pay the wage set by the board. The hospital, along with others, brought suit to challenge the authority of the board to set wages.

136

The case was argued before the Court by Harvard Law School professor Felix Frankfurter in collaboration with the National Consumers League. Frankfurter would later take a seat on the Court as an associate justice in 1939. In this case, Frankfurter stressed that the law had not harmed local industry or reduced the level of employment and in fact had improved the welfare of the district's women and children. He and his supporters submitted a large volume of documentary evidence in support of their arguments but ultimately failed to convince the Court that minimum wage legislation was valid. The opponents of the legislation held to a basic conservative argument of the need to protect private property and stressed the importance of freedom of contract.

Writing for the majority, Justice George Sutherland held that the 1918 law not only disrupted the right of a private contract but also violated the right of property protected by the due process clause of the Fifth Amendment. He argued that the right of private contracts could be restrained only in exceptional cases and that in the view of the Court, at least for the time being, labor relations were largely beyond the police powers and regulatory powers of the states, Congress, and the courts.

Since earlier rulings had given mixed signals about when and where it was appropriate to set maximum work hours, the opinion in *Adkins* drew a sharp distinction between minimum wage laws and maximum hour laws. In *Adkins*, the Court held that contractual wages are appropriately set by the value of labor in the free market and that any attempt to fix wages placed a burden upon private employers concerning what in fact was a social issue. In *Muller v. Oregon*, the Court had ruled in 1908 that because of the state's interest in women's health it could, because of gender, legitimately set maximum hours. Because the decision in *Adkins* was handed down after the adoption of the Nineteenth Amendment in August of 1920, the Court's opinion also held that gender differences did not constitute a valid reason to ignore freedom of contract.

Chief Justice William Howard Taft, normally fairly conservative, issued a rare written dissent to the Court's decision in *Adkins*. Taft contended that laws could, in certain situations, be enacted to limit freedom of contract. It was, for example, within the police powers of the states, or Congress, to set maximum hours as well as to establish minimum wages. His dissent questioned the majority's distinction between wages and hours as a test of the liberty of contract, noting that one was as important as the other. Taft went on to note that although the adoption of the Nineteenth Amendment provided women with some political power, it did nothing to alter the physical distinctions between women and men. Constitutional issues therefore did not need to be recast simply because of its adoption.

Also dissenting in the *Adkins* decision was Justice Oliver Wendell

Holmes, Jr., who accepted the notion that Congress had the power to establish minimum wage rates for women in the District of Columbia but then questioned the constitutionality of liberty of contract. As Holmes noted, laws exist to forbid people from doing things they want to do. He questioned why labor contracts should be singled out for exemption. Holmes listed several cases in which liberty of contract had been limited by statute with validation by the Court. The attempt by Holmes to get the Court to abandon its doctrine of liberty of contract would not be accepted by a majority of the Court for some years, but in his dissent he expressed the difference in approach that the justices had concerning economic issues and labor relations. In the view of Holmes, an appointed board could be held to reasonably determine a standard for a living minimum wage. Such a standard need not come from the operations of a free market.

Impact of Event

The Court's decision in *Adkins* demonstrates the impact that laissez-faire policies had upon judicial temperaments, the economy, and the citizens of the United States in the 1920's and 1930's. The decision reflected popular, although not universal, opinion toward labor relations in the late nineteenth and early twentieth centuries. A direct impact of the Adkins decision was its use throughout the 1920's and early 1930's to overturn several states' minimum wage laws and other early New Deal legislation. The times and opinions were changing, however, and the Court's earnest endorsement of freedom of contract in *Adkins* would be overturned in 1937.

The initial reaction to the Court's ruling in *Adkins* was mixed. Those who favored a free and open market hailed it as an important and necessary endorsement of private property and the protection of freedom of contract under the due process clauses. Those who favored direct regulation of economic and social conditions attacked it as a shameful example of inhumanity. *The New Republic*, for example, ran an editorial stating that the Court had in effect endorsed the legal right to starve. Whether one agrees with the Court's ruling in *Adkins*, the case makes it clear that wages and prices are central to the operation of an economy. For that reason, various groups followed this case very closely. Groups opposed to minimum wage legislation had long stressed that these laws were potentially harmful not only to industry but also to labor itself. Harm would result as unemployment rose in response to higher legislated wages. Rising labor costs would be imposed on business and passed along to consumers. Labor groups themselves would have diminished ability to bargain. Those in favor of minimum wage legislation attempted to refute these claims. They argued that these laws protected the weak; raised standards of living, health, and welfare; improved bargaining power; and provided benefits to employers by increasing morale and worker efficiency.

Others debated the significance of an absolute power to fix wages. Did, for example, the right to set a minimum wage then also imply the ability to set a maximum wage? Was it feasible to determine and then fix a workable wage or a living wage? How would work performed at home be legislated? How would the enforcement of a minimum wage be handled?

Because of the precedence it placed on freedom of contract, this decision was a major setback to the progressive labor movement. During the early decades of the twentieth century, progressive groups sought legislative remedies for many of the inequities and problems they believed existed in labor relations. The gains made by these groups were, at least for the time being, stalled by this ruling. The Court had ruled in essence that the free marketplace and not mandated regulation would guide the decisions of society. Since minimum wage legislation was seen as a means to regulate as well as prohibit certain labor practices, progressive groups had hoped that the Court would rule to uphold the minimum wage as a means of protecting the health and welfare of women and children. Conservatives saw minimum wage legislation simply as an unconstitutional intrusion into private affairs between employers and employees.

The Court's ruling in this case, among others, provides a good deal of insight into the role of women and children in the American economy during the early years of the twentieth century. Minimum wage legislation often specified that the health and welfare of women and children were to be protected by a minimum living wage. This emphasis can be explained by the fact that gender- and age-specific legislation was more likely to be accepted, or alternatively that women and children were employed in less-productive industries, had lower wages, and had less bargaining power in the market, thus necessitating legislation on their behalf.

By ruling minimum wage legislation unconstitutional, the Court demonstrated a belief in the merits of a marketplace free from government intervention. The decision in *Adkins* affirmed the Court's belief that the freedom of contract doctrine remained, at least for the time, paramount to the operation of the free market. Moreover, if the freedom of contract doctrine were broadly applied, the nation, the economy, and labor relations would remain dominated by laissez-faire policies. The significance of this was made obvious in the *West Coast Hotel v. Parrish* decision, which upheld a Washington State minimum wage law and overturned *Adkins*. In that decision, Chief Justice Charles Evans Hughes dismissed the primacy of freedom of contract and instead argued that due process was what was in the interests of the community.

With the repudiation of the *Adkins* decision and an abandonment of a laissez-faire approach to social and economic problems, the roles of federal, state, and local governments clearly changed. The relative impact of the legislation that followed in the wake of the Court's later ruling remains a matter of considerable debate.

Bibliography

Brandeis, Louis D., and Josephine Goldmark. *Women in Industry*. Reprint. New York: Arno Press, 1969. A summary of the Supreme Court's decision upholding the constitutionality of the ten-hour workday. Helps to put labor issues and the debate on gender and the workplace into the context of the early twentieth century.

Hall, Kermit L., ed. *The Oxford Companion to the Supreme Court of the United States*. New York: Oxford University Press, 1992. A useful guide to the history of the Court, its major decisions, every justice who has served on the Court, and doctrines that have guided and influenced the Court since its founding in 1789. Concise yet detailed entries help to make landmark cases and legal terms accessible to a variety of users.

_____, ed. *The Oxford Guide to United States Supreme Court Decisions*. New York: Oxford University Press, 1999. Multiauthored collection of essays on more than four hundred significant Court decisions, with supporting glossary and other aids.

Nichols, Egbert Ray, and Joseph H. Baccus, eds. *Selected Articles on Minimum Wages and Maximum Hours*. New York: H. W. Wilson, 1936. Outlines and defines the debate on whether Congress has the power to fix minimum wages and maximum hours for workers. Reprints of editorials and comments offer a variety of legal, political, and economic interpretations.

Nordlund, Willis J. *The Quest for a Living Wage: The History of the Federal Minimum Wage Program*. Westport, Conn.: Greenwood Press, 1997.

Stigler, George J. "The Economics of Minimum Wage Legislation." *American Economic Review* 36 (June, 1946): 358-365. A concise and nontechnical discussion of the relative efficiencies of minimum wage legislation. Provides and uses evidence on employment and wages in Minnesota in the late 1930's.

Welch, Finis. *Minimum Wages: Issues and Evidence*. Washington, D.C.: American Enterprise Institute for Public Policy Research, 1978. A reexamination of the issues forty years after the enactment of the federal minimum wage law.

Timothy E. Sullivan

Cross-References

Champion v. Ames Upholds Federal Powers to Regulate Commerce (1903); The U.S. Government Creates the Department of Commerce and Labor (1903); The Triangle Shirtwaist Factory Fire Prompts Labor Reforms (1911); Labor Unions Win Exemption from Antitrust Laws (1914); The Norris-LaGuardia Act Adds Strength to Labor Organizations (1932); The CIO Begins Unionizing Unskilled Workers (1935); Roosevelt Signs the Fair Labor Standards Act (1938); Congress Passes the Equal Pay Act (1963).

IBM CHANGES ITS NAME AND PRODUCT LINE

CATEGORY OF EVENT: Foundings and dissolutions
TIME: February, 1924
LOCALE: New York, New York

By discarding its original name, Computing-Tabulating-Recording (CTR), and taking its new one, International Business Machines (IBM) signaled a new corporate direction

Principal personages:
THOMAS J. WATSON (1874-1956), the general manager of the company that became IBM
THOMAS J. WATSON, JR. (1914-1993), the general manager who took over from his father and led IBM into the computer age
CHARLES RANLETT FLINT (1850-1934), a promoter who organized CTR and selected Watson to be its leader
HERMAN HOLLERITH (1860-1929), the inventor of census tabulating machines, which became CTR's most important product
GEORGE FAIRCHILD (1854-1924), the first chairman of CTR, who left most of the real work to Watson

Summary of Event

In 1910, Charles Ranlett Flint created Computing-Tabulating-Recording (CTR). Flint was a colorful promoter who had earlier created American Woolen, United States Rubber, and American Chicle, and who was a founder of the Automobile Club of America. Today CTR would be called a conglomerate, since its divisions were largely unrelated to one another. International Time Recording manufactured time clocks and time cards onto which workers would punch their hours of arrival and departure. The Computing Scale Company of America's primary product was a scale that came equipped with a chart enabling a clerk to calculate the price of an item from its weight and price per pound. Tabulating Machine Company produced machines used to tabulate results from the 1890 census and the cards on which information was punched.

This last company was to prove the key element of CTR's success. Its founder, inventor Herman Hollerith, worked at the Census Bureau, where difficulties had developed in the tabulation of the 1880 census. It seemed clear then that unless some mechanical way was invented to speed calculations, the 1890 counting would take more than ten years to complete and would thus continue into the 1900 census year. Hollerith developed a machine that punched census information such as race, sex, age, and address onto cards. The cards could be fed into a sorter that would group them according to any desired set of data that had been punched. An operator could then count them, thus completing the task.

The machines were huge successes, but the government refused to buy them, seeking instead to lease them. Hollerith agreed, noting later that although the machines eventually turned profits, the real returns came from the sale of the punch cards on which data were recorded.

Flint considered International Time to be the most promising of the CTR divisions, so its executives dominated the first CTR board of directors. Hollerith was given the job of chief engineer and was not consulted when the company's officers were chosen. Flint arranged for a $7 million loan to get the company started. The loan had a term of thirty years at an interest rate of 6 percent, high by the standards of the time. Lenders apparently considered the company to pose a relatively high risk.

George Fairchild became CTR's first chairman. As the former president of International Time, he was a logical choice. Fairchild had been elected to the House of Representatives in 1906 and had just been named by President William Howard Taft to a ministerial post in Mexico. Fairchild thus became the firm's nominal leader, but Frank Kondolf, the former chief operating officer at International Time, performed day-to-day management. Kondolf did not impress Flint, who embarked on a search for another leader.

Flint discovered Thomas J. Watson, today considered to be one of America's premier businessmen. Watson came from the small town of Painted Post, near Corning, in upper New York. After holding several jobs in sales, in 1895 Watson accepted a trainee position at National Cash Register (NCR), whose chief executive officer, John Patterson, was a pioneering figure in the fledgling business machine industry. Patterson extolled the role of salesperson, which he considered to be the key role in the firm. At a time when salespeople were considered to be somewhat disreputable, NCR trained its sales force to be straightforward, prompt, and solicitous of customers' interests. Watson learned well and quickly rose through the ranks to become NCR's star salesman in upper New York.

In 1903, Watson was summoned to NCR's Dayton, Ohio, headquarters and told of a plan to smash the company's competition. He would establish a company, to be known as Watson's Cash Register & Second Hand Exchange, that would undersell competitors and force them out of the business. He began operating in New York City, then went on to Philadelphia and Chicago. The company was quite successful, but its secret ties with NCR were in violation of antitrust laws.

In 1910, American Cash Register filed antitrust complaints against NCR. Two years later, the federal government joined in the case, charging Patterson, Watson, and others with criminal violations. They were found guilty in 1913 and sentenced to fines and prison terms. Appeals followed, and in 1915 the courts found deficiencies and unfairness in the original trial, ordering a new one. The matter was dropped, but in the process Patterson and Watson had quarreled. Patterson had fired Watson, who now was available to Flint and CTR.

Flint offered Watson the post of general manager at a salary of $25,000 per year, until the criminal charges were settled. He accepted and began work in May, 1914. After an examination of the CTR businesses, Watson decided that Tabulating Machine Company had the most promising line of products. In addition to the general managership of CTR, he assumed the presidency of that company. After the antitrust suit against him was dropped, he became president of CTR as well.

Watson placed his own men in positions of leadership and devised new markets for tabulating machines. The Hollerith model was employed by corporations to keep inventories and by railroads to maintain schedules. They were leased, with the cards used to operate them sold outright. As with the census machines, the leases provided a steady cash flow, and the cards supplied large profits. By 1918, CTR was producing thirty million cards monthly for the Midwest alone. All the while, sales of time clocks and scales stagnated.

Fairchild died in December, 1924, whereupon Watson assumed the title of chairman along with the position of chief executive officer. Earlier in the year, he had decided to change the company's name to reflect its new business concentration. In 1917, he had christened the company's Canadian subsidiary International Business Machines. In February, 1924, he replaced CTR's corporate designation with the same name.

Impact of Event

The alteration of a company's name is hardly a major event in itself, but this one signaled a change in corporate direction. In time, scales and clocks would be discarded from the company's product lines, and Watson would concentrate on business machines.

Under Watson's leadership, IBM's engineers designed accounting and other machines, breaking through into new areas. IBM purchased a small company that manufactured electric typewriters and made it the leader in a growing field. Columbia University professors conceived a plan to develop multiple-choice tests that could be taken on standard forms and graded by machine. Watson provided the researchers with material and machines, and out of this came standardized tests graded by machines—IBM machines. The company also produced millions of forms to be used with various machines.

IBM produced large calculators capable of performing computations in minutes that previously had taken hours. It developed machines to process payrolls, with the payroll checks created on IBM cards. During World War II, IBM created machines for the military. By the war's end, IBM had annual revenues of $142 million and earnings of $10.9 million. Remington Rand, a competitor in some fields, had sales of $133 million but earnings of only $5.3 million.

Remington Rand then purchased UNIVAC, a small entity attempting to develop the first computer, from American Totalizator. Remington Rand and its large electromechanical computers won the contract for the 1950 census from a stunned IBM. Tom Watson, Jr., who had come into contact with military computers during the war, urged his father to develop an interest in them. The elder Watson demurred. Research indicated that at best only a dozen or so computers might be sold. Besides, IBM was the master in large calculators, which really were computers without programs or memories. He wondered about the wisdom of giving up a leadership position to devote more energy to an untested technology. The younger Watson persisted, and IBM entered the computer arena. With superior research and salesmanship, IBM drew close to UNIVAC and then surpassed it. In 1953, UNIVAC had most of the computer market; by 1955, IBM led in terms of placements.

Other firms soon entered the field, including Burroughs, NCR, Honeywell, General Electric, and RCA. There were some new companies to contend with, led by Control Data, Digital Equipment, and Scientific Data Systems (soon to be acquired by Xerox).

In the mid-1960's, IBM created a new line of data processing equipment known as the 360 series. Based on integrated circuits, these machines would make obsolete many highly successful machines then in production. Tom Watson, Jr., was taking the same kind of gamble as general manager of IBM that he did when entering the computer market. The line was a success, increasing IBM's lead over its rivals. Several left the field or sold off their computer operations. Some new companies appeared that attempted to emulate IBM machines and sell them at lower prices. IBM accelerated the introduction of new mainframe computers, and the upstarts faltered. They could not copy the IBM products quickly enough to earn a profit before IBM introduced a new product that made the old copies unsalable.

Watson retired in 1971 and was succeeded in turn by Vincent Learson, Frank Cary, John Opel, and John Akers. IBM remained the industry leader into the 1970's. Although rivals complained that their machines delivered more power for the buyer's dollar, IBM's support system was such that users of equipment still preferred "Big Blue."

Change was coming, however, and this time IBM faltered. In the mid-1970's, few people had heard of the small desktop computers fashioned from parts by enthusiasts. Soon, however, desktop computers were on sale to office managers. Sales to individuals followed shortly thereafter. The first buyers used them as replacements for typewriters, using their word processing capacities. As more programs were written and marketed, the small machines were used for other functions, many of which had in the past required much larger computers. Each company had its own software, or programs, which rarely worked on a competitor's machines.

IBM entered the personal computer market in 1981 and announced that its "architecture," or basic machine structure, would be available to competitors. Programs thus could be written to be compatible with machines produced by more than one company. This move was hailed by the industry but may have been an error. Using basic operating software from Microsoft and computer chips from Intel, IBM made it possible for many rivals to enter the field by purchasing components rather than seeking permission to use IBM patents.

Small computers became increasingly powerful, cutting into IBM's sales and leases of larger units. They became "commodity" products, ones for which brand name was relatively unimportant to buyers. They knew what a personal computer was supposed to do, and almost all the machines on the market performed those tasks with approximately the same proficiency and speed. IBM had a difficult time marketing its products as superior.

IBM responded by purchasing ROLM, a manufacturer of sophisticated telephonic equipment, and taking an interest in MCI Communications, a rival to American Telephone and Telegraph (AT&T) in long-line telephonics. Clearly IBM intended to branch out into areas related to data transmission. Both forays failed, and IBM abandoned the fields.

Although IBM made a promising start in the personal computer (PC) field, the company soon stumbled. Its small PC Jr. was a flop, and the company did not have a plausible entry in the laptop and notebook markets until the early 1990's, far behind competitors. By then, Akers had embarked on a series of restructurings, and it was clear that the company was foundering. In late 1992, Akers announced further cutbacks and a $6 billion charge against restructuring, hinting that more was to come, including a dividend cut.

Tom Watson, Sr., had erected a masterful company through his abilities to adjust to new markets and even to create them. His son did even better as he engaged in what economist Joseph Schumpeter called "creative destruction," forcing obsolescence by introducing new products. Whether IBM could have avoided the pitfalls of the 1980's and 1990's is sure to be debated.

Bibliography

Belden, Thomas. *The Lengthening Shadow: The Life of Thomas J. Watson.* New York: Little, Brown, 1962. The first biography of Watson, written with IBM's support. Unduly flattering but useful in showing the kind of image the company hoped to set forth.

Maisonrouge, Jacques. *Inside IBM: A Personal Story.* New York: McGraw-Hill, 1989. Maisonrouge was a senior officer at IBM who worked closely with both the Watsons.

Pugh, Emerson W. *Building IBM: Shaping an Industry and Its Technology.* Cambridge, Mass.: MIT Press, 1995. Useful history, both as a case study of IBM and as an overview of the computer industry generally. Contains an extensive bibliography and an index.

Rodgers, William. *Think: A Biography of the Watsons and IBM.* New York: Stein and Day, 1969. An early history and biography. Valuable for its point of view on the company during the early years of the computer era.

Sobel, Robert. *I.B.M.: Colossus in Transition.* New York: Times Books, 1981. A standard history of the company during its period of growth and power.

Watson, Thomas J., Jr. *A Business and Its Beliefs: The Ideas That Helped Build IBM.* New York: McGraw-Hill, 1963. Delivered as part of the McKinsey Foundation Lecture Series, sponsored by Columbia University. This is the clearest statement of the IBM philosophy available.

Watson, Thomas J., Jr., and Peter Petre. *Father, Son, and Company: My Life at IBM and Beyond.* New York: Bantam, 1990. Describes Watson's relations with his father, with some material on the early history of IBM. Watson, Thomas J., Sr. *Men-Minutes-Money.* New York: IBM, 1934. Watson's interpretation of IBM's philosophy and policies, indicating how money was spent on research and production.

Robert Sobel

Cross-References

Jobs and Wozniak Found Apple Computer (1976); CAD/CAM Revolutionizes Engineering and Manufacturing (1980's); IBM Introduces Its Personal Computer (1981); *Time* magazine Makes an E-commerce Pioneer Its Person of the Year (1999); Dow Jones Adds Microsoft and Intel (1999).

CONGRESS RESTRICTS IMMIGRATION WITH 1924 LEGISLATION

CATEGORY OF EVENT: Labor
TIME: May 26, 1924
LOCALE: Washington, D.C.

The Immigration Act of 1924 reflected widespread restrictionist sentiment after World War I, severely limiting the numbers of immigrants permitted to enter the United States from Southern and Eastern Europe each year

Principal personages:
ALBERT JOHNSON (1869-1957), a congressman from Washington, coauthor of the act
DAVID A. REED (1880-1953), a senator from Pennsylvania, coauthor of the act
WILLIAM P. DILLINGHAM (1843-1923), the chair of the Senate Immigration Committee and designer of quota systems
CHARLES EVANS HUGHES (1862-1948), the secretary of state under President Calvin Coolidge
A. MITCHELL PALMER (1872-1936), the attorney general of the United States, 1919-1921
HENRY CABOT LODGE (1850-1924), a senator from Massachusetts and opponent of "new" immigration
SAMUEL GOMPERS (1850-1924), the leader of the American Federation of Labor

Summary of Event

The Immigration Act of 1924 provided for a system of quotas for immigration into the United States, drastically limiting the numbers of people from Southern and Eastern Europe who could enter the country, especially in comparison with more "favored" national groups from Northern and Western Europe. As a result of strong pressure from American employers dependent on Latin American laborers, the measure included few restrictions on immigrants from the Western Hemisphere. Otherwise, the immigration of groups deemed by restrictionists to be not "American" enough was severely curtailed.

Immigration legislation had been passed by Congress, after contentious debate, on several occasions prior to 1924. A quota system passed in 1921 provided that people of each European nationality could enter the United States based on a percentage of their group's population in the United States in 1910. That 1921 Immigration Act allowed only about 350,000 immigrants from Europe per year, most of them from the "preferred" national groups in Northern and Western Europe. It had several loopholes. By 1924, few voices were raised against the further restriction of immigration. Some individuals called for a complete shutdown.

The Immigration Act of 1924, also known as the Johnson-Reed Act for its congressional sponsors, Congressman Albert Johnson of Washington and Senator David A. Reed of Pennsylvania, set national quotas based on estimates of the national origins of residents in the United States at the 1890 census. That the Senate Immigration Committee, headed by Senator William P. Dillingham, chose 1890 as the date from which to calculate national origins was significant. That year was prior to the most extensive immigration from Southern and Eastern Europe, particularly Italy and the Balkan countries.

Immigration to the United States from all areas rose tremendously in the late nineteenth century, but after 1896 most European immigrants came from areas different from those of previous immigrants. A large proportion of immigrants in the mid-1800's had been from Western Europe, particularly the British Isles and Germany. Pressures such as the Irish potato famine of the 1840's and the Franco-German conflicts in the third quarter of the century created these immigrant flows. The "new" immigrants, as they were called to distinguish them from immigrant groups already established in the United States by the 1890's, stood out in part simply because they came from other parts of Europe and the world, not only Southern and Eastern Europe but also, in significant numbers, Japan and the Far East.

The new immigrants could be differentiated from native-born residents of the United States and earlier immigrant groups on grounds other than their national origins. They were often physically distinguishable, with darker skin or non-"white" color (such as olive-skinned Italians or the Asian peoples), or smaller stature. They were different religiously from earlier groups, with many Southern Europeans being Catholic and Asian immigrants being non-Christians, in contrast to the Protestantism (excepting the Irish) of earlier immigrant groups. The new immigrants settled in unprecedented patterns as well. Generally, they were not as drawn to farms in the Midwest as to urban and industrial communities and mining areas in the Northeast.

Part of the purpose of the congressional legislation was to restrict the immigration of Southern Europeans, such as this Italian family. (Library of Congress)

Restriction of immigration through legislation had broad support in 1924. A few efforts to moderate the provisions of the Johnson-Reed Act, such as the attempt by Secretary of State Charles Evans Hughes to make the act comport with earlier diplomatic agreements allowing residency for certain Japanese aliens, were rebuffed by Congress. The reasons advanced for limiting or stopping new immigrant groups from coming to the United States included humanitarian concerns about urban overcrowding, arguments about preserving the purity of a supposed "Nordic" race, scientific and pseudoscientific concerns about racial characteristics, pleas to limit the labor supply, and arguments about the alleged links between the new immigrants and radical political movements. A few groups, including

151

organizations representing business such as the National Organization of Manufacturers, consistently argued against limitations on immigration, hoping that immigration would provide continued flows of inexpensive (and often nonunion) factory and unskilled labor. Their desires were drowned out in the calls for restriction.

Labor leaders such as Samuel Gompers, who in the 1910's had been uncomfortable with the tone of restrictionist proposals, became convinced of the need to ensure the "Americanism" of the labor force after World War I. The hiring of immigrant laborers as strikebreakers in several incidents increased organized labor's fear that the new immigrants were too tractable in the hands of employers and would undercut existing pay rates. The inflation and massive unemployment of the early 1920's made the labor movement even more desperate to eliminate "foreign" (that is, new immigrant) competition for jobs.

The supporters of immigration restrictions in the years prior to passage of the 1924 act found justifications for their ideas among authors who wrote about the physical classification of human beings. Such writers on race ranged from trained biologists, geologists, and geneticists such as Francis Galton of England to amateur scientists and historians such as the widely read Madison Grant of New York City. Many of the restrictionists believed that they were practicing the science of "eugenics," or "good breeding," when they recommended that "inferior" national groups such as Southern Europeans should not be allowed to "water down" the primarily whiter, Protestant, and "Nordic" groups that had arrived in the United States earlier. Such arguments found acceptance among some supporters of social Darwinism, who believed that the "Nordic" Northern Europeans were engaged in a battle for species survival. Among highly educated people in the United States, an acceptance of tenets of eugenicism and social Darwinism was widespread. Many offered it as an explanation for the success of their own well-established families. To even more extreme groups such as the Ku Klux Klan, which was at its height in influence in the postwar years, eugenics provided a "scientific" explanation for the most vicious forms of xenophobia and racism.

Nativism had been given powerful impetus by several high-profile governmental officials in the wake of World War I and the Bolshevik Revolution. U.S. Attorney General A. Mitchell Palmer launched a series of actions against radical groups and rounded up foreign agitators for deportation from the United States in 1920. Although the Palmer Raids netted only a small number of people who finally were forced to leave the country and Palmer's "Red Scare" helped discredit its instigator, a number of political leaders, including the young J. Edgar Hoover, who had been appointed head of the new General Intelligence Division in the Department of Justice, remained convinced that there was an intimate link between radicalism, disloyalty to the United States, and new immigrants. The assumption that Italians, for example, were prone to anarchism and violence pervaded the internationally famous trial of Nicola Sacco and Bartolomeo Vanzetti in the mid-1920's.

Impact of Event

The strong provisions of the Immigration Act of 1924 cut immigration to levels much lower than prior to the beginning of the new immigration, especially as supplemented by stepped-up enforcement in the late 1920's and 1930's, when fears about unemployment were even more pressing. Because some countries such as Great Britain, a "preferred" nation to the restrictionists, never filled their yearly quotas, actual annual immigration under the act was much lower than the total of 150,000 people allowed. In contrast, 1,285,000 immigrants entered the United States in 1907, the highest year of immigration. Although migration from Mexico had not been formally regulated by the 1924 act, enough small farmers began complaining about immigrants serving as cheap labor for large-scale cotton producers to pressure diplomats into restricting Mexican immigration through much stricter enforcement of visa regulations.

The fervor of restrictionist arguments moderated somewhat by the 1930's, especially as eugenics fell into disfavor because of its increasing association with fascism in Europe and as scandals smeared the reputation of the Ku Klux Klan. Ironically, however, despite Americans' mounting dismay at arguments about racial purity being advanced by Adolf Hitler, immigration restrictions (motivated in some instances by anti-Semitism) served as a powerful method for limiting immigration by Europeans seeking refuge from Nazi persecution. President Franklin D. Roosevelt refused to press for changes in immigration regulations and in the law of political asylum that would have granted admission to the United States to thousands of individuals, including children.

Immigration restriction as a national policy was severely tested by refugees from several areas of the world in the late 1940's, including people fleeing from new communist governments. The Cold War saw renewed fears within the United States that foreigners, especially from certain areas, might be spies or anti-American. Despite some administrative sympathy for refugees, notably in the administration of Harry S Truman, legislation such as the Internal Security Act of 1950 and the McCarran-Walter Act of 1952 (both passed over presidential veto) contained strict regulation of potential subversives, strengthened the authority of government agencies to enforce immigration legislation, and kept the quota system in place.

The quota system remained as a guiding principle in U.S. immigration policy until 1965, when new grounds for establishing a person's suitability for entry into the country as a resident were established. Incremental changes in immigration law in the 1950's and early 1960's had provided for the reuniting of some immigrant families, but sweeping reforms of the quota system were blocked for a time by key members of Congress who still advocated restriction. Wholesale reform of immigration law was urged by organized labor, which long since had absorbed "new" immigrants as members, and by religious and intellectual groups that viewed the quota system as needlessly discriminatory. The authors of the Immigration Act of 1965 allowed for a "brain drain" of skilled and professional immigrants from the rest of the world into the United States, in part as a compromise with congressional restrictionists to assure them that immigrants would be productive additions to American society.

With the passage of the act of 1965, no longer would one's national origin be the primary determinant of ability to enter the United States. The usefulness of an individual's occupation, which first was provided as a consideration in the McCarran-Walter Act, and the necessity for political asylum could count in favor of a potential immigrant. The total number of immigrants was increased to 170,000 annually. Much as had been the case prior to 1924, legal immigration after 1965 stemmed more from Mediterranean countries, Asia, and Mexico.

Bibliography

Calavita, Kitty. *U.S. Immigration Law and the Control of Labor, 1820-1924*. London: Academic Press, 1984. A theoretical discussion of United States immigration policy, heavily informed by neo-Marxist analysis of the role of the state in promoting capitalism. Argues that pressure for the 1924 act was widespread and not attributable to any single group or set of interests.

Higham, John. *Strangers in the Land: Patterns of American Nativism, 1860-1925*. New York: Atheneum, 1974. Exploration of reasons for nativism among an assortment of groups in American society. Subtly explains the existence of xenophobia in some religions' traditions and the appeal of restrictionist and racist organizations such as the Ku Klux Klan. Full bibliographic essay, including references to ethnic and specialized newspapers.

Hutchinson, E. P. *Legislative History of American Immigration Policy, 1798-1965*. Philadelphia: University of Pennsylvania Press, 1981. Encyclopedic discussion of all major pieces of immigration legislation considered and passed by Congress. Chronicles changes in the form of various bills as they passed through committees and floor discussions.

Kessner, Thomas. *The Golden Door: Italian and Jewish Immigrant Mobility in New York City, 1880-1915*. New York: Oxford University Press, 1977. Uses a variety of local records, including census materials, to argue that "new" Italian and Jewish immigrants in New York City were upwardly mobile, despite the fears of nativists.

LeMay, Michael, and Elliott Robert Barkan. *U.S. Immigration and Naturalization Laws and Issues: A Documentary History*. Westport, Conn.: Greenwood Press, 1999. Collection of primary documents on immigration history, with bibliographical references and index.

Taylor, Philip. *The Distant Magnet: European Emigration to the U.S.A.* New York: Harper & Row, 1971. Vivid and readable account of the motivations for and experience of immigration to the United States, drawn from diverse source material including photographs. Captures the pathos and richness of a variety of cultures and the venom of restrictionist arguments.

Elisabeth A. Cawthon

Cross-References

The U.S. Government Creates the Department of Commerce and Labor (1903); The United States Begins the Bracero Program (1942); The Immigration Reform and Control Act Is Signed into Law (1986); The North American Free Trade Agreement Goes into Effect (1994).

THE TEAPOT DOME SCANDAL PROMPTS REFORMS IN THE OIL INDUSTRY

CATEGORY OF EVENT: Government and business
TIME: December 18, 1924
LOCALE: Washington, D.C.

The Federal Oil Conservation Board, established in the wake of the Teapot Dome scandal, increased federal regulation of the U.S. petroleum industry

Principal personages:
ALBERT B. FALL (1861-1944), the secretary of the Interior, 1921-1923
JOSEPHUS DANIELS (1862-1948), the secretary of the Navy, 1913-1921
ROBERT M. LA FOLLETTE (1855-1925), a U.S. senator, (1906-1925)
THOMAS J. WALSH (1859-1933), a U.S. senator, 1913-1933
CALVIN COOLIDGE (1872-1933), the president of the United States, 1923-1929
GIFFORD PINCHOT (1865-1946), the chief of the Division of Forestry in the Department of Agriculture, 1898-1905
HARRY F. SINCLAIR (1876-1956), the president of the Mammoth Oil Company
EDWARD DOHENY (1856-1935), the president of the Pan-American Petroleum and Transport Company

Summary of Event

In 1921 and 1922, Secretary of the Interior Albert B. Fall, after transferring federal lands designated for naval oil reserves from the Secretary of the

Navy's jurisdiction to his own department, awarded leases on the Teapot Dome area in Wyoming and Elk Hills, California, to the Mammoth Oil Company and the Pan-American Petroleum and Transport Company. Senate investigations in October, 1923, of Fall's actions revealed that Fall had accepted $400,000 in loans from executives of those companies. The resulting political scandal forced Fall to resign and heightened public concerns over federal regulation of petroleum resources. President Calvin Coolidge, under pressure from public opinion, conservationists, and a number of leaders from the petroleum industry, on December 18, 1924, created the Federal Oil Conservation Board (FOCB), composed of the secretaries of War, Navy, Interior, and Commerce. The FOCB was to bring greater federal involvement in petroleum conservation regulation, but it also provided a forum for the industry to voice its concerns to the federal government.

The idea of reserving petroleum-bearing lands for exclusive federal use, especially for the military, went back to the early twentieth century. The U.S. Navy had changed its coal-burning engines to petroleum-based internal combustion engines in 1904, and the army would increasingly use trucks and automobiles. Thus the U.S. military was becoming dependent upon petroleum products. On September 27, 1909, President William H. Taft issued an executive order that withdrew from private use 3,041,000 acres of land in California and Wyoming for exclusive federal use. From late 1909 through 1910, the federal government withdrew lands in western states for the maintenance of petroleum reserves.

The issue of federal petroleum reserves came to the forefront during World War I. American oil played a crucial part in the war effort, and thus petroleum was established as a commodity of strategic importance. Secretary of the Navy Josephus Daniels, seeking to ensure that the Navy had an adequate supply of oil during and after the war, in 1917 planned to have lands set aside for exclusive federal petroleum reserves. In 1920, as the Navy faced a shortage of oil and as pressure from private interests to open up federal lands for oil production intensified, Daniels drafted an amendment to the general Mineral Lands Leasing Act of 1920 allowing the Secretary of the Interior to grant leases to private companies to produce crude oil on federal lands, thus making petroleum supplies available to the Navy.

High production levels during the war, fed by rising prices and endless federal demand, heightened concerns over waste, exhaustion of oil reserves, price, and industrial stability. Production across the nation rose from 265 million barrels of oil in 1914 to 355 million in 1918. Oil production continued to increase, at an even greater rate, after the war, rising from 472

million barrels in 1921 to 732 million in 1923. Oil prices fell from $3.08 per barrel in 1920 to $1.78 in 1921, then to $1.34 in 1923. The price remained around $1.30 for the rest of the decade before declining precipitously with the economic depression of the 1930's. Leaders of the oil industry feared an immediate and severe price deflation and consequent economic collapse in the industry. In addition, with production levels reaching new highs each year, conservationists, government officials, and a number of oil executives be-

After the death of Warren G. Harding, it was left to his successor, Calvin Coolidge (pictured) to resolve the problems caused by Teapot Dome. (Library of Congress)

gan to fear exhaustion of domestic petroleum reserves in the near future. During the early 1920's, fears of oil shortage were overshadowed by concerns of oversupply, price deflation, and economic chaos for the petroleum industry. Conservation of petroleum increasingly came to be seen as an answer to each of these problems. It was in this context that pressure from the Teapot Dome scandal led to creation of the FOCB.

When Albert B. Fall became Secretary of the Interior under President Warren G. Harding, he faced immediate suspicion from conservationists. Fall, a former U.S. senator from New Mexico, represented southwestern interests that advocated unrestrained development of natural resources by the private sector. In May, 1921, using the amendment that Daniels wrote to the Mineral Lands Leasing Act of 1920, Fall had authority over federal reserves transferred from the Secretary of the Navy to his Department of the Interior. In July, 1921, Fall leased federal lands in Elk Hills, California, to Edward Doheny of the Pan-American Petroleum and Transport Company. In April, 1922, Fall leased the Teapot Dome tract in Wyoming to Harry F. Sinclair of Mammoth Oil Company.

The transfer of naval reserves to private interests not only further enraged Fall's critics but also gave them something to focus on. Fall already had been branded as anticonservationist by critics such as senator Robert

M. La Follette (R-Wisconsin) and Gifford Pinchot, former chief forester under Theodore Roosevelt. Daniels, who had drafted the amendment allowing the Secretary of the Interior to oversee the naval supply, distrusted Fall's intentions. With Daniels' support, in 1923 Pinchot and La Follette investigated Fall's actions. Ultimately, La Follette persuaded Senator Thomas Walsh (D-Montana), a member of the Senate Public Lands Committee, to open Senate hearings on the matter.

A rising tide of protest against Fall forced him to resign even before the hearings began in October, 1923. The Senate investigation revealed that Fall had accepted $400,000 in loans from Sinclair and Doheny in return for the public land leases. Historians have noted that had Fall truly desired to profit by exploiting his office, he could have obtained much larger loans from oil interests. Both Doheny and Sinclair were acquitted of bribery, but Sinclair spent several months in jail in 1929 for contempt of the Senate and of court. Fall was later found guilty of accepting a bribe while Secretary of the Interior and was sentenced to a year in jail.

The Teapot Dome scandal, coming to attention during the presidential election campaign of 1924, occurred in the context of a public arena of heightened political rhetoric. The scandal resulted in much more focus being placed on federal regulation of the petroleum industry. Calvin Coolidge, who became president after Harding's death in 1923, created a Naval Petroleum Reserve office in the Department of the Navy in March, 1924. He attempted to shift federal policy from private exploitation back to federal conservation. Coolidge also came under pressure from public opinion, conservationists, and a number of leaders from the petroleum industry to increase federal regulation of the oil industry.

On December 18, 1924, Coolidge created the Federal Oil Conservation Board (FOCB). The purpose of the FOCB was to study the government's responsibilities, with cooperation from representatives of the oil industry. The FOCB was to focus on the three main industry concerns: the size of crude oil reserves, the technical conditions of production, and the economic disruption caused by overproduction. Coolidge commented upon the direct relationship between oil conservation and economic stability, stating that overproduction encourages low prices, which in turn led to wastefulness. The FOCB would also advise the president on the best policy to ensure the future supply of fuel oil for the Navy and to safeguard national security through conservation of oil. From its inception the FOCB was cooperative with and even deferential to the petroleum industry, especially to the American Petroleum Institute (API), the major trade association for the industry.

Impact of Event

In 1926, the FOCB held hearings and attempted to build a consensus among the representatives of various concerns within the petroleum industry on the conservation issue. The FOCB encountered an industry divided on the issue of production controls but united against federal intervention. Larger integrated companies traditionally supported production controls, and smaller companies opposed restrictions. Representatives from the API stated to the FOCB during these hearings that there was no danger of exhausting petroleum reserves, that waste was negligible, and that the government should let the oil industry determine its own prices.

The hearings and subsequent actions of the FOCB focused on technical problems of petroleum production. The API's assertions of the industry's ability to regulate itself were undermined by continued heavy production in the mid-1920's. Nevertheless, there were no significant federal production controls imposed in the 1920's.

As production levels increased across the nation in the 1920's, oil prices continued to fluctuate but primarily fell. The industry and the API abandoned the policy of relying solely on the market to determine prices, realizing that more stringent cooperative private efforts at production control were needed. In early January, 1929, the API announced a policy of voluntary production controls to limit production for the next three or four years, based on 1928 levels. The FOCB approved a version of this code on May 28, 1930. In December, 1928, industry leaders and members of the API set out to institute an industrywide code of ethics designed to eliminate price and nonprice competition in an attempt to bring stability. In July, 1929, the Federal Trade Commission approved this code, with deletions of restrictions on price cutting and extension of credit. The FOCB still refused to implement federal production controls, stating that voluntary efforts would have to be the largest part of any production control program. In March, 1930, the FOCB initiated a program of demand forecasts to help the petroleum industry project market need and produce accordingly. In 1932, the FOCB worked out a system of voluntary informal restrictions with the leading oil importers in the United States. In all these actions, the FOCB helped the petroleum industry to regulate itself.

These efforts at industrial self-regulation and production control were swamped by new and even more productive fields in Oklahoma City in late 1929 and East Texas in late 1930. President Herbert Hoover, formerly a member of the FOCB as Secretary of Commerce under Coolidge, took an even stronger laissez-faire approach, stating that the FOCB had no legal power to control production. Hoover believed that responsibility for such actions lay with the Congress, not the executive branch. The FOCB ultimately urged various forms of self-regulation and left the industry to solve its own problems. The problem of oil conservation regulation was left to the industry itself and to state governments until Franklin D. Roosevelt came into office. The Teapot Dome scandal returned federal policy on naval reserves back toward conservation and preservation. Ironically, despite the political scandal Fall created, his policy may have been the more correct one. Within a decade after the scandal, planners for the Navy realized that some of their reserves had been depleted as a result of drainage. This occurred when production crews drilled on private property adjacent to the federal lands and drained the neighboring petroleum reservoirs.

With the New Deal programs of President Franklin D. Roosevelt, the federal government generally increased its regulatory role. The Petroleum Administration Board (PAB) continued in the manner that the FOCB had established. The PAB replaced the FOCB, assuming its duties and taking over its files. The PAB came to an end in May, 1935, when the Supreme Court ruled the National Industrial Recovery Act unconstitutional. The PAB had been created under that act. The Bureau of Mines then began forecasting demand for the oil industry. In response to continuing problems of overproduction, Congress passed the "Hot" Oil Act of 1935, restricting interstate shipment of oil. It also set up, under the Department of the Interior, the Federal Petroleum Board (FPB), which enforced the prohibition against "hot" oil. This federal regulatory agency, like the ones before it, worked closely with the industry and with the state regulatory commissions.

The concept of maintaining strategic petroleum reserves was renewed during World War II and the Korean War. Concerns again rose over exhaustion. President Roosevelt created the Petroleum Reserves Corporation (PRC), a government corporation that would exploit Saudi Arabian oil reserves, to conserve petroleum in the United States and counteract British influence in that region. The PRC was short-lived, however, because of opposition from U.S. oil companies, which did not want federal interference in their private efforts to produce oil in the Middle East. During the Korean War, Congress passed the Defense Production Act of 1950, which enabled President Harry Truman to establish the Petroleum Administration for Defense (PAD), which, like the FOCB, made demand forecasts for the industry. The PAD facilitated collective voluntary efforts from nineteen of the largest oil companies to coordinate petroleum supplies. The PAD was dissolved after the war, but in 1954 President Dwight D. Eisenhower began to implement a policy of maintaining reserves equal to 20 percent of domestic annual production. Also in 1954, Eisenhower created the Committee on Energy Supplies. Composed of the secretaries of State, Treasury,

Interior, and Commerce, this committee studied the extent of available domestic petroleum resources as well as the growing problem of U.S. dependence on oil imports from the Middle East.

As the United States grew increasingly dependent on oil imports from the Middle East in the 1960's and 1970's, the idea of national strategic petroleum reserves was again revived. The Strategic Petroleum Reserve was begun in 1973. In 1990, these reserves held approximately 600 million barrels of oil. Both Germany and Japan adopted similar national petroleum reserves.

Bibliography

Bates, J. Leonard. *The Origins of Teapot Dome: Progressives, Parties, and Petroleum, 1909-1921.* Urbana: University of Illinois Press, 1963. This work focuses more on the political events leading up to and including the Teapot Dome scandal than on the actions and policies of the Federal Oil Conservation Board. Useful for its thorough account of the development of the Mineral Lands Leasing Act of 1920, the political debates over federal lands policy, the naval reserves issue, and pressures for legislation during this period.

Davis, Margaret L. *Dark Side of Fortune: Triumph and Scandal in the Life of Oil Tycoon Edward L. Doheny.* Berkeley: University of California Press, 1998. Biography of one of the leading figures in the Teapot Dome scandal.

Melosi, Martin V. *Coping with Abundance: Energy and Environment in Industrial America.* New York: Alfred A. Knopf, 1985. An excellent overview of the growth of the major energy industries in the United States. Contains a concise yet detailed account of the Teapot Dome scandal and the formation and actions of the Federal Oil Conservation Board.

Nash, Gerald D. "After Teapot Dome: Calvin Coolidge and the Management of Petroleum Resources, 1924-1929." In *United States Oil Policy, 1890-1964.* Pittsburgh, Pa.: University of Pittsburgh Press, 1968. Probably the best work for an introduction and overview of the development of the petroleum industry and the growth of federal and state regulations. Deals especially well with the relationship between the industry and the federal government. Thorough treatment of the Teapot Dome scandal and the Federal Oil Conservation Board.

Noggle, Burl. *Teapot Dome: Oil and Politics in the 1920's.* Baton Rouge: Louisiana State University Press, 1962. Deals with the politics of petroleum and the federal government. Focuses mostly on the Teapot Dome scandal. Gives only slight attention to the Federal Oil Conservation

Board and the concerns of the petroleum industry in oil conservation regulation.

Williamson, Harold F., Ralph L. Andreano, Arnold R. Daum, and Gilbert C. Klose. *The American Petroleum Industry: The Age of Energy, 1899-1959*. Evanston, Ill.: Northwestern University Press, 1963. Perhaps the most comprehensive study of the national petroleum industry in the twentieth century. Excellent account of the development, actions, and policies of the Federal Oil Conservation Board.

Yergin, Daniel. *The Prize: The Epic Quest for Oil, Money, and Power*. New York: Simon & Schuster, 1991. Deals only briefly with Teapot Dome and the Federal Oil Conservation Board but provides a useful, informative, and readable account of the growth of the oil industry in the United States and in the international arena.

Zimmerman, Erich W. *Conservation in the Production of Petroleum*. New Haven, Conn.: Yale University Press, 1957. Excellent monograph on the development of petroleum conservation policies in the United States. Deals at some length with the Federal Oil Conservation Board. Assumes some familiarity with conservation issues.

Bruce Andre Beauboeuf

Cross-References

Discovery of Oil at Spindletop Transforms the Oil Industry (1901); The Supreme Court Decides to Break Up Standard Oil (1911); Atlantic Richfield Discovers Oil at Prudhoe Bay, Alaska (1967); Arab Oil Producers Curtail Oil Shipments to Industrial States (1973); The United States Plans to Cut Dependence on Foreign Oil (1974); The Alaskan Oil Pipeline Opens (1977).

THE RAILWAY LABOR ACT PROVIDES FOR MEDIATION OF LABOR DISPUTES

CATEGORY OF EVENT: Labor
TIME: May 20, 1926
LOCALE: Washington, D. C.

The 1926 Railway Labor Act set up mechanisms for mediating labor disputes acceptable both to organized labor and to the railroad companies, in the process guaranteeing the right to collective bargaining for workers

Principal personages:
CALVIN COOLIDGE (1872-1933), the president of the United States, 1923-1929
HARRY DAUGHERTY (1860-1941), the U.S. attorney general who secured the sweeping injunction that broke the 1922 strike
WARREN G. HARDING (1865-1923), the president of the United States, 1921-1923
HERBERT HOOVER (1874-1964), the secretary of commerce under Harding and Coolidge
DONALD RICHBERG (1881-1960), a lawyer who served as counsel for the railroad unions in the 1920's and who held the responsibility for preparing the 1926 Railway Labor Act

Summary of Event

The 1926 Railway Labor Act brought peace to an industry plagued by strikes and violence. It created machinery acceptable to the railroad carriers and labor to mediate their disputes while guaranteeing labor's long-sought goal of collective bargaining. The carriers submitted to these terms in exchange for excluding specific bargaining agents (unions) for labor from the act. This enabled the railroads to maintain their company unions, despite the intent of the act.

The origins of the Railway Labor Act lie in a fiercely contested strike in 1922. That action stemmed from wage cuts ordered by the Railroad Labor Board (RLB), an agency charged by the 1920 Transportation Act with monitoring and regulating wages and rates in the railroad industry. Staffed by appointees of President Warren G. Harding, who held strong antilabor views, the RLB rescinded wage increases granted in 1920. This action hit hardest the shopcraft and other workers not directly included in operating the railroads. At the same time, the RLB tolerated the Pennsylvania Railroad's defiance of the RLB's orders that carriers restore union contracts that they had unilaterally abrogated and that the carriers also dismantle recently established company unions. Fearing for their long-term survival, the shopcraft and nonoperating unions struck the railroad carriers on July 1, 1922, primarily over the issues of wages and hours. Hurt least by the reductions and conciliated by the RLB's promise of no further wage cuts, the operating employees remained on the job.

Soon the strike took a new turn, as the carriers demanded an end to seniority rights, the very heart of union strength. In order to sustain operations, the companies recruited scores of strikebreakers to fill the positions held by striking workers. By eliminating seniority, the carriers eased their task of rehiring strikers and, as the unions asserted, created a massive surplus of railroad workers. By this measure, the railroad companies had raised the stakes from mere wages to union survival. The unions complained bitterly about the RLB's decision to urge the carriers to try to break the strike and to allow the companies to broach the seniority issue.

Working behind the scenes, Secretary of Commerce Herbert Hoover proved unable to persuade the carriers to negotiate. The refusal angered Harding. By the fall of 1922, Harding had reversed his early stand. Frustrated by the unions' continued rejection of the RLB demands for wage cuts, the president placed the blame for the prolonged strike squarely on the shoulders of organized labor. By the late summer, he had embraced Attorney General Harry Daugherty's position of the strike's illegality and agreed that only drastic action could prevent the country's transportation system from grinding to a halt. With presidential backing, Daugherty used a sweeping injunction to end the strike action, forcing compliance with the RLB wage cuts. The injunction, issued by Judge James Wilkerson of the District Court of Chicago on September 1, 1922, exceeded past judicial orders by prohibiting picketing and even minimal communications among the strikers and their supporters. The measure outraged many moderate

The Railroad Labor Board created by the Railway Labor Act was staffed by appointees of President Warren G. Harding, who held strong antilabor views. (Library of Congress)

Republicans such as Hoover, who had advocated a cooperative rather than confrontational solution to the strike.

Faced with a hostile government and determined carriers, the unions had no choice but to return to work. Most unions followed the Baltimore & Ohio plan suggested by Hoover ally Daniel Willard, president of that railroad. The plan entailed negotiating with the companies on a separate basis in exchange for salvaging their seniority rights.

In the wake of this massive confrontation, union members and moderate Republicans agreed hat the industry needed a new mechanism to cope with grievances and disputes. The Special Committee Representing Railroad Labor Organizations prepared an initial report that outlined labor's objectives in its relationships with the carriers. Union representatives turned this document over to Donald Richberg, who had earned a reputation as the leading labor attorney for his work in the 1922 strike. Charged with resolving the problems inherent in the carrier-union relationship, Richberg integrated these recommendations into his proposed legislation aimed at establishing new negotiating procedures.

Richberg's early drafts inevitably sparked controversy. The original proposal, known as the Howell-Barkley Bill, contained a provision that the carriers found particularly objectionable. It designated sixteen railroad labor organizations as specific bargaining agents for the rail employees. Acceptance of this condition would acknowledge carrier recognition of the unions, a position the railroad companies fiercely resisted. The two parties worked out a compromise, which President Calvin Coolidge signed on May 20, 1926.

The final version of the act disbanded the RLB and substituted new procedures for settling disputes. As a first step, these included conferences between the two parties to iron out differences on wages, hours, and other items in the contract. If the parties remained deadlocked, an adjustment board, which would handle disputes over interpretation of the terms of a contract, assumed jurisdiction. The act was vague as to whether a national board (favoring the unions) or a systemwide board (implicitly allowing for company unions) would hear the grievances. The carriers seized upon the ambiguity of the act to maintain their employee representation schemes and bring grievances to systemwide boards. As late as 1933, 147 of the 233 largest carriers still maintained company unions that predated the 1926 law. The law included neither the means to enforce decisions nor the power to inflict penalties on guilty parties, therefore emboldening the railroad carriers. The weaker shopcraft and nonoperating workers proved most vulnerable to the company union strategy.

A National Mediation Board was to intervene in disputes involving changes in a contract. The act required either party to provide a thirty-day prior notice before such changes went into effect. Once that period elapsed, the board would step in to negotiate a settlement. Arbitration stood as the absolute last choice of the board and occurred only if both parties agreed. If the mediation board perceived that the dispute endangered the transportation system, it could so inform the president, who could appoint an emergency board to deal with the crisis. The emergency board lacked enforcement power. The National Mediation Board's course of moderation and accommodation contrasted sharply with the aggressive and hostile character of the RLB.

The Railway Labor Act of 1926 established industrial peace throughout the railroad industry and acted as a model for other industries seeking accommodation between company owners and union advocates. Its recognition of collective bargaining as an employee right opened alternatives for workers throughout the economy who had no access to any form of bargaining procedure.

Impact of Event

The 1926 Railway Labor Act marked an important turning point in organized labor's drive for recognition and the right to collective bargaining. It drew on earlier legislation such as the Erdman and Newlands Acts and would play a critical role in the formulation of the 1933 Bankruptcy Act, the 1934 amendments to the Railway Labor Act, and the 1935 Wagner Act.

The Erdman Act of 1898 attempted to restore equality to the bargaining process between the railroad carriers and organized labor. The act applied only to operating employees—specifically engineers, firemen, conductors, and trainmen—yet it moved toward establishing mediation procedures that dealt fairly with unions. It banned the "yellow dog" contract, which threatened workers engaged in union activity with dismissal. The act also outlawed blacklisting, which permanently barred union supporters from employment through a system of files that carriers maintained on dissidents. A court test struck down these last two provisions. The 1913 Newlands Act sought to keep alive the negotiation process by setting up the U.S Board of Mediation and Conciliation, which again dealt only with the operating workers.

World War I created an atmosphere more favorable to union demands. The urgency of continued production, the need for industrial peace, and the government's desire to placate unions sparked administrative and legislative decisions that favored organized labor. Even before the declaration of war, the railroad unions had won the eight-hour day with the passage of the Adamson Act in 1916. During the conflict, the federal government assumed control of the nation's rail system. The government promoted standard wages and hours, long favored by the rail unions, and ensured that union members remained free of discriminatory practices by the carriers.

The unions found federal control far more in tune with their interests than was private ownership. The end of the war and the specter of company interests reclaiming their control worried the unions. Quickly, their representatives brought forth the Plumb plan, which outlined a scenario in which the unions, the bondholders, and the shippers exercised administrative control of the industry. Organized labor clearly wished to hold on to the gains made during the war and sustain what it perceived as favorable conditions.

The war's end proved disappointing to organized labor. Collective bargaining faced a sustained assault by carriers. Railroads pushed for open shops, in which workers did not have to belong to unions, and workers saw a resurgence of yellow dog contracts. The passage of the Railway Labor Act transformed the hostile environment that menaced the very existence of unions. The act salvaged the union goals first articulated in the Erdman Act and pursued through World War I. It revived collective bargaining and ended yellow dog contracts in the rail industry while guaranteeing the long-term survival of unions. Its success provided a model that greatly influenced subsequent legislation regarding labor relations through the mid-1930's and acted as a beacon for pro-union forces in the economy.

The revision of the 1890 Bankruptcy Law in June of 1933 demonstrated the continued influence of the Railway Labor Act. The Great Depression forced many railroads to the brink of ruin. Bankruptcy offered one alternative for troubled companies. It also opened the possibility of companies suspending all union contracts. To prevent such an action, the unions insisted on amendments that enabled the terms of the Railway Labor Act to prevail despite economic contingencies and secured the right to self-organization free from carrier intrusion. The Emergency Transportation Act of 1933, with a one-year life, reiterated these provisions. Designed to promote efficiencies and reduce waste in the industry, that act ensured that no workers would lose their jobs as a result of measures enacted under this law.

In 1934, the unions sought permanent legislation to create a more stable workplace. Specifically, they intended to change the conditions that allowed company unions to persist in more than half the carriers. The 1934 amendments to the Railway Labor Act guaranteed employees the right to organize independent of carrier influence. The act also established a National Board of Adjustment, which acknowledged the unions as bargaining agents for the workers and created a new board of national mediation. The act gave the president the power to appoint members to this board, subject to congressional confirmation. The mediation board also exercised the authority to certify representatives from either side, a measure that preserved the autonomy of the unions. As important, workers had the right to select their representatives through secret ballots, which isolated them from company pressures.

The success of the rail workers was illustrated most prominently in the formulation of the Wagner Act of 1935, which culminated a drive for collective bargaining throughout the economy. Already the National Industrial Recovery Act (NIRA) had incorporated boards of mediation and arbitration that had assumed a central role in the rail industry. Donald Richberg, who oversaw the writing of the Railway Labor Act, participated in the preparation of the NIRA, so similarities between the 1926 measure and the NIRA come as no surprise.

The Wagner Act, or National Labor Relations Act, replaced the NIRA, which was found to be unconstitutional. It repeated many of the staples of the Railway Labor Act and its 1934 revisions. Company unions and yellow dog contracts fell by the wayside, and the law recognized the right of workers to organize free of company interference throughout all industries. Collective bargaining assumed a central role in labor-company relations. The Wagner Act, unlike the Railway Labor Act, acknowledged closed shops, in which workers had to belong to the union before beginning work. By the mid-1930's, the unions had achieved their long-sought autonomy.

Bibliography
Babson, Steve. *The Unfinished Struggle: Turning Points in American Labor, 1877-Present.* Lanham, Md.: Rowman & Littlefield, 1999.
Bernstein, Irving. *The Lean Years: A History of the American Worker,*

1920-1933. Baltimore: Penguin Books, 1960. One of the most thorough accounts of labor's activities in the 1920's and early 1930's. It provides a complete account of the railway union-carrier relationship and explains the positions of the participants in the 1926 legislation. Contains one of the best and most detailed descriptions of the various parts of the Railway Labor Act.

_____. *Turbulent Years: A History of the American Worker, 1933-1941*. Boston: Houghton Mifflin, 1970. Chapters 5 and 7 discuss the amendments to the Railway Labor Act and the Wagner Act. The chapters pinpoint the influence of the original legislation in the formulation of national labor policy. One of the most thorough accounts available on the labor-company debates of the 1930's.

Breen, W. J. *Labor Market Politics and the Great War: The Department of Labor, the States, and the First U.S. Employment Service, 1907-1933*. Kent, Ohio: Kent State University Press, 1997. History of the federal government's involvement in labor issues through the critical period from before World War I through the early years of the Great Depression. Contains a lengthy bibliography and an index.

Fleming, R. W. "The Significance of the Wagner Act." In *Labor and the New Deal*, edited by Milton Derber and Edwin Young. New York: Da Capo Press, 1972. A concise description of the various influences on preparation of the NIRA and the Wagner Act. Serves as a useful introduction to the debates of the era.

Foner, Philip S. *On the Eve of America's Entrance into World War I, 1915-1916*. Vol. 6 in *History of the Labor Movement in the United States*. New York: International Publishers, 1982. Provides a systematic description of labor conditions on the eve of World War I. Includes a succinct description of the legislative history of labor relations in the rail industry from the Erdman Act of 1898 through the Adamson Act of 1916.

Jacoby, Daniel. *Laboring for Freedom: A New Look at the History of Labor in America*. Armonk, N.Y.: M. E. Sharpe, 1998.

Keller, Morton. *Regulating a New Economy: Public and Economic Change in America, 1900-1930*. Cambridge, Mass.: Harvard University Press, 1990. Chapter 3 contains a brief discussion of the development of the federal government's transportation policies from the beginning of the twentieth century through the 1920's. Stresses the complexity of the rail industry, which is subject to the multiple influences of shippers, organized labor, manufacturers, and other interest groups. Indispensable for grasping the importance of regulation throughout society.

Locklin, D. Philip. *Economics of Transportation*. 3d ed. Chicago: Richard

D. Irwin, 1947. Chapter 12 lists all the relevant railroad legislation for the period, outlining each act in a concise fashion and providing the reader with a clear guide to its legal history. The description of the Railway Labor Act excludes comments on the ambiguity of the law that enabled carriers to maintain their company unions.

Montgomery, David. *The Fall of the House of Labor: The Workplace, the State, and American Labor Activism, 1865-1925*. New York: Cambridge University Press, 1987. The most analytical and detailed description of labor relations in general, includes much information on the rail industry, particularly the activities of the operating unions and their role in the debates on national transportation policy both before and after World War I.

Tomlins, Christopher L. *The State and the Unions: Labor Relations, Law, and the Organized Labor Movement in America, 1889-1930*. New York: Cambridge University Press, 1985. Chapter 4 traces the legal origins of collective bargaining, including brief descriptions of legislation in the rail industry.

Vadney, Thomas E. *The Wayward Liberal: A Political Biography of Donald Richberg*. Lexington: University of Kentucky Press, 1970. Chapter 3 explains in detail Richberg's role in the formation of pro-union railroad legislation. Provides a thorough account of Richberg's motivations.

Zieger, Robert H. *Republicans and Labor, 1919-1929*. Lexington: University of Kentucky Press, 1969. The best analysis of the influence of the Republican Party in shaping labor's position in its relationship with the carriers. Particularly effective in explaining the reversal of the Republican Party from hostility toward the rail unions under President Harding and Attorney General Daugherty to the cooperative spirit promoted by Herbert Hoover under President Coolidge and embodied in the Railway Labor Act.

Edward J. Davies II

Cross-References

Labor Unions Win Exemption from Antitrust Laws (1914); The Norris-LaGuardia Act Adds Strength to Labor Organizations (1932); The National Industrial Recovery Act Is Passed (1933); The Wagner Act Promotes Union Organizations (1935); Roosevelt Signs the Fair Labor Standards Act (1938).

CONGRESS PASSES THE AGRICULTURAL MARKETING ACT

CATEGORY OF EVENT: Government and business
TIME: June 15, 1929
LOCALE: Washington, D.C.

The Agricultural Marketing Act of 1929 established the Federal Farm Board to make loans to farm cooperatives and to control surpluses of farm commodities

Principal personages:
HERBERT HOOVER (1874-1964), the president of the United States, 1929-1933
ALEXANDER LEGGE (1866-1933), the first chairperson of the Federal Farm Board
ARTHUR M. HYDE (1877-1947), the secretary of agriculture under Herbert Hoover
CHARLES MCNARY (1874-1944), a senator from Oregon, coauthor of the McNary-Haugen bills
GILBERT HAUGEN (1859-1933), a representative from Iowa, coauthor of the McNary-Haugen bills

Summary of Event

In order to understand the impact of the Agricultural Marketing Act of 1929, it is necessary to understand what happened to the American farm sector early in the twentieth century. The second decade of the twentieth century was a good one for farmers. The world had experienced rapid industrial expansion, causing incomes and spending to rise. Demand for agricultural commodities had expanded, giving farmers high prices for their crops. Farmers in the United States were producing large crops and exporting large parts of them to foreign markets. A fixed quantity of good agricultural land caused land prices to go up, making farmers feel wealthier. There was no end in sight to the prosperity.

Things began to change in 1919. European farmers were producing more as they recovered from World War I, and prices started to fall. In 1921, wheat and cotton were selling for half their 1920 prices, and farmers realized that hard times had returned. By 1923, agricultural commodity prices had started to rise slowly, and farm conditions began to improve. Things were getting better, but conditions for farmers still were unfavorable. Mechanization of farm work promised to help farmers by cutting production costs but was soon to contribute to problems of overproduction.

Agriculture was an important sector in the United States economy in the early 1920's, and Congress believed that help was needed for farmers, even though farm prices were edging up after the drastic drop in the early 1920's. A major attempt to help was embodied in the five McNary-Haugen bills introduced in Congress from 1924 to 1928. These bills called for an export corporation, which would purchase agricultural crops in large enough amounts to keep their prices at acceptably high levels. These purchases were not to be sold domestically but were to be sold in foreign markets. The bills also called for an import tariff to discourage foreign farmers from sending agricultural goods to the United States to compete with domestic products. The first three McNary-Haugen bills did not pass Congress. The last two bills passed Congress but were vetoed by President Calvin Coolidge. Herbert Hoover, Coolidge's secretary of commerce, was influential in advising Coolidge to veto the bills.

The Agricultural Marketing Act of 1929 differed from these bills in that it focused on improved marketing as a means of aiding farmers. The government, under this act, would encourage formation of national cooperative marketing organizations but would not run them.

As director of the Food Administration and as secretary of commerce, Hoover had participated in the many agricultural policy debates of the late 1910's and the 1920's. In 1928, he campaigned for president, promising to call a special session of Congress to deal with farm problems. Hoover had grown up on an Iowa farm and believed that an improved marketing process was the solution to the farm problem. Despite his strong feelings about the issue, once in the office of president he sent no specific legislation of his own to Congress, not wanting to interfere with Congress' legislative prerogative. Even so, Congress had a good idea what Hoover wanted. It passed the Agricultural Marketing Act, which became law on June 15, 1929.

The overall goal of the act was to put agriculture on an equal footing with other business sectors in the country. The objectives specified to carry this out were to decrease agricultural surpluses, stabilize prices for agricultural commodities and thereby cut down on speculation, and provide help in marketing of agricultural commodities. The act called for the establishment of the Federal Farm Board, which was to have a budget of $500 million.

The Federal Farm Board was directed to set up national farmer cooperatives as a means of achieving its goals. These cooperatives were to be controlled by farmers and were to be used primarily to improve the marketing of crops. It was believed that the coming together of farmers into a comprehensive organization that could bargain on behalf of farmers would give farmers the power to prevent drastic price declines. The Federal Farm Board was authorized to make loans to the cooperatives to increase their size and efficiency. These loans could be used to build new facilities or for expenses of marketing agricultural crops. Farmers could obtain loans at low rates of interest.

President Hoover persuaded Alexander Legge to leave his $100,000-per-year job as chairman of International Harvester to become the first chairman of the Federal Farm Board. Seven other board members were appointed, representing the major farm commodities. Arthur M. Hyde, as Hoover's secretary of agriculture, was an ex officio member.

By October of 1929, the Federal Farm Board had succeeded in setting up the Farmers National Grain Associations, which were stock companies in each of the major commodities. Stock in the associations was owned by the larger local grain cooperatives. The goal of each of these corporations was to become a large, centralized organization to facilitate marketing for the particular commodity it represented. It was hoped that their sheer size and the coordination of the marketing process they offered would increase the efficiency of marketing ag-

As president of the United States, Herbert Hoover had primary responsibility for implementing the provisions of the Agricultural Marketing Act. (Library of Congress)

ricultural crops, thus stabilizing prices at the desired high levels. The National Grain Associations were also supposed to control agricultural surpluses. Unfortunately, the government also had in place county extension agents, whose job was to help increase production. Getting farmers to control production was difficult, and the Federal Farm Board never succeeded in this task. The government thus, to some extent, operated at cross purposes, trying to keep prices high while also encouraging production.

Impact of Event

In 1930, the Federal Farm Board decided that its efforts were not succeeding. A surplus of major commodities kept agricultural prices low. Several factors contributed to the surpluses. The United States and Europe had had a few years of abundant harvests, and other countries were restricting imports from the United States and imposing tariffs in retaliation for the Smoot-Hawley Tariff of 1930. Farmers were particularly hurt by these retaliatory tariffs because they had long used exports as a means for eliminating agricultural surpluses. Finally, the Great Depression caused everyone to suffer. Low incomes meant that people were buying less of everything, including farm products.

The surplus in wheat was particularly troubling. Wheat prices fell dramatically, and in response the Federal Farm Board set up Grain Stabilization Boards in February of 1930. The Grain Stabilization Boards hoped to control grain prices by encouraging farmers to reduce their output. Chairperson Legge of the Federal Farm Board and Secretary of Agriculture Hyde toured the country trying to get farmers to participate in the production control process. They were unsuccessful in getting farmers to cooperate with these programs, so the Grain Stabilization Boards started buying surplus wheat. The purchase program was intended to be temporary, as no one recognized that the Great Depression was going to last for many years. Grain prices continued to fall, and by 1931 farm incomes were at the lowest levels of the century. The Federal Farm Board decided that it could no longer afford to buy grain or to store the grain it had already purchased. Fearing that the grain already purchased would rot in storage, the Federal Farm Board began to sell the grain it owned. This had a further dampening effect on prices and enraged farmers. The public outcry against the sale was so large that Legge resigned as chair of the Federal Farm Board.

The national cooperatives never emerged as the force that Hoover had hoped they would be. They were poorly managed and suffered from the same inefficiencies as the rest of the agricultural sector. They had little lasting effect on American agriculture, and most of them did not survive to the end of the 1930's.

The price stabilization portion of the Federal Farm Board's efforts fared no better than did the national cooperatives. The Federal Farm Board found that it could not stop the slide in agricultural prices by buying surplus grains, as illustrated by the case of wheat. Not only did it fail to keep prices from going down, it spent $400 million in taxpayers' money and disrupted commodity markets. Stabilization was a relatively new idea that was to be used in later legislation; some credit needs to be given to the Federal Farm Board for innovative thinking.

Production controls similarly failed. Hoover thought that if farmers voluntarily cut back on production, surpluses could be eliminated. Legge and Hyde toured the country to try to get farmers to cooperate with this plan. Primarily because the plan was voluntary, farmers did not participate in it. The Federal Farm Board made a special report to Congress in late 1932 in which it stressed that farm policy should include a system that would control the acreage planted. Future farm legislation made this recommendation part of production control programs.

Hoover did not recognize immediately that his farm plans were not working, so no adjustments to the plans were made during his presidential administration. His top farm advisers, Legge and Hyde, shared Hoover's vision of how to help the farmers and so did not offer alternative plans. In Hoover's defense, it is likely that the McNary-Haugen plans introduced in the 1920's would not have fared much better. The onset of the Great Depression, coinciding with increased production made possible by the mechanization of farm production, made the Federal Farm Board's goals nearly impossible to achieve.

Hoover had high hopes for solving farm problems with voluntary participation by farmers. He had seen what had happened to farmers in the Soviet Union and did not want the government to intervene on such a large scale. Farmers did not choose to participate in Hoover's plans, however, and even if they had, the low budgets available to the Federal Farm Board doomed the stabilization plans to failure.

Congress became disenchanted with the Federal Farm Board and cut its 1932-1933 budget by 60 percent. Hoover lost the 1932 election, in which Franklin D. Roosevelt was elected president. Roosevelt had his own ideas about what should happen in the farm sector. He abolished the Federal Farm Board in 1933, effectively ending the influence of the Agricultural Marketing Act of 1929. In 1933, Congress passed the Agricultural Adjustment Act, which was the New Deal's attempt to help farmers.

By 1935, farm income was 50 percent higher than it had been in 1932. Key elements of the 1933 act were declared unconstitutional in January of 1936. Later that year, new farm legislation was passed. As was suggested by the Federal Farm Board, production controls were a key element in the new plans.

Bibliography

Benedict, Murray. *Farm Policies of the United States, 1790-1950.* New York: Twentieth Century Fund, 1953. A detailed discussion of farm policy, starting during the period when the United States was primarily an agricultural country. Useful for illustrating the fine points of farm legislation.

Davis, Joseph S. *On Agricultural Policy 1926-1938.* Stanford, Calif.: Food Research Institute, 1939. A series of presentations and articles written during this time period. Not a systematic presentation, but interesting because of when it was written and because Davis was a Federal Farm Board economist.

Hamilton, David. *From New Day to New Deal.* Chapel Hill: University of North Carolina Press, 1991. Focuses on the farm policies of the Hoover and Roosevelt administrations. Attributes the failed Hoover policies to the Depression as well as to misconceptions about the nature of the farm problem.

Kirkendall, Richard. *Social Scientists and Farm Politics in the Age of Roosevelt.* Ames: Iowa State University Press, 1982. Shows how the events of the 1920's, including the Agricultural Marketing Act of 1929, led to the farm policies of the Roosevelt Administration.

Nourse, Edwin G. *Marketing Agreements Under the AAA.* Washington, D.C.: Brookings Institution, 1935. Has a short summary of the Agricultural Marketing Act of 1929 and goes on to show how the Agricultural Adjustment Act, the legislation that replaced the 1929 act, resembled legislation of the early 1920's.

Rasmussen, Wayne, and Gladys Baker. "A Short History of Price Support and Adjustment Legislation and Programs for Agriculture, 1933-65." *Agriculture Economics Research* 18 (1966): 68-79. A short, insightful, nontechnical discussion of the Agricultural Marketing Act of 1929 and the agriculture programs that followed it.

Tweeten, Luther. *Foundations of Farm Policy.* 2d rev. ed. Lincoln: University of Nebraska Press, 1979. A basic book for understanding farm policy. There is only a short section on the Agricultural Marketing Act of 1929, but the remaining material allows the reader to place the act in perspective.

Eric Elder

Cross-References

The U.S. Stock Market Crashes on Black Tuesday (1929); The Banking Act of 1933 Reorganizes the American Banking System (1933); Eisenhower Begins the Food for Peace Program (1954); The North American Free Trade Agreement Goes into Effect (1994).

THE U.S. STOCK MARKET CRASHES ON BLACK TUESDAY

CATEGORY OF EVENT: Finance
TIME: October 29, 1929
LOCALE: New York, New York

The boom of the 1920's ended in a dramatic crash of the stock market in late October, 1929, that signaled the beginning of the Great Depression of the 1930's

Principal personages:
HERBERT HOOVER (1874-1964), the president of the United States, 1929-1933
ROGER W. BABSON (1875-1967), an economist who warned of a crash
IRVING FISHER (1867-1947), an optimistic economics professor
CHARLES E. MITCHELL (1877-1955), the president of the National City Bank
THOMAS W. LAMONT (1870-1948), a senior partner at J. P. Morgan
RICHARD WHITNEY (1888-1974), the vice president of the New York Stock Exchange

Summary of Event

October 29, 1929, "Black Tuesday," is remembered as the most devastating day in American stock market history. Stock prices fell in a selling frenzy that began the moment the opening bell sounded. When the trading day was over, the Dow Jones Industrial Average had dropped more than thirty points, with some leading stocks plummeting $30-$60 a share. Billions of dollars of fortunes and the life savings of many small investors were wiped out as the decline of the market, which had begun in September, culminated on Black Tuesday. Few people had foreseen the coming of the Great Crash. The country had been riding on the boom of the 1920's.

The decade of the 1920's is often called the "Roaring Twenties." The American economy remained strong after World War I. Technological advances and mass production brought conveniences and a sense of prosperity to the average American family. With the advent of a new financial arrangement called the installment plan, the public could easily buy on credit such luxury items as automobiles, radios, vacuum cleaners, and electric iceboxes, all of which were just coming into widespread use. In his presidential campaign in 1928, Herbert Hoover promised "a chicken in every pot and two cars in every garage" and won the election in a landslide. Growing optimism and a sense of prosperity were reflected in the stock market.

The 1920's saw a broader participation of ordinary people in the stock market. As the glamorous lives of some successful stock speculators were publicized, many people became infected with the desire to make a quick fortune. Buying stocks was made easy by brokerage firms, which allowed customers to buy stocks "on margin," paying a fraction of the total value in cash and borrowing the rest from the broker. As long as the stock price rose, this speculation was safe. If the price fell, however, an investor could get a "margin call," meaning that more cash had to be put up to cover any further losses. If the money was not paid, the broker would sell the stock at the prevailing market price. Since stock prices were rising steadily in the 1920's, many investors thought that buying stocks on margin was safe speculation. Many ordinary people who had little knowledge about investments became investors in the stock market.

The stock market in the 1920's, however, was dominated by a few powerful, wealthy investors. Some of them engaged in manipulation of stock prices, often using insiders' information. They would first artificially inflate the price of a target stock, then, when other unsuspecting investors hopped on the bandwagon, sell the stock at a profit. Michael J. Meehan, for example, successfully manipulated the stock of Radio Corporation of America (RCA) in March, 1929, making $100 million in a week. In many cases, the surge in stock prices had to do with speculative momentum rather than with company profits. In fact, there were ominous signs in the American economy in 1929. The credit burden on consumers was heavy. Automobile sales were down. Steel production was falling. Few people were worried about these signs amid the increasing optimism, although some were concerned about the inflated stock investment. Economist Roger W. Babson, for example, predicted the coming of a crash in the stock market.

Stock prices reached a record high on September 3, 1929, following a decade of steady increase. There was no sign of pessimism in the air. Few investors suspected that the day marked the peak of the bull market and that from then on stock prices would steadily decline, collapsing in October. The market began a long slide. Stock prices fell slowly but relatively steadily during the month of September. Tumbles in prices were often followed by small rallies. By the end of the month, the stock index hit its lowest mark for the year up to that point. This decline continued through the month of October. Fear and apprehension began to mount among both large and small investors, amid confusion and uncertainty. As margin calls went out, more and more investors had to scramble to cover their losses, often drawing from their life savings. Sales of stock when margin calls could not be met put further downward pressure on prices. Still, investors were consoled by sporadic upward movements in stock prices. There were some optimistic analysts as well. For example, Irving Fisher, a respected economics professor, dismissed the selling trend of the market as a "shaking out of the lunatic fringe." He implied that eliminating marginal speculators would bring stability to the market. Stock prices, however, continued to decline.

The stock market began to crash in heavy liquidation beginning on October 23. The price of General Electric stock, for example, fell $20 from the previous day, while Auburn Auto's stock lost $77. By now, brokers and investors began openly to express their pessimism. Fear and anxiety prevailed. Few had any idea of what the next day, "Black Thursday," would bring.

Prices began to plummet at the opening bell on October 24. Thousands of investors had received margin calls the night before and had no choice but to sell their shares to cover their debts. The stock ticker carrying current stock price information began to run behind as the frenzied selling continued. Furthermore, price quotations printed on the ticker were confusing, as prices were tumbling in the double digits while the ticker tape showed only one-digit changes. Frustrated brokers scrambled to carry out their clients' sell orders but were often unable to find buyers. At lunch time, Thomas W. Lamont, the acting head of J. P. Morgan, called several bankers in an attempt to control the situation. This so-called bankers' pool met and agreed to pour a large sum of money into the market to support stock prices in an attempt to avoid catastrophe. In the early afternoon, Richard Whitney, the vice president of the New York Stock Exchange, walked onto the exchange floor and in a loud voice began to place buy orders at prices higher than actual selling prices. He and other brokers representing the bankers continued this, going from post to post. The prices of major stocks immediately began to recover. In fact, by the time the market closed, many stocks had recovered some of their earlier losses. RCA stock, for example, closed at

58¼, well above the lowest level of the day, recorded at 44½. The Dow Jones Industrial Average fell 6.3 points on a record trading volume of more than twelve million shares. The situation could have been much worse if the bankers had not supported stock prices.

The market remained relatively calm on Friday and Saturday. Some prices rose slightly on Friday, and the Dow Jones Industrial Average was down only a few points in Saturday morning's trading. Fear and anxiety, however, were building among investors over the weekend. When the market opened on Monday, October 28, prices began to drop at an accelerating speed. This time, there was no support from the bankers. The Dow Jones Industrial Average lost more than 38 points on a trading volume of more than nine million shares. The panic continued on the next day, Black Tuesday, when the bottom fell out of the market. The great bull market of the 1920's had crashed. The crash would continue until mid-November of 1929. For the next two and a half years, stock prices would continue to slide.

Panicked investors crowd Wall Street as news of the stock market's collapse spreads. (Library of Congress)

Impact of Event

The stock market crash of 1929 was followed by the Great Depression of the 1930's. Investors suffered massive losses. Many businesses and banks that had invested heavily in the stock market failed as a result of losses. The collapse in stock prices was followed by the banking panic of 1931. The crash was a harbinger of economic malaise that lasted through the 1930's. National output plunged by 30 percent between 1929 and 1933, and the nation's unemployment rate climbed to more than 24 percent.

Although some have argued that the crash was a prime cause of the Depression, that claim is widely disputed. The Great Crash and the Great Depression may be only tangentially related. It is generally accepted, however, that the crash was caused in part by various abusive practices in the securities markets in the 1920's including manipulation of securities prices, extensive speculation made possible by purchases on margin, trading by company officials using insiders' information, and the sale of risky securities while withholding important information about them.

The crash triggered a series of reforms in securities markets. At first, the Hoover Administration was reluctant to add federal regulations to the already existing state rules for the securities exchanges. Some people, particularly in the financial circle, feared that such measures would jeopardize the capitalistic mechanism in the financial markets. President Hoover hoped that Wall Street would reform itself in order to prevent future disasters. Many people argued, however, that strict measures to safeguard investors were necessary.

In late 1931, the Senate voted to begin a major investigation of the securities markets in an attempt to unearth the manipulative practices in securities trading that were believed to have caused the crash. The hearings conducted by the Senate Committee on Banking and Currency lasted for two years and produced thousands of pages of testimony. The inquiry gave an impetus for Congress to pass several legislative measures to regulate the securities market on the federal level. When President Franklin D. Roosevelt took office in 1933, he closed the banks in an attempt to restore order in banking. The Emergency Banking Act of March 9, 1933, declared a bank holiday, and a program to reopen the banks was initiated. As part of the bank holiday, the New York Stock Exchange was closed from March 6 to March 14.

The Securities Act of 1933 was based on the idea that the securities markets needed to be regulated by the federal government in order to protect investors. Underwriters of various securities were required to register new issues with the Federal Trade Commission before they could be offered to the public. The Banking Act of 1933, also called the Glass-Steagall Act, gave more power to the Federal Reserve Banks in controlling member banks' speculative activities. Furthermore, the act mandated that commercial banks separate themselves from investment functions in order to prevent them from using depositors' funds for speculation. As a result, commercial banks were detached from the stock market by the mid-1930's. The Federal Deposit Insurance Corporation was established to safeguard depositors and to avoid widespread bank failures.

In 1934, Congress went one step further to regulate the securities markets. The Securities and Exchange Act of 1934 established a federal agency called the Securities and Exchange Commission (SEC) to oversee the securities markets and to enforce provisions designed to guard against manipulations and fraud. This legislation was much broader in scope than in the Securities Act of 1933, in that the Securities and Exchange Act regulated securities trading at any time, even after initial distribution, while the Securities Act dealt only with stocks and bonds at their initial offering stages. Every aspect of securities trading was addressed. The SEC began to enforce the margin rules set by the Federal Reserve System in order to regulate the buying of securities on credit. Broad provisions were established for the collection and transmission of information and for investigation of securities. Penalties for violators were also established.

These new legislative measures brought sweeping changes in Wall Street practices, ensuring better market safeguards and procedures. Regulations prohibited stock manipulation using pool operations, or the combined powers of two or more operators. More stringent requirements were established for buying stock on margin. Underwriters of securities were obliged to disclose all important information about their issues. Limits were placed on the amount of speculation allowed by insiders in the stocks and bonds of their own companies. These and other measures helped the securities markets to recover in the years to come. The Great Crash had inflicted much pain on the nation, but the lesson learned from the experience was a valuable one. Even so, crashes could still occur, as illustrated by the drop in the Dow Jones Industrial Average of 508 points that occurred on October 19, 1987.

Bibliography

Beaudreau, Bernard. *Mass Production, the Stock Market Crash, and the Great Depression: The Macroeconomics of Electrification.* Westport, Conn.: Greenwood Press, 1996.

Coben, Stanley, ed. *Reform, War, and Reaction: 1912-1932.* Columbia: University of South Carolina Press, 1972. A collection of forty-two papers. The last five chapters deal with the economy of the 1920's, including the crash. Suitable for a general audience.

Galbraith, John K. *The Great Crash, 1929.* Boston: Houghton Mifflin, 1955. A readable book that describes the dramatic days before, during, and after the Crash of 1929.

Hiebert, Ray, and Roselyn Hiebert. *The Stock Market Crash, 1929: Panic on Wall Street Ends the Jazz Age.* New York: Franklin Watts, 1970. This book recounts events of September through November, 1929, in and

around the New York Stock Exchange. Accessible to a general audience.
Patterson, Robert T. *The Great Boom and Panic: 1921-1929*. Chicago: Henry Regnery, 1965. This book describes various aspects of the boom of the 1920's and the stock market collapse. Human aspects of the crash and the Great Depression are also discussed. Accessible to a general audience.
Sobel, Robert. *The Big Board: A History of the New York Stock Market*. New York: Free Press, 1965. A detailed history of the New York stock market from its birth to the early 1960's. Suitable for a general audience.
Wigmore, Barrie A. *The Crash and Its Aftermath: A History of Securities Markets in the United States, 1929-1933*. Westport, Conn.: Greenwood Press, 1985. A detailed history of the stock and bond markets between 1929 and 1933. Political and economic influences on the securities markets are analyzed. Accessible to a general audience.

Daniel Y. Lee

Cross-References

The Wall Street Journal Prints the Dow Jones Industrial Average (1897); The Banking Act of 1933 Reorganizes the American Banking System (1933); The Securities Exchange Act Establishes the SEC (1934); The Banking Act of 1935 Centralizes U.S. Monetary Control (1935); The U.S. Stock Market Crashes on 1987's "Black Monday" (1987); Dow Jones Adds Microsoft and Intel (1999).

THE NORRIS-LaGUARDIA ACT ADDS STRENGTH TO LABOR ORGANIZATIONS

CATEGORY OF EVENT: Labor
TIME: March 23, 1932
LOCALE: Washington, D.C.

By curbing the use of injunctions in labor disputes, extending unions' exemption from antitrust laws, and prohibiting "yellow dog" contracts, the Norris-LaGuardia Act made it easier to organize and operate labor unions

Principal personages:
GEORGE W. NORRIS (1861-1944), a United States senator from Nebraska, 1913-1943
FIORELLO HENRY LA GUARDIA (1882-1947), a United States representative from New York, 1917-1933
LOUIS D. BRANDEIS (1856-1941), a United States Supreme Court Justice, 1916-1939
JOHN L. LEWIS (1880-1969), the president of the United Mine Workers union, 1920-1960

Summary of Event

The Norris-LaGuardia Act of March 23, 1932, was passed in order to free labor unions from antiunion actions involving three related elements: the Sherman Antitrust Act, the injunction, and the "yellow dog" contract. As industry developed rapidly in the United States in the late nineteenth century, widespread efforts were undertaken to organize labor unions and to engage employers in collective bargaining. Many employers resisted these efforts. One instrument for such resistance was the Sherman Antitrust

186

Act of 1890, which outlawed "every contract . . . or conspiracy, in restraint of trade or commerce . . . ." Union actions such as strikes and boycotts could be penalized through employer lawsuits for triple damages, as in the Danbury Hatters' (*Loewe v. Lawlor*) case of 1908. Antiunion employers often were able to obtain court injunctions against union actions. An injunction is a court order primarily intended to forbid someone from taking actions that could cause severe injury to another. Courts had wide latitude in issuing injunctions. Violating an injunction could bring the offender under severe penalties for contempt of court, again with wide discretion for the court.

Another antiunion instrument was the so-called "yellow dog" contract, whereby a worker was required, as a condition of employment, to explicitly agree not to join a union and to renounce any current union membership. Efforts by legislatures to outlaw such contracts had been overruled by the United States Supreme Court. A company whose workers had signed such contracts could seek an injunction against any union organizer who might try to persuade workers to breach their contracts.

The Clayton Antitrust Act of 1914 ostensibly established the principle that the existence and operation of labor unions were not illegal under the Sherman Act. Further, the law forbade the federal courts to issue injunctions against a long list of union activities, vaguely worded but clearly referring to strikes and boycotts. Union jubilation that the Clayton Act would expand labor's scope of organized activity was short-lived. In 1917, the Supreme Court held in the *Hitchman Coal Company v. Mitchell* case that issuing an injunction was an appropriate remedy against a union organizer trying to persuade workers to breach their "yellow dog" contracts. Even more striking was the *Duplex Printing Company v. Deering* case of 1921. The Duplex company had attempted to obtain court action against a system of union boycotts intended to force it to become unionized. Federal district and appeals courts refused to uphold the Duplex claim, but the Supreme Court overruled them in 1921. The decision held that the union's actions could be in violation of the Sherman Act and did not constitute a "labor dispute" protected by the specific terms of the Clayton Act. Furthermore, issuing an injunction was appropriate to prevent harm to the employer. In a dissenting opinion, Justice Louis D. Brandeis pointed out that the majority opinion appeared to deny the intent of the Clayton Act.

A strong antiunion trend persisted in Supreme Court decisions during the 1920's. In 1921, the Court upheld use of an injunction against picketing when there were elements of intimidation and when "outsiders" to the direct dispute were involved, in *American Steel Foundries v. Tri-City Central Trades Council*. Also in 1921, the Court held unconstitutional an

Arizona statute establishing the right to peaceful picketing in *Truax v. Corrigan.* The case of *Bedford Cut Stone Company v. Journeymen Stone Cutters' Association* (1927) involved concerted refusal by union stonecutters to work on the products of a nonunion firm. The Court held that this action could be considered a violation of the Sherman Antitrust Act and that an injunction was an appropriate form of relief. In a vigorous dissent, Justice Brandeis pointed out the lack of parallel between the union activities and the business monopoly actions against which the antitrust laws were directed.

The prosperous conditions of the 1920's did not produce much union militancy; in fact, union membership showed a declining trend. After 1929, the economy headed into severe depression. As workers faced wage reductions, layoffs, or reduced hours, many perceived an increased need for the protection of union members and collective bargaining. Workers brought increasing political pressure to overrule the antiunion legal doctrines. In the United States Congress, their cause was taken up by Senator George W. Norris, a Republican progressive from Nebraska. With the aid of a panel of distinguished labor law experts, including Felix Frankfurter of Harvard Law School, Norris drafted a bill to achieve the intent of the Clayton Act. Fiorello Henry La Guardia of New York, also a progressive, introduced the bill into the House of Representatives. As the worsening depression created a sense of panic among many legislators who became eager to show concern for workers, the Norris-LaGuardia Act passed both houses of Congress by overwhelming margins and became law on March 23, 1932.

Sections 3 and 4 of the law stated that contracts whereby workers agreed not to join a union were not to be enforced and could not be the basis for injunctions. Section 4 directed federal courts not to issue injunctions against concerted refusals to work (that is, strikes), joining or remaining in a union, giving financial or other aid to a union or strike, publicizing a labor dispute by picketing or other methods, or assembling peaceably to organize or promote a labor dispute. Further, such actions were not to be held to constitute violations of the antitrust laws. Section 13 gave a broad definition of a labor dispute, allowing disputes to involve persons other than an employer and his or her workers, thus broadening the range of union activities protected by the law. Section 6 provided that no union officer or member could be held liable for financial damages for the separate and independent actions of other union members or officers.

Impact of Event

The Norris-LaGuardia Act removed obstacles to the formation of unions and to their activities, particularly organizing, striking, and boycotting. The law did not commit the government directly to the promotion of unions. Such promotion, however, was soon forthcoming. After the election of 1932, Franklin D. Roosevelt's New Deal swept aside the Republican administration and many Republican members of Congress, including La Guardia. One of the first acts of the New Deal was passage of the National Industrial Recovery Act (NIRA) of 1933.

Its section 7a guaranteed workers the right to form and join unions of their own choosing and obliged employers to bargain with those unions. Similar provisions were contained in the Railway Labor Act of 1934. When the NIRA was held unconstitutional in 1935, Congress enacted the National Labor Relations Act (Wagner Act) of 1935. This affirmed a "right" to unionize and created the National Labor Relations Board (NLRB) to make this right effective. Whereas the Norris-LaGuardia Act merely protected union activities from damage suits and injunctions, the Wagner Act protected unions from a long list of "unfair" labor practices. These included employer interference with union organizing activities or union operations, discrimination against union members, and refusal to bargain collectively "in good faith" with certified unions. The NLRB was authorized to conduct elections to determine if a group of workers should be represented by a union.

As a consequence of this legislation, much of the focus in labor relations shifted away from the private lawsuits with which the Norris-LaGuardia Act was concerned. Union organizers undertook vigorous campaigns for new members, sparked by the Congress of Industrial Organizations (CIO) under the leadership of John L. Lewis. Union membership, which had fallen below three million in 1933, passed ten million in 1941. Organizing efforts continued to meet with strong opposition, and employers still tried to enlist the courts to assist them, without much success. In 1938, the Supreme Court upheld the constitutionality of the Norris-LaGuardia Act in the case of *Lauf v. E. G. Shinner and Company*. The Court affirmed the legality of union picketing activities directed against a nonunion employer. In the case of *Apex Hosiery Company v. Leader*, the Supreme Court in 1940 refused to consider a union sitdown strike to be a violation of the antitrust laws. The case arose from a violent incident in 1937 when union members broke into the company's plant and physically took possession of it. The Court noted that the union's actions were clearly unlawful but argued that the appropriate remedies lay in channels other than the antitrust laws. In the case of *United States v. Hutcheson* (1941), the Supreme Court again refused to permit antitrust prosecution to be brought against union officials. The carpenters' union that was the target of the lawsuit was trying to use a boycott to induce Anheuser-Busch Brewing Company to reverse a decision that certain work should be performed by machinists. It was a no-win situation for the company, since it could be similarly attacked by the machinists if it reversed its decision. The Supreme Court simply affirmed that the union actions should not be viewed as a violation of the Sherman Antitrust Act.

The great spread of unionization in the late 1930's helps explain why hourly wage rates in manufacturing increased about 30 percent between 1935 and 1941 at a time when more than 10 percent of workers remained unemployed. Some economists noted that while union workers were benefiting, their gains were raising business costs and thus slowing the rise of job openings for the unemployed.

Union membership continued to increase during World War II, but developments led many observers to believe that unions held too much power. Strikes by coal miners led by John L. Lewis during the war were particularly damaging to the image of unions. In November, 1946, Lewis provoked a confrontation with the government, which was then nominally operating the mines under wartime legislation. A federal court issued an injunction against a work stoppage by the union and then imposed heavy fines on Lewis and the union when they did not comply. In March, 1947, the Supreme Court upheld the injunction, ruling that the Norris-LaGuardia Act did not apply when the government was in the role of employer. In 1945, the Supreme Court established that some labor union actions could be considered to violate the Sherman Antitrust Act, if the union acted in collusion with employers in a manner that promoted monopoly conditions in markets for business products.

The belief that unions had gained too much power ultimately led to adoption of the Taft-Hartley Act in 1947. That act prohibited a long list of "unfair" practices by unions. By that time, many of the issues confronted by the Norris-LaGuardia Act had faded from significance. Under the protection of the Wagner Act, unions had been organized and certified in most of the areas in which workers wanted them. "Yellow dog" contracts had disappeared, and harassment of union organizers had diminished. A major consequence of the Norris-LaGuardia Act was to shift the bulk of litigation involving labor union activities to state courts. Picketing and related activities associated with strikes and other labor disputes often primarily involved state laws, local ordinances, and local police. Private business firms largely lost the opportunity to bring civil lawsuits to halt or penalize nonviolent strikes and other labor union activities.

Bibliography
Babson, Steve. *The Unfinished Struggle: Turning Points in American Labor, 1877-Present*. Lanham, Md.: Rowman & Littlefield, 1999.

Bernstein, Irving. *The Lean Years: A History of the American Worker, 1920-1933*. Boston: Houghton Mifflin, 1960. First volume of two-volume history; see below.

_____. *Turbulent Years: A History of the American Worker, 1933-1941*. Boston: Houghton Mifflin, 1970. Taken in combination, these two volumes provide an excellent detailed narrative of a colorful and dramatic period in labor history.

Breen, W. J. *Labor Market Politics and the Great War: The Department of Labor, the States, and the First U.S. Employment Service, 1907-1933*. Kent, Ohio: Kent State University Press, 1997. History of the federal government's involvement in labor issues through the critical period from before World War I through the early years of the Great Depression. Contains a lengthy bibliography and an index.

Daugherty, Carroll R. *Labor Problems in American Industry*. Boston: Houghton Mifflin, 1941. An older college textbook that deals at length with all aspects of labor relations. Pages 880-918 present information on Norris-LaGuardia and many court cases subsequent to it.

Gregory, Charles O., and Harold A. Katz. *Labor and the Law*. 3d ed. New York: W. W. Norton, 1979. Detailed but readable account of the legislation and court actions relating to unions. Chapter 7 focuses on Norris-LaGuardia and related litigation.

Jacoby, Daniel. *Laboring for Freedom: A New Look at the History of Labor in America*. Armonk, N.Y.: M. E. Sharpe, 1998.

Lieberman, Elias. *Unions Before the Bar*. New York: Harper and Brothers, 1950. Devotes a chapter apiece to twenty-six major court cases involving unions. Excellent background on the events. Summarizes litigation at all court levels.

Limpus, Lowell M., and Burr Leyson. *This Man La Guardia*. New York: E. P. Dutton, 1938. A good review of La Guardia's colorful career, including tenure as New York City's mayor.

Mason, Alpheus T. *Brandeis: A Free Man's Life*. New York: Viking Press, 1946. This very detailed account of the life of a powerful liberal thinker and activist puts his Supreme Court role in a broad context. His labor dissents are particularly noted in pages 539-547.

Norris, George W. *Fighting Liberal*. New York: Macmillan, 1945. Norris' autobiography demonstrates the impressive array of liberal causes he supported. A chapter entitled "Yellow Dog Contract" gives a narrative of the evolution of the Norris-LaGuardia Act.

Paul B. Trescott

Cross-References

Labor Unions Win Exemption from Antitrust Laws (1914); The National Industrial Recovery Act Is Passed (1933); The Wagner Act Promotes Union Organization (1935); The CIO Begins Unionizing Unskilled Workers (1935); The Taft-Hartley Act Passes over Truman's Veto (1947).

THE U.S. GOVERNMENT CREATES THE TENNESSEE VALLEY AUTHORITY

CATEGORY OF EVENT: Government and business
TIME: May 18, 1933
LOCALE: Washington, D.C.

The Tennessee Valley Authority, a massive federal experiment, sought to upgrade the economies of seven southern states and curtail abuses by private power utilities

Principal personages:
FRANKLIN D. ROOSEVELT (1882-1945), the president whose New Deal administration launched the TVA
GEORGE W. NORRIS (1861-1944), a liberal senator who helped lay the foundations of the TVA
ARTHUR E. MORGAN (1878-1975), a hydraulic engineer, educator, and utopian who became the TVA's first chairman
HARCOURT B. MORGAN (1868-1950), a soil expert and a TVA director
DAVID ELI LILIENTHAL (1899-1981), a TVA director and its most influential chairman

Summary of Event

During the memorable first hundred days of his first administration, President Franklin D. Roosevelt, aware that the United States expected immediate action to combat the Great Depression, placed before Congress a series of reconstruction measures. One of these called for incorporation of the Tennessee Valley Authority (TVA). The TVA received congressional approval on May 18, 1933, and its three-person board of directors was confirmed on June 13, 1933. Of all Roosevelt's early New Deal legislative

President Franklin D. Roosevelt (behind microphone), Eleanor Roosevelt, and Arthur E. Morgan during an inspection tour of TVA projects in late 1934. (Tennessee Valley Authority)

initiatives, the TVA was closest to his heart. The president passionately believed in the rehabilitation of America's farms and the restoration of its rural cultures as means of encouraging better social balance in a predominantly urban civilization.

The TVA's missions focused upon the economic and social underdevelopment of seven southern states, or portions of them, that formed parts of the Tennessee River watershed. Fourth among American rivers in the volume of water that it carried, the eight-hundred-mile Tennessee River drained an area of more than forty-one thousand square miles. Within a few years, the TVA became the country's largest power utility and emerged as the Roosevelt administration's most ambitious regional social experiment. It is doubtful that any other early New Deal legislative action, certainly no enduring one, elicited more reverential praise or loosed more bitter animosities than did establishment of the TVA.

Proposed by President Roosevelt as "a corporation clothed with the power of government but possessed of the flexibility and initiative of a private enterprise," the TVA as a semiautonomous federal corporation was charged with a variety of missions, foremost—and explicitly—the unified conservation and rehabilitation of a region's intertwined human and physical resources. Attainment of this sweeping, almost visionary objective was contingent, as Congress demanded, upon the TVA's successful pursuit of the specific practical objectives of flood control, navigation development, and the production of electric power. Growing out of these major responsibilities, if ancillary to them, emerged a number of other important activities such as soil conservation, forest and wildlife restoration, the provision and expansion of recreational facilities, fertilizer production, community and industrial development, air pollution control, control of aquatic weeds, coal and solar energy research, construction of dams and steam plants, environmental education programs, acquisition of uranium supplies, assistance to small coal operators, wildlife management, and woodland analysis.

Fulfillment of these tasks was placed in the hands of the three people, technically the TVA's "incorporators," who constituted its board of directors. Presidential appointees subject to Senate approval, they served overlapping nine-year terms. They were virtually autonomous, free to function beyond the pale of regulations governing other federal bodies. They had no need to petition Congress for annual appropriations since TVA operating revenues came from commercial sales of power. Although administrative expenses were tied to the Bureau of Budget's sanction and to the Treasury's approval for any borrowing, the directors were left untrammeled otherwise by the rulings of state or federal utility commissions. Neither the hiring nor the management of personnel fell under civil service guidelines. The heads of private utilities, as well as many other business leaders, were appalled and angered by the power lodged with the TVA's board, just as they would be by some of the board's principal policies, which they soon decried as "creeping socialism."

Soon after their appointment, the first directors agreed among themselves to a division of labor. Arthur E. Morgan, the board's first chairman, was charged with planning, overseeing the construction of dams, and formulating educational programs, duties for which he was well qualified. Morgan was an idealistic progressive, a thoughtful utopian who had served as a reform-minded college president. He had earned high repute, first in Minnesota, then throughout the Mississippi Valley, as a hydraulic engineer. Another director, Harcourt A. Morgan, an entomologist by specialization, was entrusted with agricultural plans and problems along with the production and distribution of badly needed chemical fertilizers. He was both prominent and respected throughout the South as a land-grant university educator and agricultural expert.

David E. Lilienthal, thirty-four years old, was the youngest of the directors. Ambitious, brilliant, alternately ingratiating or ruthless as the occasion suggested to him, he would by 1941 become the most influential, the most controversial, and the most famous member of the board. Born in Indiana, a lawyer by profession and a progressive by persuasion, Lilienthal had developed political credentials as the reformist chairman of Governor Philip La Follette's Wisconsin Public Service Commission. He undertook the planning and execution of the TVA's power policies, seeing his tasks as revitalizing democracy in an impoverished region.

The prologue to the careers of the two Morgans and Lilienthal had been written by Nebraska's George W. Norris. Senator Norris, always a maverick, long had fought for the extension of federally sponsored public power. Before Roosevelt entered the White House, he had been defeated by three previous administrations. Pivoting his battles on the troublesome disposition of the federal government's World War I power and nitrate facilities at Muscle Shoals, Alabama, Norris drafted and fought for the legislation that made the TVA possible.

Impact of Event

The threats posed, both philosophically and practically, to private utilities in particular and to American businesses in general by the TVA appeared to be clear ones. Asked by a reporter if the TVA was socialistic, President Roosevelt acknowledged that indeed it was. TVA was owned entirely by the federal government. Its directors were neither elected officials nor accountable to Congress or dependent on Congress for appropriations. They were almost invulnerable to normal political or public scrutiny. The TVA was entrusted with bringing not only electrical power but a wide range of other services to the people of a specific region, the functional bounds of which kept expanding. Seen in context with the dictatorial actions of Italy's Fascist regime and its government-run corporate economy, Germany's National Socialism, and the Soviet Union's Stalinist brand of Communism, the TVA presented menacing prospects to those who believed in a free marketplace dominated by private enterprise.

Fears of socialism were exacerbated after controversy erupted among the directors. The disagreements produced distinct shifts in the accenting of the TVA's primary goals. The TVA's first chairman, Arthur Morgan, in order to safeguard the comprehensive vision he entertained for the TVA, wanted straightforward, friendly cooperation with private power companies, notably with Wendell Wilkie's Commonwealth and Southern Power

Company. He wanted to sell TVA electricity to them directly. By choosing to avoid conflict, Morgan hoped to prevent a costly duplication of facilities. More important, he wanted to save the TVA from disaster by taking a pacific approach to its enemies and competitors while the TVA was snarled in litigation that threatened its existence. Eventually Morgan, a high-minded man who in critical circumstances allowed his moral righteousness to emerge in baseless accusations against his colleagues' integrity, lost their confidence as well as the president's.

Lilienthal emerged from this internecine struggle as the arbiter of the TVA's power policies. They were strikingly different from Arthur Morgan's. Lilienthal's intent was to emphasize the TVA's mandate to use its production of electric power as a yardstick against which the presumptively exorbitant rates charged by private utilities could be measured—and thereby reduced.

Prior experience had nourished Lilienthal's distrust of private utilities. Because they were often owned by Wall Street financial interests, they tended, in his estimate, to function by remote control, distant from the needs of the people or regions that they serviced. Rather than selling the TVA's output directly to Commonwealth and Southern, to Alabama Power, or to lesser regional utilities, Lilienthal hoped to decentralize the distribution of electric power while increasing the number of outlets available to the TVA's consumers. To accomplish this, he first tried to stimulate municipalities to construct and operate their own power facilities. Construction would be supported by federal loans, and operations would be encouraged by access to the TVA's relatively inexpensive electricity. Lilienthal worked to secure this goal of decentralization by bringing other nonprofit organizations, such as farmers' cooperatives, into the TVA net and by educating small industries and farmers about the advantages of cheap electricity, just one of the many benefits that the TVA afforded them.

Underlying Lilienthal's emphasis on such tactics lay his conviction that although the utilization of modern technology could not in itself make people better, it could help them improve themselves. Furthermore, when used under the guidance of an agency of their own government, namely the TVA, he believed that modern technology would bring renewed vitality to their perceptions of American democracy.

The TVA, like many early New Deal programs, was swiftly brought to court by its opponents. It survived assaults on its constitutionality before the U.S. Supreme Court. It won a limited victory in 1936 in *Ashwander v. Tennessee Valley Authority*, a decision confirming the government's right to build dams to serve national defense and improve interstate commerce. The government also could sell surplus power generated by its dams, as the

Constitution granted to the federal government the right to sell property it had lawfully acquired.

Two more sweeping decisions followed shortly thereafter. Several state-chartered utilities complained that TVA-sponsored federal loans to municipalities for construction of their own power facilities confronted the private utilities with unfair competition and misappropriated tax dollars. These complaints were dismissed by the Supreme Court in 1938 in *Alabama Power Co. v. Ickes.* Similarly, mounting a more direct and potentially deadly attack, eighteen state-chartered utilities attempted to enjoin the TVA from the sale and distribution of electric power, charging that congressional uses of the commerce clause and war powers to justify the TVA were unconstitutional. The Supreme Court rejected the charges in *Tennessee Electric Power Company v. T.V.A.* in 1939, thereby effectively removing the TVA from constitutional challenge.

By the 1940, the TVA had become a New Deal icon as well as one of the monumental testaments to the vision and practical achievement of liberal America. Its champions boasted that the TVA's production of electric power had driven down the rates of private and state-chartered utilities to honest and competitive levels while directly and indirectly distributing affordable electricity to millions who were previously without it. In addition, they credited the TVA with controlling a complex regional water system, without precedents to guide it, through its thirty-three dams and its locks. They further lauded notable increases in the tonnage of barge traffic on rivers with navigation improved by the TVA. Pointing to still more dramatic results, they credited the TVA with saving a previously flood-plagued region from the huge losses in lives and property that it once seemed fated to bear almost annually. They also cited evidence of the region's agricultural and industrial gains following the TVA's assumption of responsibility for rehabilitating the region.

Others have been more critical of the TVA. Embarrassed by it, moderately conservative President Dwight D. Eisenhower and later President Richard M. Nixon wanted to sell the TVA's major facilities to private enterprise. Utilities and other businesses continued objections to what they charged were the TVA's subsidized power rates. By the mid-1980's, cost-benefit analyses of each of the TVA's major activities had raised serious questions about the TVA's asserted achievements. Many such studies concluded that all of the TVA's claimed achievements in power production, flood control, navigation, and regional economic recovery resulted from complex factors that would have operated without government interference and without the cost of so many billions of dollars. More than six decades after the TVA's establishment, politicians, conservationists, businesspeople, and academicians still saw the TVA as controversial.

Bibliography
Chandler, William U. *The Myth of TVA: Conservation and Development in the Tennessee Valley, 1933-1983*. Cambridge, Mass.: Ballinger, 1984. A clearly presented cost-benefit analysis of the TVA's performance. Critical of the TVA. Seventeen tables, page and chapter notes, appendices, valuable index.
Colignon, Richard A. *Power Plays: Critical Events in the Institutionalization of the Tennessee Valley Authority*. Albany: State University of New York Press, 1997.
Ginzberg, Eli. *New Deal Days, 1933-1934*. New Brunswick, N.J.: Transaction Publishers, 1997.
Lilienthal, David Eli. *TVA: Democracy on the March*, New York: Harper & Brothers, 1944. Intended for general readers, this is an idealistic, enthusiastic estimate of the TVA's objectives and accomplishments by its chairman. Contains a map, a bibliography, and a good index. Informative and full of the spirit that guided the early TVA.
McCraw, Thomas K. *Morgan v. Lilienthal: The Feud Within TVA*. Chicago: Loyola University Press, 1970. Describes the battle of conflicting visions and objectives. Notes, bibliography, useful index.
Neuse, Steven M. *David E. Lilienthal: The Journey of an American Liberal*. Knoxville: University of Tennessee Press, 1996. Biography of one of the TVA's most influential directors.
Owen, Marguerite. *The Tennessee Valley Authority*. New York: Praeger, 1973. Clear, informative, and substantive praise of the TVA by an author who served the agency. Very brief bibliography, useful index.
Schlesinger, Arthur M., Jr. *The Coming of the New Deal*. Vol. 2, in *The Age of Roosevelt*. Boston: Houghton Mifflin, 1958. A classic liberal narrative. Brilliantly written and informed. Part 5 is pertinent to the origins of the TVA. Page notes serve as a bibliography. Fine index. Well worth reading in its entirety.
_____. *The Politics of Upheaval*. Vol. 3 in *The Age of Roosevelt*. Boston: Houghton Mifflin, 1960. Superb narrative. Chapter 20 deals with court challenges to the TVA. Wonderful historical work on a dramatic subject. Page notes function as a bibliography. Excellent index.
Wilcox, Clair. *Public Policies Toward Business*. Homewood, Ill.: Richard D. Irwin, 1966. Superb for essentials on the TVA as a government authority and its effects on the business community. Clear basic presentation, objectively handled. Many page notes, excellent index.

Clifton K. Yearley

Cross-References

The Teapot Dome Scandal Prompts Reforms in the Oil Industry (1924); The Banking Act of 1933 Reorganizes the American Banking System (1933); The National Industrial Recovery Act Is Passed (1933); The Securities Exchange Act Establishes the SEC (1934).

THE BANKING ACT OF 1933 REORGANIZES THE AMERICAN BANKING SYSTEM

CATEGORY OF EVENT: Finance
TIME: June 16, 1933
LOCALE: Washington, D.C.

The Banking Act of 1933 established deposit insurance, regulated interest paid on deposits, prohibited underwriting of corporate securities by commercial banks, and restricted loans to buy securities

Principal personages:
CARTER GLASS (1858-1946), a former secretary of the treasury, a powerful member of the Senate Banking Committee
FERDINAND PECORA (1882-1971), the counsel to the Senate Banking Committee and an original member of the Securities and Exchange Commission
HENRY BASCOM STEAGALL (1873-1943), a congressman from Alabama, 1915-1943
ARTHUR HENDRICK VANDENBERG (1884-1951), a senator from Michigan, 1928-1951

Summary of Event

Failure of hundreds of American banks each year in the 1920's, and then thousands of them in the period from 1930 to 1933, dramatized the inadequacies of the existing banking and financial oversight system. Senator Carter Glass began pushing for reform of the system in 1931. The Senate Banking Committee, when it reported out the bill that became the Banking

Act of 1933, explained that "a completely comprehensive measure for the reconstruction of our banking system" had been deferred. The purposes of the committee's emergency bill were more modest: "to correct manifest immediate abuses, and to bring our banking system into a stronger condition." The new law significantly amended the Federal Reserve Act (1913) and the National Bank Act (1864) and added the Federal Deposit Insurance Corporation (FDIC) to those agencies already regulating and monitoring the banking system.

The collapse of the stock market, with share prices on average falling to one-sixth of their 1929 value by 1932, was blamed in large part on excessive loans to stockbrokers and, through them, to stock speculators. Generous credit to stock speculators had fueled the Wall Street boom in the late 1920's. A major purpose of the Banking Act of 1933, signed into law on June 16 of that year, was to prevent the "undue diversion of funds into speculative operations."

Banks belonging to the Federal Reserve System (member banks) were forbidden to act as agents to brokers and dealers on behalf of nonbank lenders. The Federal Reserve Board, a presidentially appointed group that governed the Federal Reserve System, was to ascertain whether bank credit was being used unduly for speculative purposes. It could limit the amount of member banks' loans that could be secured by stock and bond collateral. Member banks fostering speculation through their lending policies would be denied the privilege of borrowing from the Federal Reserve Bank of their district. Congress was concerned that businesses engaged in agriculture, industry, and commerce would be deprived of adequate credit. Most of the loans financing speculation in stocks and bonds had been made by banks in financial centers; there is no evidence that these banks turned down requests by business firms for short-term loans. Moreover, corporations could finance expansion through the sale of new securities.

Commercial banks in the 1920's began large-scale development of affiliates that dealt in securities. By 1930, these affiliates brought more than half of all new securities issues to market, in successful competition with established investment banks. Extensive hearings on affiliates' practices conducted by Ferdinand Pecora, counsel to the Senate Banking Committee, generated negative publicity regarding abuses. One section of the Banking Act of 1933, often referred to as the Glass-Steagall Act (although this name was originally attached to the entire Banking Act of 1933), ordered the separation of deposit taking from investment banking activities within a year. Financial institutions had to choose to be either commercial banks or investment houses; investment banks could no longer accept deposit accounts and member banks could no longer underwrite securities issues of business corporations. Banks with national charters were, however, permitted to underwrite and deal in securities issued by all levels of government in the United States for resale to the investing public. Separation of commercial banking and investment banking was expected to contribute to the soundness of commercial banks and to increase the overall stability of the economy.

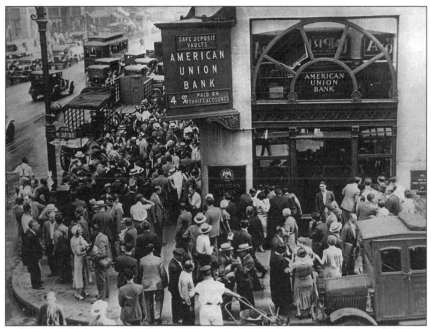

Worried depositors gather outside a New York City bank after it was closed in April, 1932. (National Archives)

There is little evidence to support the idea, which prevailed in 1933, that many bank failures were the result of the securities activities of affiliates. Many failures of small banks were blamed on the poor results of their securities portfolios, purchased on the advice of larger "correspondent" banks eager to promote issues held by their affiliates. As a result of this perception of blame, member banks were forbidden to invest in corporate stock. They could continue to buy corporate bonds for their investment portfolios, provided that those bonds were of investment, rather than speculative, quality.

Senator Glass was convinced that banks should confine their activities to short-term lending to businesses. His belief in short-term lending stemmed from the fact that the deposits of banks were largely payable on demand. He believed that banks should not lock themselves into long-term loans when their deposits, the source of funding for loans, could be withdrawn quickly.

Banks were believed to have taken on riskier loans and investments than in the past so that they could offer higher interest rates to their depositors (a situation believed to have recurred in the 1970's and 1980's). To encourage safer portfolios, Congress resorted to regulating interest rates. For deposits payable on demand, no explicit interest was allowed. The ban on interest was also intended to discourage interbank deposits with correspondent banks, with the funds going instead to local borrowers. Small banks, however, continued to hold deposits with correspondent banks. Rather than paying interest, the correspondent banks offered various services free of charge.

The Federal Reserve Board set ceilings on the rates that member banks were permitted to pay on time and savings deposits. In 1935, the FDIC was empowered to do the same for all other insured banks. Regulation Q, issued by the Federal Reserve Board, established a ceiling of 3 percent as of November 1, 1933. The rate was well above what most banks paid.

Congressman Henry Bascom Steagall was responsible for the deposit insurance provisions of the Banking Act of 1933. For fifteen years he had battled for the reform, which he saw as benefiting community banking, as it allowed the banking public to have confidence in the safety of deposits made in local banks. Senator Arthur Hendrick Vandenberg pushed for deposit insurance to take effect immediately, but President Franklin D. Roosevelt was opposed. As a compromise, a temporary plan covering the first $2,500 in insured accounts went into effect on January 1, 1934. In the meantime, infusions of capital strengthened the banks that were permitted to reopen after Roosevelt's banking holiday from March 6 to March 13, 1933.

Between 1920 and 1933, thousands of minuscule small-town banks failed. The Banking Act of 1933 imposed a $50,000 minimum capital requirement to open a national bank; the minimum had been $25,000. Capital for each branch of a national bank had to at least match that required for a one-office bank in the same location. To prevent unhealthy competition resulting from bank proliferation, the Banking Act of 1935 later tightened the requirements for a bank to obtain a charter. The FDIC stood ready to deny insurance if excessive competition threatened.

Banks in the United States were overwhelmingly undiversified institutions doing business at a single location, and their fates were thus tied to the fortunes of local economies. To provide some banking services to localities in which banks had closed, states began to ease restrictions on branch banking in the early 1930's. The battle for permission to operate branches was fought hard in state legislatures and in Congress. Federally chartered national banks were authorized in 1927 to branch in the same community as their head offices if the state in which they were located did not prohibit branching. The Banking Act of 1933 permitted branches beyond the head-quarters community, so that national banks could branch to the same extent as allowed for state banks. Interstate branches remained forbidden.

In 1922, the Federal Reserve Banks began to coordinate their purchases and sales of government securities (known as open market operations). The 1933 act placed open market operations under Federal Reserve Board regulation; the board could now disapprove policies recommended by the Federal Open Market Committee. Further, all relationships and transactions of the Federal Reserve Banks with foreign institutions were placed under control of the Federal Reserve Board. Both measures diminished the policy roles previously played by the twelve Federal Reserve Banks, particularly the powerful one in New York City.

The 1933 act also, for the first time, gave the Federal Reserve System some authority over bank holding companies that owned shares in member banks. A bank holding company could avoid this supervision if control over a member bank was exerted without the need to vote shares. Involvement of the Federal Reserve System with bank holding companies remained limited.

Impact of Event

Exercise of authority over banking by individual states had led to a "competition in laxity" with federal regulators. Over the years, restrictions on national banks, under federal jurisdiction, had been eased in order to prevent them from switching to state charters and to encourage state banks to convert to national charters. Many states had weak or inadequate banking supervision. State banks failed at a much higher rate than national banks between 1920 and 1933.

Supporters of states' rights had succeeded in preventing a federal take-over of chartering, supervision, and regulation of all commercial banks. After the Banking Act of 1933, however, states had to share jurisdiction with the FDIC for nonmember banks covered by that agency's insurance. States retained the power to decide policy on branch banking. Some persisted in prohibiting all branches, but more broadened the territory in which branching was authorized. In no case was interstate branching permitted.

Deposit insurance, fiercely opposed by some bankers in 1933, became permanent with the Banking Act of 1935. Advocates hoped that deposit insurance would stimulate bank lending to the private sector as deposits increased. Bank deposits increased by more than 46 percent between 1934 and 1939, surpassing the record 1930 total by more than $2.6 billion. Total loans, however, failed to increase significantly, reflecting the weak recovery of business investment spending and the timidity of bank lending officers.

The FDIC had been organized in September, 1933. All member banks were required to join; solvent nonmember banks were also eligible. Banks paid an initial premium of .25 percent of insurable deposits. By the beginning of 1934, 87 percent of all commercial banks had joined the FDIC, and more than 96 percent of all deposits were covered. By the end of that year, 93 percent of commercial banks had joined, and 98 percent of deposits were covered. All but about 1 percent of applicant banks qualified for deposit insurance.

To remain insured, nonmember banks were expected to become member banks by mid-1936. This deadline was first extended and then abandoned in 1939. A majority of American banks continued to be nonmembers, enjoying the lower minimum capital and lower reserve requirements demanded by many state charters as opposed to the requirements imposed by the Federal Reserve Board.

The FDIC later proved successful in one of its goals, that of preventing a new wave of bank failures triggered by depositors' fears. Even as hundreds of banks were forced to close in the 1980's, depositors did not panic and rush to remove their funds.

Ceilings on interest rates did not hamper the gathering of deposits by banks until the 1950's. Thereafter, competition with other investment outlets that offered returns higher than those permitted under Regulation Q caused some hardships for banks. Interest rate regulations for time and savings deposits were eliminated in 1986.

The separation of commercial from investment banking called for in the Banking Act of 1933 had already begun before the act was passed. The two leading American banks, Chase National Bank and National City Bank, announced plans to eliminate their affiliates in March, 1933. The Morgan investment banking business, sharply reduced by the Depression, was continued by several partners who left to form Morgan, Stanley & Company. The historic name of J. P. Morgan & Company now belonged to a commercial bank that became Morgan Guaranty Trust Company in 1959. Other large investment banks chose to eliminate their deposit-taking activities.

The 1933 act began the process of diminishing the autonomy of the twelve Federal Reserve Banks and centralizing power in the Federal Reserve Board in Washington. The Banking Act of 1935 completed that shift. In many significant ways, however, the American banking system was unchanged by New Deal legislation. Major problems left unresolved involved the dual banking system of state and national banks, the division of responsibilities among federal agencies, and limited ability of banks to branch and thus to diversify their lending and deposit bases. The 1933 act also created some problems by failing to make deposit insurance premiums related to risk and by banning interest on demand deposits, making it more difficult for banks to get those deposits.

Bibliography

Benston, George J. *The Separation of Commercial and Investment Banking: The Glass-Steagall Act Revisited and Reconsidered.* New York: Oxford University Press, 1990. A well-argued case for the repeal of separation of the two types of banking.

Burns, Helen M. *The American Banking Community and New Deal Banking Reforms, 1933-1935.* Westport, Conn.: Greenwood Press, 1974. Useful background material and a detailed exposition of the attitudes of bankers regarding proposals that led to the banking acts of 1933 and 1935.

Chandler, Lester Vernon. *American Monetary Policy, 1928-1941.* New York: Harper & Row, 1971. A leading economic historian discusses banking issues as well as central bank policy.

_____. *America's Greatest Depression, 1929-1941.* New York: Harper & Row, 1970. Provides the economic setting of the era.

Friedman, Milton, and Anna Jacobson Schwartz. *A Monetary History of the United States, 1867-1960.* Princeton, N.J.: Princeton University Press, 1963. Masterful and comprehensive. Covers the banking collapse and legislation of the 1930's in great detail, from a monetarist perspective.

Ginzberg, Eli. *New Deal Days, 1933-1934.* New Brunswick, N.J.: Transaction Publishers, 1997.

Kennedy, Susan Estabrook. *The Banking Crisis of 1933.* Lexington: The University Press of Kentucky, 1973. Carefully researched, authoritative treatment of events of the period after 1929 and measures to deal with the banking crisis.

Klebaner, Benjamin J. "Banking Reform in the New Deal Era." *Quarterly Review (Banca Nazionale de Lavoro)* 178 (September, 1991): 319-341. An analysis of the limited changes made between 1933 and 1939 in commercial and central banking.

Krooss, Herman Edward, comp. *Documentary History of Banking and Currency in the United States.* 4 vols. New York: Chelsea House Publishers, 1969. Volume 4 contains the text of the Banking Act of 1933 and useful commentary by an eminent financial historian.

Studenski, Paul, and Herman Edward Krooss. *Financial History of the*

United States. 2d ed. New York: McGraw-Hill, 1963. Excellent, concise treatment of developments since 1789 by two leading experts.

Westerfield, Ray B. *Money, Credit, and Banking.* New York: Ronald Press, 1938. The most comprehensive treatise of the period. Well written. A less-detailed second edition appeared in 1947.

Wicker, Elmus. *The Bank Panics of the Great Depression.* New York: Cambridge University Press, 1996.

Benjamin J. Klebaner

Cross-References

The Federal Reserve Act Creates a U.S. Central Bank (1913); The U.S. Stock Market Crashes on Black Tuesday (1929); The Banking Act of 1935 Centralizes U.S. Monetary Control (1935); Congress Deregulates Banks and Savings and Loans (1980-1982).

THE NATIONAL INDUSTRIAL RECOVERY ACT IS PASSED

CATEGORY OF EVENT: Government and business
TIME: June 16, 1933
LOCALE: Washington, D.C.

The National Industrial Recovery Act temporarily replaced the market system with a system of planning boards, under which labor and management would decide on wages, prices, and output levels

Principal personages:
FRANKLIN D. ROOSEVELT (1882-1945), the thirty-second president of the United States
HUGH S. JOHNSON (1882-1942), the first head of the National Recovery Administration
REXFORD GUY TUGWELL (1891-1979), an economist and Roosevelt adviser
ROBERT F. WAGNER (1877-1953), the chief congressional sponsor of the bill
WILLIAM E. BORAH (1865-1940), the leader of opposition to the bill in the Senate
CLARENCE DARROW (1857-1938), a famous criminal lawyer, appointed by Roosevelt to head the National Recovery Review Board

Summary of Event

The National Industrial Recovery Act was passed by Congress on June 16, 1933, in an attempt to bring relief from the Depression by overhauling the way in which American industry was organized. The experiences of the War Industries Board during World War I had convinced many in Washing-

As scenes such as these unemployed men lining up for bread during the early years of the Great Depression became more common, there were increasing calls for government intervention in the economy. (Library of Congress)

ton that it was possible to greatly expand production if the competitive system were replaced with a system of industrial cooperation, guided by government. By the spring of 1933, the severity of the Depression was such that even the U.S. Chamber of Commerce was urging the new administration of Franklin D. Roosevelt to expand government's role in the economy. Rexford Guy Tugwell, an economist at Columbia University and a member of Roosevelt's "brain trust," had sketched out a plan for peacetime governmental direction of production through the use of industry codes in his book *The Industrial Discipline and the Governmental Arts*, published in early 1933.

The National Industrial Recovery Act (NIRA) as sent by President Roosevelt to Congress on May 15, 1933, was divided into two parts. Title I closely followed Tugwell's recommendations. It authorized a suspension of antitrust laws to allow management and labor in each industry to write binding codes specifying standards of fair competition. The National Recovery Administration (NRA) was established to administer the codes. Section 7a of Title I was aimed at securing the rights of labor by guaranteeing the right to collective bargaining and by including minimum wage and maximum hour stipulations. Title II of the bill established the Public Works Administration and appropriated $3.3 billion for the carrying out of public works.

The bill was passed quickly by the House of Representatives with little dissent, but it ran into trouble in the Senate. Many senators feared that suspending antitrust laws would give industry free rein to fix prices and restrict output. A group led by Senator William E. Borah of Idaho attempted to amend the bill to preclude price fixing, but the bill's Senate sponsor, Robert F. Wagner of New York, arguing that the drafters of the industry codes should be given maximum flexibility, was able to defeat the amendment. The Senate finally passed the bill on June 13, 1933, by a vote of forty-six to thirty-nine. Roosevelt signed the bill on June 16.

Roosevelt chose Hugh S. Johnson to head the National Recovery Administration and decided to place the Public Works Administration under the control of Secretary of the Interior Harold Ickes. Johnson had had considerable relevant administrative experience serving as an aide to Bernard Baruch on the War Industries Board during World War I. Although Johnson appeared to have considerable authority to impose codes of fair practice on industry, he chose instead to attempt to obtain voluntary cooperation. He hoped to establish a system of industrial self-government not dissimilar to the European doctrine of syndicalism, although Johnson saw himself as building on the industry trade associations that had arisen and grown during the 1920's. Johnson's reliance on voluntary cooperation was reinforced by doubts about the constitutionality of the NIRA and fear that disgruntled industrialists might bring lawsuits against it.

The process of writing codes took place largely in offices at the Department of Commerce, with NRA administrators mediating between delegations of owners and workers from each industry. The reliance on voluntary cooperation resulted in few codes being drawn up during the early months. In July, Johnson persuaded Roosevelt to agree to a stopgap proposal under which essentially every business in the country would adopt NRA standards on minimum wages and maximum hours immediately. Businesses in compliance with what was called the President's Reemployment Agreement would be allowed to display a sign featuring the NRA's Blue Eagle and the motto We Do Our Part. Gradually, NRA administrators began to hammer out the industry codes. By June, 1934, codes covering 450 industries with twenty-three million workers had been drawn up.

The industry codes all included provisions establishing minimum wages and maximum hours and guaranteeing the collective bargaining rights of workers. Employment of children under the age of sixteen was also generally prohibited. Most codes specified minimum prices and otherwise attempted to restrict competition. Examples of restrictions on competition included production quotas, under which individual companies would be assigned a specified share of total industry output, which would itself be limited; restrictions on the installation of new machinery; and restrictions on the hours during which existing machinery could be operated.

Supporters of the NIRA in Congress and in the Roosevelt Administration had always been ambivalent concerning the wisdom or necessity of allowing business to restrict output and fix prices. The ambivalence is evident in a parenthetical phrase included in the following passage from section 1, Title I of the act, where the purpose of the legislation is explained: "[The Act is] to promote the fullest possible utilization of the present productive capacity of industries, [and] to avoid undue restriction of production (except as may be temporarily required)." In practice, it became clear during the negotiations for drawing up the codes that industry saw output restrictions and price fixing as a quid pro quo for agreeing to the restrictions on wages and hours and guarantees of collective bargaining.

Support for the NRA began to wane as it became clear to what extent the industry codes allowed the code authorities to replace determination of wages, prices, and output through the market with determination by administrative fiat. Support was also undermined by the mercurial and erratic behavior of Johnson as administrator. Responding to criticism, Roosevelt set up the National Recovery Review Board, chaired by attorney Clarence Darrow, to review the industry codes. Johnson was finally obliged to resign in late September, 1934. He was replaced as the administrative authority by a five-person National Industrial Recovery Board (NIRB). The NIRB, particularly under the influence of Leon Henderson, the NRA's chief economist, attempted to scale back the regulation of smaller industries and to modify the price fixing and output-restricting provisions in existing codes.

The original act was set to expire in June, 1935. In February, Roosevelt formally asked for a two-year extension. Privately, however, Roosevelt appeared to have been ready to abandon the NIRA as having done little to help economic recovery. Many in Congress were also skeptical. In the end, congressional consideration of an extension of the NIRA was rendered moot when the Supreme Court ruled in the case of *Schechter Poultry Corp. v. United States* (1935) that the NIRA was unconstitutional. The Court was unanimous in ruling that the act was an unconstitutional delegation of legislative authority to the executive branch and that the commerce clause of the Constitution did not allow the federal government to control the details of the operations of businesses that had only a slight involvement in interstate commerce.

Impact of Event

Following the Supreme Court decision, the vast apparatus of industrial codes and industrial authorities was rapidly dismantled. Congress preserved the labor legislation embodied in the NIRA by passing the National Labor Relations Act (NLRA, popularly known as the Wagner Act), which actually went beyond section 7a of the NIRA in attempting to ensure fair labor practices. Under the NLRA, the National Labor Relations Board was set up to police labor relations.

In the years since the demise of the NIRA, the law's impact has been debated by economists and historians. Economists have generally viewed the NIRA as having retarded recovery from the Great Depression. Economists have tended to be critical of the industry codes for having artificially raised wages and prices and authorized—in fact, often promoted—output restrictions. Some historians have been kinder to the NIRA, inclined to view favorably the social consequences of the labor law reforms contained in the act. Arthur Schlesinger, for example, although conceding that the NIRA contributed little economically to the recovery, has argued that legislative sanction for maximum hours, minimum wages, and collective bargaining and against child labor would have been difficult to obtain any other way.

Editorial cartoon satirizing the proliferation of New Deal legislation in 1934. (Library of Congress)

A careful analysis of the economic impact of the act has been carried out by Michael Weinstein, who argues that the codes had a substantial effect on wages and prices. The NIRA's impact on wages resulted, first, from the enactment of minimum wage regulations that raised the wages of workers who previously had been earning below the minimum, and second, from increases in the wages of those who had been earning more than the minimum in order to restore previous wage differentials. Weinstein estimates that in the absence of the NIRA, average hourly earnings in manufacturing in May, 1935, would have been less than $.35 per hour, rather than almost $.60 per hour. The act resulted in higher prices as a result of its effect on wage costs and its encouragement of collusive behavior and price fixing. Weinstein estimates that in the absence of the NIRA, the price level in May, 1935, would have been more than 20 percent lower than it actually was.

Higher prices reduced the purchasing power of the existing stocks of money and wealth. This resulted in lower levels of consumption than would otherwise have occurred. The lower real value of the money stock also resulted in higher interest rates than would otherwise have existed. These higher interest rates, in turn, retarded borrowing by businesses to finance new machinery and equipment and borrowing by households to finance houses and, to a lesser extent, automobiles, furniture, and other consumer durables.

In fact, industrial production had increased, on a seasonally adjusted basis, by more than 50 percent between March and July, 1933, before the NRA had begun operations. During the operating life of the NRA, industrial production actually declined slightly. Perhaps most damning is the fact that from the time of the Supreme Court's ruling in May, 1935, that the NIRA was unconstitutional until the end of that year, industrial production increased by almost 15 percent.

Investment spending performed somewhat better during the NRA period. Spending by businesses on new machinery and equipment and new factories and office buildings rose more than 40 percent between the depressed second quarter of 1933 and the second quarter of 1935. This still left business investment spending more than 60 percent below its level in 1929 and further still below the level necessary if the economy was to return to full employment. Similarly, spending by consumers on new houses more than doubled during the time of the NRA, but residential construction remained more than 70 percent below its peak level of the late 1920's.

Peter Temin has provided an interesting argument that reinforces the view that the NRA retarded recovery from the Depression. Temin notes that there are a number of parallels between the course of the early years of the Depression in the United States and in Germany. After 1933, however, the paths of the two countries diverged economically. Germany experienced very rapid employment gains, while employment recovered only slowly in the United States. Temin argues that the recovery in Germany was spurred, in part, by the determination of the Nazis, who came to power in January, 1933, to hold down the growth of wages. In the United States, in contrast, the NRA acted to keep wages far above market-clearing levels. Although there are many striking contrasts between U.S. and German economic policy in the post-1933 period, Temin believes that differences in wage policies are central in understanding the differing pace of employment recovery in the two countries. The NRA effectively precluded the possibility that the large numbers of unemployed workers in the United States would be able to find jobs by competing on the basis of wage rates.

Bibliography
Filipetti, George, and Roland S. Vaile. *The Economic Effects of the NRA: A Regional Analysis*. Minneapolis: University of Minnesota Press, 1935. Explores in detail the impact of the NRA on the Minneapolis-St. Paul area. Although fairly short, it provides a revealing account of some aspects of the industry codes in operation.

Ginzberg, Eli. *New Deal Days, 1933-1934*. New Brunswick, N.J.: Transaction Publishers, 1997.

Hawley, Ellis W. *The New Deal and the Problem of Monopoly: A Study in Economic Ambivalence*. Princeton, N.J.: Princeton University Press, 1966. Attempts to place the NIRA in the context of New Deal attitudes toward big business. Interesting discussion of the turn toward enhanced antitrust enforcement in the post-NIRA period.

Lyon, Leverett S. *The National Recovery Administration: An Analysis and Appraisal*. Washington, D.C.: The Brookings Institution, 1935. At more than nine hundred pages, much too long for the general reader, but worth skimming for an interesting contemporary appraisal of the NRA. Completed in the spring of 1935, before the *Schechter* decision, when the future of the NRA was still in doubt.

Rosenof, Theodore. *Economics in the Long Run: New Deal Theorists and Their Legacies, 1933-1993*. Chapel Hill, University of North Carolina Press, 1997. Examination of the New Deal and its theorists from the perspective of their impact on later years. Contains an extensive bibliography and index.

Schlesinger, Arthur M., Jr. *The Coming of the New Deal*. Vol. 2 in *The Age of Roosevelt*. Boston: Houghton Mifflin, 1958. Chapters 6-10 provide a sympathetic treatment of the formulation and administration of the NRA by one of the best-known biographers of Roosevelt.

Temin, Peter. *Lessons from the Great Depression*. Cambridge, Mass.: MIT Press, 1989. Chapter 3 presents Temin's argument that the high wages resulting from the NRA retarded economic recovery in the United States. Contains references to fairly advanced economic theory, but the basic argument is easily understood.

Tugwell, Rexford G. *The Industrial Discipline and the Governmental Arts*. New York: Columbia University Press, 1933. Contains Tugwell's rationale for the sort of system embodied in the NRA codes. Reveals the extent to which confidence in the free market system had declined by 1933.

Weinstein, Michael M. "Some Macroeconomic Impacts of the National Industrial Recovery Act." In *The Great Depression Revisited*, edited by Karl Brunner. Boston: Martinus Nijhoff, 1981. A brief analysis of the economic impact of the NIRA. Relatively nontechnical, but some knowledge of elementary economics is presumed.

Anthony Patrick O'Brien

Cross-References

The Banking Act of 1933 Reorganizes the American Banking System (1933); The Wagner Act Promotes Union Organization (1935); Roosevelt Signs the Emergency Price Control Act (1942); Truman Orders the Seizure of Railways (1946).

THE SECURITIES EXCHANGE ACT ESTABLISHES THE SEC

CATEGORY OF EVENT: Finance
TIME: June 6, 1934
LOCALE: Washington, D.C.

The Securities Exchange Act of 1934 created a quasi-judicial administrative body, the Securities and Exchange Commission, with broad powers to regulate the securities markets and protect the public interest

Principal personages:
FRANKLIN D. ROOSEVELT (1882-1945), the president of the United States, 1933-1945
FERDINAND PECORA (1882-1971), a Senate investigator who documented capital market transgressions
SAM RAYBURN (1882-1961), a congressman from Texas who cosponsored the Securities Exchange Act
DUNCAN FLETCHER (1859-1936), a senator from Florida who cosponsored the Securities Exchange Act
RICHARD WHITNEY (1888-1974), an influential president of the New York Stock Exchange during the 1930's

Summary of Event

The Securities Exchange Act of 1934 (Public Law 291) solidified the expanding role of the federal government in protecting the investing public. Passed in the aftermath of the greatest stock market collapse in history, this legislation established a new administrative agency with broad powers to ensure that many of the financial abuses and deceptive practices of the past would not recur.

Historically, as economic activity increases in volume, complexity, and sophistication, the corporation emerges as the dominant form of business organization. Corporate entities thrive because of the continued and expanding capital investment of people willing to accept the risks and rewards of ownership but unwilling or unable to actually participate in management of the business operation. Through the issuance of securities by corporations, ownership can be spread over a broad base of individuals, thus maximizing the potential for invested resources.

In order to facilitate this capital exchange process, organized marketplaces have developed throughout the world. These capital markets provide the mechanism for the corporate distribution of debt and equity securities as well as the subsequent transfer of these securities between individuals.

Because of the inherent separation of corporate management from ownership, current and potential investors operate under a distinct informational disadvantage. Capital contributors are at the mercy of claims made by the "insiders." Exploitation of unwary investors inevitably occurs, and securities markets merely serve to provide an organized forum within which to execute such schemes on a broad scale.

Government, concerned with ensuring an adequate supply of available capital in order to sustain economic growth, has a natural interest in protecting investors and maintaining public confidence in these securities markets. In the United States, attempts at regulation of securities were first made at the state level. In response to widespread fraudulent activities of stock promoters, Kansas enacted a statute in 1911 to protect the public interest. In the first year following enactment of this law, approximately fifteen hundred applications to sell securities in Kansas were filed. Only 14 percent were accepted, the rest being judged fraudulent (75 percent) or too highly speculative (11 percent).

Other legislatures followed Kansas' lead, and by 1913, twenty-two other states had passed laws similar in intent but widely varying in approach. These state securities laws are often called blue-sky laws, since the speculative schemes they attempted to foil often involved little more than selling "pieces of the sky," or worthless securities.

For various reasons, the individual state attempts to regulate securities markets were not very effective. Perhaps the greatest problem arose from the tactic of "interstate escape." Individuals or companies could continue deceptive and fraudulent practices merely by moving across state lines (physically or through the mails) to another jurisdiction where regulations were inadequate, poorly enforced, or perhaps even nonexistent. To limit such evasion, some form of federal intervention was needed.

During the 1920's, there was a veritable explosion in securities market activity. Small investors entered the market in numbers larger than ever before. National brokerage firms doubled the number of their branch offices and reported phenomenal increases in business. Despite the vigorous trading and investing activity, the strength of the market was quickly eroding as a result of a number of prevailing traditions.

First, stock price manipulation was common. This was often executed by means of a manipulation pool, in which a syndicate of corporate officials and market operators join forces and, through a succession of equally matched buying and selling orders ("wash sales") among themselves, create the false impression of feverish activity, thus driving up the price of the stock. At the height of this artificial activity, the stock is sold, huge profits are reaped by the syndicate, and the stock price then subsequently plummets. As an example of the success of this gambit, a pool formed in March, 1929, to trade in Radio Corporation of America stock operated for only a seven-day period and netted a profit of almost $5 million.

The excessive use of credit to finance speculative stock transactions (that is, buying stocks "on margin") was another tradition that undermined the stability of the market. An investment as small as $100 could purchase $1,000 in securities (with a 10 percent margin), and there were no limits to the level of credit a broker could extend to a customer. This practice effectively lured potential capital away from productive economic investment and toward mere market speculation.

A third practice that hindered the efficient operation of the securities market relates to the misuse of corporate information by insiders. Corporate officials could withhold information, either positive or negative. By timing its release after they had already positioned themselves in the market, they could benefit from the price fluctuation when the news finally became public.

The weight of these traditions finally culminated in the stock market crash of October, 1929. This was a financial earthquake of dramatic proportions. The aggregate value of all stocks listed on the New York Stock Exchange (the largest capital market in the United States, handling 90 percent of all stock transactions on a dollar basis) declined from $89 billion before the crash to only $15 billion by 1932. The economic depression that rapidly deepened following the crash was the worst economic crisis in U.S. history.

In March, 1932, the Senate Banking and Currency Committee was empowered to investigate the securities industry. This inquiry was continued and greatly expanded in scope after the election of Franklin D. Roosevelt as president in November, 1932. Roosevelt had been on record since his tenure as governor of New York as being highly critical of various stock market activities. The 1932 Democratic national platform on which he ran explicitly called for federal supervision of securities transactions.

Ferdinand Pecora served as legal counsel to this committee during its extensive investigations in 1933 and 1934. He compiled an impressive body of evidence concerning financial corruption and malpractice. Pecora personally elicited much of the damaging evidence from the most prestigious financial leaders of the time and was invaluable in documenting the need for securities regulation. For example, his investigation disclosed that of the $50 billion of new securities issued during the decade after World War I, half had proved to be worthless.

With the passage of the Securities Act in 1933 (signed into law on May 5, 1933, soon after Roosevelt's inauguration), the federal government finally entered the arena of securities regulation. This bill was championed in Congress by Representative Sam Rayburn of Texas and Senator Duncan Fletcher of Florida. The 1933 act is primarily a disclosure statute, concerned only with the initial distribution of a security. Although it was an important first step and forerunner to more ambitious efforts in securities regulation, this legislation failed to adequately address many of the practices in the capital market that contributed to the 1929 collapse.

Fletcher and Rayburn once again introduced bills in Congress, based in large part on drafts written by investigator Pecora. At the time, there was significant and widespread opposition to stock market regulation. Government interference, it was argued, would likely upset the delicate workings of Wall Street. Richard Whitney, president of the New York Stock Exchange (NYSE), was at the vanguard of this resistance. Whitney organized a well-financed protest campaign and mobilized forces to defeat the proposed legislation. Overt threats were even made to relocate the NYSE to Montreal, Canada, which offered a less obtrusive regulatory environment. Intense lobbying efforts did result in some modifications of the original bills, but finally, on June 6, 1934, Roosevelt signed the Securities Exchange Act.

Impact of Event

The major provisions of the Securities Exchange Act deal with three broad areas of regulation in an attempt to prevent the abuses previously cited and thereby protect the public interest: full and fair disclosure, supervision of capital market practices, and administration of credit requirements. This act requires that all national securities exchanges register with and be subject to the regulations of the Securities and Exchange Commission (SEC), an administrative agency with quasi-judicial powers that was created by this legislation. The immediate result was the closing of nine stock exchanges that could not meet the new requirements, including a one-man exchange operating out of an Indiana poolroom.

All corporations with securities listed on a national exchange must file detailed registration statements with the SEC and are required to disclose financial information on a periodic basis, in a form that meets standards. The SEC retains discretionary power over the form and detail of such disclosures. SEC also required periodic audits of these firms by independent accountants.

This last requirement has had a dramatic impact on the growth and development of the accounting profession. Certified public accountants were effectively granted a franchise to audit corporations with publicly traded securities. There was a substantial cost involved in terms of increased risk exposure. By expressing an opinion on the veracity of financial statements filed with the SEC, the auditor becomes legally liable to third parties (including investors) who may subsequently be harmed by reliance on that information.

In the area of actual market practices, the SEC had immediate and far-reaching impact. Because of the relative informational advantage that market participants have over the public, the SEC now closely scrutinizes their activities. Exchanges, brokers, and dealers must all register with the SEC and file periodic disclosure reports. Corporate insiders are subject to especially strict rules designed to prevent unfair profit-taking. Certain stock market manipulation schemes (for example, wash sales) were prohibited. In fact, any fraudulent, manipulative, or deceptive securities dealings, whether specified by the act or not, are prohibited for all market participants. The penalties for infraction include fines, imprisonment, or both.

Finally, in the area of credit, the 1934 act authorizes the Federal Reserve System to administer the extension of margin credit in securities trading, with the SEC as ultimate enforcer. This important component of government economic and monetary policy was no longer to be left in the hands of individual brokers.

The first commission was composed of a presidentially appointed five-member bipartisan panel that included Ferdinand Pecora. Ironically, Pecora was passed over as chairman in favor of Joseph Kennedy, who the year before had participated in a pool syndicate operation. Since its inception, the SEC has progressed through a number of different phases. The first decade of operation was an innovative period in which the permanent machinery and procedures necessary to carry out the functions and responsibilities of the SEC were established. This period was also marked by a concerted effort on the part of the early commissioners to promote the agency to both the public and the business community as a powerful partner in the quest for honest financial activity, not as a mere enforcement arm of the government.

It was during this early period that a philosophy of operation began to evolve. Rather than merely coercing compliance through enforcement actions, the SEC often adopted the policy of encouraging self-regulation within a framework of governmental constraints. By inspiring confidence in the laws that it administered, the SEC hoped to foster a heightened sense of social responsibility and ethics among the private sector, leading to development of self-monitoring systems.

This pragmatic approach was perhaps most evident in the area of establishing accounting and reporting standards. Although the SEC had been empowered to develop and maintain standards and principles of accounting practice, it generally deferred to the accounting profession. Such concession did not occur automatically. The SEC first had to satisfy itself that the private sector's system of establishing accounting and auditing standards had progressed to an acceptable level.

The next twenty-year period was characterized by very little significant legislation or innovation. Investor confidence in the capital markets was generally high, and the SEC routinely carried on the mission that had been developed. Revitalization of the SEC came in the early 1960's, after a rash of litigation related to the civil and criminal liability issues involved in inaccurate financial disclosures. Various amendments to legislation administered by the SEC followed. In the 1970's, major legislation was passed to combat corporate bribery and other illegal business practices.

During the 1980's, the SEC was guided by a doctrine of facilitation. Major efforts to expand full and fair disclosure and to streamline and standardize reporting requirements demonstrated the SEC's commitment to improving the efficiency of the flow of information and ultimately the flow of capital investment in the economy. Continuation of this tradition will likely ensure that the SEC remains a potent regulatory force in the mission of protecting the public interest.

Bibliography

Chatov, Robert. *Corporate Financial Reporting*. New York: Free Press, 1975. A scholarly, yet readable, study of the broad regulatory process and the various social and political controls used in public policy formation and implementation. The SEC serves as the focal point for this detailed analysis of independent regulatory agency behavior.

De Bedts, Ralph F. *The New Deal's SEC*. New York: Columbia University Press, 1964. Provides an interesting historical perspective on the origins of the SEC and a description of its early, formative years of operation.

Offers a depth of coverage and understanding not normally found in writings on New Deal reforms. Relaxed narrative form.

Ginzberg, Eli. *New Deal Days, 1933-1934.* New Brunswick, N.J.: Transaction Publishers, 1997.

Pointer, Larry Gene, and Richard G. Schroeder. *An Introduction to the Securities and Exchange Commission.* Plano, Tex.: Business Publications, 1986. Designed as a supplemental text for undergraduate accounting students, this booklet is nontechnical and serves as a good, brief overview of the SEC for the general reader. Some historical perspective is provided, but the emphasis is on the SEC's structure and operation.

Previts, Gary John, and Alfred R. Roberts, eds. *Federal Securities Law and Accounting, 1933-1970: Selected Addresses.* New York: Garland, 1986.

Rappaport, Louis H. *SEC Accounting Practice and Procedure.* 3d ed. New York: Ronald Press, 1972. An exhaustive reference work and guide to the broad range of financial reporting requirements of the SEC. Often very technical in presentation, a natural outcome of the inherent complexity of the subject matter. Provides numerous illustrative examples.

Tyler, Poyntz, ed. *Securities, Exchanges, and the SEC.* New York: H. W. Wilson, 1965. Provides the general reader with background information essential to an understanding and appreciation of more complex writings in the area of investing, capital markets, and regulation. Contains reprints of short articles, excerpts from books, and other documents. An interesting compendium that is very readable.

Jon R. Carpenter

Cross-References

The U.S. Stock Market Crashes on Black Tuesday (1929); The Banking Act of 1933 Reorganizes the American Banking System (1933); Insider Trading Scandals Mar the Emerging Junk Bond Market (1986); The U.S. Stock Market Crashes on 1987's "Black Monday" (1987); Drexel and Michael Milken Are Charged with Insider Trading (1988).

CONGRESS ESTABLISHES THE FEDERAL COMMUNICATIONS COMMISSION

CATEGORY OF EVENT: Government and business
TIME: June 10, 1934
LOCALE: Washington, D.C.

Following President Franklin D. Roosevelt's desire to consolidate regulatory powers over communications, Congress created the Federal Communications Commission

Principal personages:
FRANKLIN D. ROOSEVELT (1882-1945), the president of the United States, 1933-1945
DANIEL C. ROPER (1867-1943), the secretary of commerce
FRANK MCMANAMY (1870-1944), the chairman of the legislative committee of the Interstate Commerce Commission
E. O. SYKES (1876-1945), the chairman of the Federal Radio Commission
LIONEL VAN DEERLIN (1914-   ), the chairman of the House Subcommittee on Communications

Summary of Event

The Radio Act of 1927 created the Federal Radio Commission (FRC), the purpose of which was to ensure that public interest, convenience, or necessity was served by radio broadcasting. The FRC had the central authority to grant licenses to radio stations. The FRC soon faced a regulatory nightmare. Radio broadcasters with long histories enjoyed a favored status that they vigorously fought to retain, many radio stations were broadcasting on frequencies reserved for Canada, and several unregulated amateurs had ventured into radio broadcasting. To add to these problems, the FRC had been created on a temporary basis, with authority for one year. As a result, its life had to be extended annually through a congressional renewal process that was used to impose restrictions on the FRC. For example, the Davis Amendment to the 1928 congressional renewal of the Radio Act severely restricted the FRC by requiring it to divide licenses and broadcast frequencies equally across five geographic zones.

Although such congressional mandates elicited protests from President Herbert Hoover, the regulation of broadcasting remained in this unsatisfactory state until 1933, when President Franklin D. Roosevelt directed Daniel C. Roper, the U.S. secretary of commerce, to study radio broadcasting. In January, 1934, a committee chaired by Roper recommended that the communications-oriented regulatory activities of the FRC (radio frequencies), the Interstate Commerce Commission (telephone, telegraph, and cable), the postmaster general, and the president be consolidated into a single regulatory body. Extensive congressional hearings on this subject followed. Witnesses offering testimony included Frank McManamy, chairman of the legislative committee of the Interstate Commerce Commission, and E. O. Sykes, chairman of the Federal Radio Commission. As a result of the hearings, Congress enacted the Communications Act of 1934, which established the Federal Communications Commission (FCC).

Congress directed the FCC to uphold the "public interest, convenience, and necessity" in regard to broadcasting, the same mandate that it had imposed on the FRC. This mandate had the potential to curb the free speech rights of broadcasters guaranteed by the First Amendment to the U.S. Constitution. For example, a central theme of the Communications Act was that the airwaves should serve the needs and interests of the public. As a result, broadcast licensees are expected to be "socially responsible," a goal that has found expression in many FCC policies relating to broadcast media content. Such policies include the fairness doctrine, stipulating that opportunities be provided for expression of opposing viewpoints about any topic of public importance, and FCC policy statements on scheduling television programs for children. Such policies were applied only to the broadcast media context. In contrast, these policies would be construed as illegal censorship in a print media context. Court rulings have reconciled this apparent anomaly by perpetuating the view that government supervision of broadcast content is more acceptable than review of print outlets. This interpretation underscores complaints that the broadcast media enjoy less First Amendment protection than do the print media.

A basic justification for the "socially responsible" orientation of broadcast regulations enforced by the FCC is that the right of the public to receive useful and unbiased information should outweigh the First Amendment rights of broadcast licensees to be free of government control over the content of broadcast material. According to this view, the broadcasting media are "scarce" because of the finite range of airwave frequencies available for licensing. In addition, the ability to reach mass audiences bestows substantial power on broadcast licensees that can be used to influence public opinion. Under these circumstances, some form of government control to ensure that broadcasts serve the public interest, as opposed to granting unbridled First Amendment protection to the broadcast media, was deemed appropriate.

The first president to understand the power of radio communication, Franklin D. Roosevelt won public support for his New Deal programs through regular "fireside chats" broadcast over the radio networks. (FDR Library)

Impact of Event

The organizational structure of the FCC consisted of seven commissioners and several professional or middle-level staff personnel. Over the years, both these groups have substantially influenced the direction and thrust of

FCC policies. Analysis has suggested that the education and occupational background of FRC and FCC commissioners were key variables that affected decisions in these administrative agencies. In contrast to the commissioners, who directly administer broadcast policy, FCC staff members influence policy matters indirectly by controlling the content and flow of information provided to commissioners prior to decision making.

Broadcast regulation is an intensely political enterprise. Studies have also found that the political orientation of FCC commissioners has strongly affected FCC regulation activities. For example, the speeches of Commissioner Newton Minow in the early 1960's reflected the political stance of the John F. Kennedy Administration toward enforcing stricter regulation of broadcast programming. In the 1980's, under the leadership of Chairman Mark Fowler, the FCC reflected a deep commitment to follow President Ronald Reagan's political philosophy that government should make regulations less intrusive. Although the FCC has played a significant role in administering broadcast regulation, its policies and actions have changed over time to accommodate the philosophies of elected officials. Because commissioners are political appointees and because the Communications Act requires that no more than four commissioners share a party affiliation, virtually every president has tried to select commissioners who agree with the administration's philosophy and policy objectives, regardless of party identification.

The following illustration shows how politically driven changes in FCC policy were instrumental in the evolution of a new form of commercial communication labeled "program-length commercials" or PLCs, also called "infomercials." PLCs are commercials that usually resemble regular television talk show or documentary programs in both content and length. In the early 1970's, the FCC expressed concern over broadcast of PLCs because they potentially subordinate programming in the public interest to programming in commercial interests. The commission launched two policy initiatives to outlaw PLCs. First, widespread concern over television advertising directed toward children led the FCC to stress the need for distinguishing between program content and advertising material. The FCC expressed concern over children's shows that focused on particular toys, which sometimes were characters in animated shows. Second, the commission adopted a limit of sixteen minutes of commercial matter per broadcast hour. The FCC reversed this policy in 1984 by eliminating quantitative advertising guidelines for television broadcasting on the grounds that marketplace forces were adequate to regulate the level of advertising. As part of the broadcast deregulation effort launched by the Reagan Administration, the FCC rescinded its earlier policy banning PLCs. By underscoring the acceptability of PLCs, these developments also enhanced their popularity. As a result, PLC programming registered impressive growth in the late 1980's and early 1990's. The "infomercial" industry, which barely existed in the early 1980's, accounted for an estimated annual sales volume of $750 million in 1992.

Broadcast regulation in the United States is a dynamic and complex process, and the FCC is only one of the participants in that process. Other key participants include industry groups such as the National Association of Broadcasters (NAB), various citizens' groups, the courts, Congress, and the White House. It is important to understand how the FCC is influenced by each of these participants. The NAB commanded substantial lobbying power until the mid-1960's, and other organizations such as the Association of Maximum Service Telecasters, Clear Channel Broadcasting Service, and Daytime Broadcasters Association emerged as specialist lobbying groups. The broadcast industry has influenced FCC policies through successful lobbying efforts directed at Congress. This industry's substantial political clout in Congress stems from its control over electronic media exposure, an important resource for politicians.

Citizens' groups also have influenced FCC activities. In 1966, a landmark decision by the U.S. Court of Appeals for the District of Columbia recognized the right of responsible civic groups to object to license renewal applications that were under the FCC's consideration. In this instance, the Office of Communication of the United Church of Christ was allowed to challenge the license renewal of WLBT-TV in Jackson, Mississippi, because this broadcaster discriminated against black audiences. Groups such as the National Citizens Committee for Broadcasting and Action for Children's Television actively sought to influence the FCC on policy matters relating to the content of broadcast material. During the 1960's, several citizens' groups sought to protest against and settle differences with specific broadcasters via petitions to the FCC requesting denial of license renewal for these broadcasters. In the 1970's, the first black commissioner was appointed to the FCC at the urging of such groups, which also actively participated in congressional hearings to urge funding support for consumer group activities.

Although the courts do not adjudicate every decision of administrative agencies such as the FCC, they generally influence policy-making. Effective policy formulation entails careful deliberation to ensure its ability to withstand any eventual judicial scrutiny. The continual threat of judicial review tends to have an impact on policies of the FCC even when these policies are not formally adjudicated. The Communications Act stipulates that appeals concerning FCC decisions on broadcasting licensing should be filed with the U.S. Court of Appeals for the District of Columbia Circuit and that the decisions of that court are final, except for review by the U.S. Supreme Court.

Congress exercises substantial control over federal administrative agencies such as the FCC. The FCC has often been targeted for special congressional investigations. Investigations supervised by Congressman Oren Harris (D-Arkansas) in the early 1960's provided insights into "payola" problems widely prevalent in the recording and broadcast industries and led to revisions in the Communications Act. Several powerful standing committees in Congress continuously review FCC performance and the adequacy of the broadcasting regulatory framework. This is accomplished through general oversight hearings and hearings designed to evaluate any germane proposed legislation. A 1981 decision by Congress to change the FCC's status from a permanently authorized agency to one requiring congressional reauthorization every two years underscores the power of the standing committees, which ultimately have the authority to approve such reauthorization. Finally, Congress and the White House together influence the FCC through the nomination and confirmation process for commissioners. In addition, the White House Office of Management and Budget exercises authority through reviewing and revising the annual FCC budget.

In 1976, Congressman Lionel Van Deerlin (D-California) proposed a major revision to the Communications Act. The motivation for the proposal was that the law had become antiquated because new technologies such as cable television had transformed broadcasting. Van Deerlin introduced a bill in 1978 proposing abolition of the FCC and its replacement with a Communications Regulatory Commission. This proposal was abandoned in 1979. In retrospect, the proposal was beneficial to the FCC because it pushed the agency toward major deregulation decisions involving the radio and cable television industries.

Bibliography

Krasnow, Erwin G., Lawrence D. Longley, and Herbert A. Terry. *The Politics of Broadcast Regulation.* New York: St. Martin's Press, 1982. An authoritative account of the laws and policies that govern broadcasting in the United States. This work traces the history of both the FRC and the FCC and offers insights into the political factors that shaped their creation and growth. The arguments and perspectives offered in the book are forceful, thought provoking, and well researched. This work also includes five case studies on diverse topics including ultrahigh frequency television, commercials, and congressional efforts to rewrite the Communications Act during the 1970's.

Lichty, Lawrence. "The Impact of FRC and FCC Commissioners' Back-grounds on the Regulation of Broadcasting." *Journal of Broadcasting* 6 (Spring, 1962): 97-110. Suggests that factors such as the education, occupational history, and personal experience of commissioners affect policies.

Robinson, Glen O. "The Federal Communications Commission: An Essay on Regulatory Watchdogs." *Virginia Law Review* 64 (March, 1978): 169-262. A former FCC commissioner offers some rare and useful perspectives on the FCC.

U.S. Congress. House. Committee on Interstate and Foreign Commerce. *Federal Communications Commission: Hearings Before the Committee on Interstate and Foreign Commerce, House of Representatives, Seventy-third Congress, Second Session on H.R. 8301, a Bill to Provide for the Regulation of Interstate and Foreign Communication by Wire or Radio, and for Other Purposes.* 73d Congress, 2d session, 1934. Contains verbatim transcripts of hearings on H.R. 8301.

Williams, Wenmouth, Jr. "Impact of Commissioner Background on FCC Decisions: 1962-1975." *Journal of Broadcasting* 20 (Spring, 1976): 244-256. Extends Lichty's work on how the backgrounds of FCC com-missioners have influenced FCC policy.

Siva Balasubramanian

Cross-References

The Federal Trade Commission Is Organized (1914); The A. C. Nielsen Company Pioneers in Marketing and Media Research (1923); The 1939 World's Fair Introduces Regular U.S. Television Service (1939); The U.S. Government Bans Cigarette Ads on Broadcast Media (1970); Cable Televi-sion Rises to Challenge Network Television (mid-1990's).

CONGRESS PASSES THE FEDERAL CREDIT UNION ACT

CATEGORY OF EVENT: Finance
TIME: June 26, 1934
LOCALE: Washington, D.C.

By establishing a federal credit union system, the Federal Credit Union Act of 1934 encouraged savings and made credit more available to people of limited means

Principal personages:

ROY F. BERGENGREN (1879-1955), the first manager of the Credit Union National Association

EDWARD A. FILENE (1860-1937), a Boston merchant and philanthropist who established and financed the Credit Union National Extension Bureau, which in 1934 became the Credit Union National Association

ALPHONSE DESJARDINS (1854-1920), a legislative journalist who helped to organize the first legally chartered cooperative credit society in the United States

F. HERMANN SCHULZE-DELITZSCH (1808-1883), a German urban cooperative credit founder

FRIEDRICH WILHELM RAIFFEISEN (1818-1888), a German rural cooperative credit founder

ARTHUR CAPPER (1865-1951), a Republican senator from Kansas and chairman of the committee that held hearings on the Federal Credit Union Act

Summary of Event

A federal credit union is a nonprofit, member-owned cooperative organized to encourage its members to put money into savings and to use these accumulated savings to make loans to members. It also has the function of educating members on how to manage their own finances. The federal government, through the National Credit Union Administration (NCUA), charters credit unions as corporations as well as supervising and insuring them.

In order to generate and maintain a feeling of mutual responsibility, members of a federal credit union must have a common bond of employment, association, or residence. The members, with one vote each, elect a volunteer board of directors from the membership at an annual meeting. The board has authority to determine the maximum limits on loans and the interest rates to be charged. Interest rates tend to be favorable in comparison to those offered by other lenders because of the lower labor costs in volunteer organizations, lower losses on defaulted loans, and lower marketing costs. In addition to an unpaid board of directors, credit unions have officers who are generally unpaid or receive nominal salaries. The ratio of delinquent to outstanding loans in the early 1990's stood at half that of federally insured commercial banks. Personal contact and personal credit judgments play a large role in keeping this ratio low. Two major marketing advantages are the bond of clients to the credit union through membership and the close proximity of clients, with the credit union often located at an employee's place of work.

Loans can be designed to meet the needs of individual members. Federal credit unions must comply with all federal consumer protection laws, such as the Truth in Lending Act (1980) and the Equal Credit Opportunity Act (1975).

Deposits by members are in the form of shares in the credit union and are frequently made through payroll deductions. Each account as of the early 1990's was insured up to $100,000 by the NCUA. Profits from lending money and other sources may be distributed to the members as dividends.

The development of credit unions resulted from the needs of lower income groups. Prior to the existence of credit unions, there were a limited number of outlets for small savings or loans. In 1948, the first credit union was organized in Belgium. At the same time in Germany, F. Hermann Schulze-Delitzsch organized cooperative credit societies and developed the principle that the funds to be loaned to members would come from the savings of members. By 1880, about three thousand cooperative credit societies had been organized in Germany.

Friedrich Wilhelm Raiffeisen also organized cooperative credit societies in Germany but put greater emphasis on unselfish service to the organization. By 1920, his model for the earliest credit unions was being used in most countries in the world.

The credit union movement spread to the North American continent with the help of Alphonse Desjardins, a legislative journalist who was studying economic conditions in Europe in the late 1890's. In 1900, Desjardins used ideas from the Schulze-Delitzsch and Raiffeisen financial cooperatives to establish the first cooperative bank, La Caisse Populaire (the people's bank), in the city of Levis in the province of Quebec, Canada.

Edward A. Filene, a wealthy Boston merchant and philanthropist, was influential in bringing credit unions to the United States. His interest in the subject resulted from extensive travel throughout the world. He convinced Pierre Jay, commissioner of banking for Massachusetts, to work toward establishing a cooperative credit society in that state. Jay asked Desjardins to assist in passing a credit union act in Massachusetts. The Massachusetts Credit Union Act, the first complete credit union act in the United States, was enacted in 1909. In the same year, in Manchester, New Hampshire, Desjardins helped to organize the first legally chartered cooperative credit society in the United States.

Growth in the credit union movement was slow during the decade after passage of the Massachusetts act. By 1919, however, Filene believed that there was a sufficient number of credit unions to justify an organized move toward national legislation. He organized the National Committee on People's Banks to spearhead this task. The development of credit unions was aided by favorable conditions during the 1920's. General prosperity and development of new consumer goods resulted in higher savings by workers and greater demand for consumer credit.

Three factors were necessary to expand the movement: legislation allowing the chartering (incorporation) of credit unions, education of the general public regarding the movement, and voluntary associations of credit unions at the state level to further expand the movement. To facilitate each of these, the Credit Union National Extension Bureau (which became the Credit Union National Association in 1934) was created and financed by Filene. He hired Roy F. Bergengren as manager and Thomas W. Doig as assistant manager. Bergengren had started as the managing director of the Massachusetts Credit Union Association in 1920. He used the extension bureau to promote enabling legislation authorizing credit unions and helped organize individual credit unions.

The Great Depression had a favorable impact on the movement. In 1932, Congress authorized credit unions in the District of Columbia and allowed them to borrow from the Reconstruction Finance Corporation. By 1934, thirty-eight states had enacted credit union laws and more than twenty-four hundred credit unions were in operation.

Bergengren became increasingly convinced that national legislation was necessary. He argued that a federal law would permit the organization of credit unions in states that had refused to pass such legislation; that there was some possibility that other states might repeal their credit union laws, as West Virginia had done in 1931; that a federal statute would be useful as a basis of organization in those states that had weak or defective laws; and that federal legislation should be complete before credit unions formed a national association.

The culmination of the legislative efforts of the Credit Union National Extension Bureau came on June 26, 1934, when the United States Congress enacted the Federal Credit Union Act. The act provided for the chartering, supervision, and examination of federal credit unions by the United States government. The writers of the act tried to incorporate the best ideas from state laws.

In the same year, Congress chose the Farm Credit Administration (FCA) to supervise credit unions because of its expertise in examining other types of financial cooperatives chartered by the U.S. government. Claude R. Orchard was appointed the first director of the Credit Union Section, FCA. More than eighty-seven hundred federal credit unions were chartered during the nineteen years he served as director. Also in 1934, Bergengren and Filene held a national meeting of credit union delegates that led to the development of the Credit Union National Association (CUNA).

Impact of Event

The most important impact of the Federal Credit Union Act of 1934 was the confidence it inspired in the American public regarding credit unions. Involvement by the federal government played a major role in the growth of credit unions, from almost 2,500 credit unions when the act was passed to 3,372 by the end of 1935. In 1937, Congress passed legislation prohibiting the taxation of federal credit unions except on the basis of real or personal property. This legislation further supported growth in the number of entities, which approached 8,000 by 1939.

Individual credit unions were also growing at an impressive rate. By March, 1936, Armour and Company employee credit unions had more than 22,000 members, had $1.25 million in assets, and had made loans up to that date of almost $7 million. There were twenty-four credit unions among Sears, Roebuck and Company employees, with 7,982 members, and credit unions associated with the U.S. Steel Corporation had almost 23,000 members. A credit union served employees of the United States Senate. Another credit union at the studios of Twentieth Century-Fox had more than 1,000 members.

Many employers considered a credit union to be an important fringe benefit, with the advantage of involving no necessary cost to them. Space for the credit union offices often was provided on the premises, perhaps at reduced cost. Payroll withholding both for regular savings and for installment collection of loans was another common service by employers.

In 1935, CUNA's national board of directors agreed to establish the CUNA Mutual Insurance Society. The society provided only borrowers' protection insurance to credit unions at first, adding life insurance for officers and families associated with CUNA in August, 1936. At the same time, the society considered writing automobile insurance but took no action. By the end of 1936, 437 credit unions in thirty states were members of the society. A total of twenty-three thousand loans were insured, with a total coverage of $2,425,000. The reserves of the society for payment of claims amounted to $11,000. Deposit insurance did not begin until 1970.

The Credit Union Modernization Act of 1977 and 1978 revised much of the Federal Credit Union Act of 1934. The new legislation extended loan maturities, expanded real estate and home improvement loans, authorized self-replenishing credit lines to borrowers, and standardized participation loans with other credit unions. It also made many other changes in the technical operation of credit unions that expanded lending and investment authority.

The Financial Institutions Reform Act of 1978, as part of the Modernization Act, established the Central Liquidity Facility as part of the National Credit Union Administration. This organization added safety to credit union lending by providing liquidity for emergency needs. It was not intended to provide permanent financing. This legislation also restructured the National Credit Union Administration and set up a new administrative board with increased supervisory functions.

The Depository Institutions Deregulation and Monetary Control Act was passed in 1980. This law affected credit unions directly by increasing deposit insurance coverage. It affected them indirectly by legalizing share drafts for banks and savings and loans, increasing competition for the credit union industry, which already offered share drafts. The act also required that depository institutions maintain some level of reserves with the Federal Reserve System. Most credit unions did not maintain these reserves because the requirement was not implemented for any institution with deposits of less than $2 million. The Garn-St. Germain Act of 1982 suspended the monetary reserve requirement for the first $2 million in reservable accounts. This act also gave credit unions more flexibility and authority to handle their own affairs, including greater freedom in mortgage markets.

In general, all this legislation, combined with favorable regulatory changes, made credit unions more competitive with banks and savings and loans. The industry was permitted to use a greater variety of sources for both assets and liabilities, and a greater range of financial activities was allowed. The interest rates that credit unions could pay on savings and charge for loans were relatively free from government control. Finally, credit unions still enjoyed the political and economic benefits of being nonprofit organizations.

Bibliography

Bergengren, Roy F. "Achievement: United States." In *Credit Union, North America*. New York: Southern Publishers, 1940. Gives a detailed summary of the growth of credit unions by state.

_____. *Crusade: The Fight for Economic Democracy in North America, 1921-1945*. New York: Exposition Press, 1952. A detailed history of the credit union movement, written by the man who had the greatest influence in passage of the Federal Credit Union Act and growth of credit unions. Reads like an autobiography in parts. Includes a six-page photograph section of early crusaders and administrators in the movement.

_____. *CUNA Emerges*. Madison, Wis.: Credit Union National Association, 1935. Summarizes the functions and operations of credit unions one year after passage of the Federal Credit Union Act of 1934. Discusses the organization of the Credit Union National Association (CUNA). The final chapter offers an interesting, almost philosophical, explanation of how credit unions can lead to a better society.

Croteau, John T. *The Economics of the Credit Union*. Detroit: Wayne State University Press, 1963. Credit unions have many unique economic characteristics because they do not maximize profits as their sole goal. After analyzing data from credit union questionnaires, the author recommends ways to improve financial efficiency in large credit unions. Topics include reserves, liquidity, growth, and investment yields. Written to be comprehensible by noneconomists.

_____. *The Federal Credit Union: Policy and Practice*. New York: Harper & Brothers, 1956. An analytical study of the growth, policies, and practices of credit unions on a national scale from 1934 to 1954. Provides statistics on assets and liabilities, operating costs, earnings, and dividends. Includes an interesting chapter on structural change and suggested improvement.

Ginzberg, Eli. *New Deal Days, 1933-1934*. New Brunswick, N.J.: Transaction Publishers, 1997.

Isbister, John. *Thin Cats: The Community Development Credit Union Movement in the United States*. Davis: Center for Cooperatives, University of California, 1994.

Moody, J. Carroll, and Gilbert C. Fite. *The Credit Union Movement: Origins and Development, 1850-1970.* Lincoln: University of Nebraska Press, 1971. Traces and analyzes the history of credit unionism as a national social movement, with a focus on the founders and leaders. Detailed and comprehensive. Source of many of the statistics in this article.

Pugh, Olin S., and F. Jerry Ingram. *Credit Unions: A Movement Becomes an Industry.* Reston, Va.: Reston Publishing Company, 1984. A comprehensive look at the growth of the credit union movement. Describes the structure of the industry, regulations, financial management, and role in the financial marketplace. Also discusses the future of the industry from an early 1980's perspective, including likely effects of legislation of that era.

U.S. National Credit Union Administration. *Development of Federal Credit Unions.* Washington, D.C.: Author, 1972. Focuses on the role of the U.S. government in the credit union movement. Explains the benefits of federal government participation in the movement. Also describes the Credit Union National Association, Inc. (CUNA) and organizations associated with it.

Richard Goedde

Cross-References

The Federal Reserve Act Creates a U.S. Central Bank (1913); The U.S. Stock Market Crashes on Black Tuesday (1929); Congress Passes the Consumer Credit Protection Act (1968); Congress Prohibits Discrimination in the Granting of Credit (1975); Congress Deregulates Banks and Savings and Loans (1980-1982).

THE WAGNER ACT PROMOTES UNION ORGANIZATION

CATEGORY OF EVENT: Labor
TIME: July 5, 1935
LOCALE: Washington, D.C.

The National Labor Relations Act (Wagner Act) of 1935, one of the most significant American labor laws, placed positive federal authority behind labor organizing and collective bargaining

Principal personages:
ROBERT F. WAGNER (1877-1953), a New York labor reformer and principal author of the National Labor Relations Act
FRANKLIN D. ROOSEVELT (1882-1945), a reform president who helped guide national recovery from the Depression and supported prolabor legislation
WILLIAM GREEN (1872-1952), the leader of the traditionally organized American Federation of Labor
JOHN L. LEWIS (1880-1969), a leader of the United Mine Workers and first president of the Congress of Industrial Organizations
CHARLES EVANS HUGHES (1862-1948), the Chief Justice of the United States who rendered a key decision supporting the Wagner Act

Summary of Event

Passage of the National Labor Relations Act (the Wagner Act) on July 5, 1935, signaled the beginning of a national labor policy, a prolabor reform policy that the first administration of President Franklin D. Roosevelt, then preoccupied with the nation's economic recovery, initially had not anticipated and about which it was ill informed. The Wagner Act was one of the most significant pieces of labor legislation ever enacted in the United States. Moreover, unlike the Norris-LaGuardia Act of 1932, which was pro-labor in spirit and removed unions and their organizers from the danger of court injunctions, the Wagner Act actively placed that authority of the federal government behind economic coercions, such as strikes, believed to be essential to a vigorous and expansive labor movement. The Wagner Act also instantly provoked heated controversy both in the ranks of organized labor and in the boardrooms of many employers.

Senator Robert F. Wagner around the time he introduced his National Labor Relations bill. (Library of Congress)

The novel presumption of the Wagner Act was that the profound labor unrest from 1933 into early 1935—much of it attended by bitter strikes, violence, critical disruptions of interstate commerce (a factor vital to federal jurisdiction), and in some quarters fears of civil war—was largely attributable to employers' general refusal to recognize organized labor's conviction that collective bargaining was a prerequisite to union survival. The ability to organize unions that could bargain more equally with employers in regard to individual workers' wages, hours, and working conditions was perceived not only as a necessity but as a right. Accordingly, the act carried into public law an explicit acknowledgment that employers, especially the nation's giant corporations, enjoyed disproportionate shares of bargaining power relative to those of their employees. These imbalances were perceived to be large enough to allow employers to slash employment and wages almost at will, drastically reducing much of the nation's purchasing power and thus contributing directly to the unprecedented and persisting Depression of the 1930's. The act represented, therefore, the federal government's mandate to redress the imbalance of power.

Such were the assumptions and rationales confirmed in the act's introductory section and mortised into its substantive portions, most notably in section 7. It was this section that guaranteed workers the right to self-organization, or the forming, joining, or assisting of union organizations, as well as the right to bargain collectively through their chosen union representatives and to collaborate in their efforts to achieve collective bargaining. The Wagner Act provided more than guarantees to labor. It further recognized the intense antiunion hostilities of corporate employers in the partially or entirely unorganized mass-production industries and consequently specified and prohibited practices that were deemed unfair to labor. Employers were prevented, for example, from interfering with, restraining, or coercing workers trying to exercise the rights extended to them by section 7. Similarly, employers could no longer with impunity interfere with the formation of unions or dominate their operations, nor could they contribute to unions' support. Hiring or tenure policies could neither encourage nor discourage workers' union membership. Workers involved in lawful strikes against employers' unfair practices, moreover, had to be reinstated when reapplying for their jobs, even when employers had replaced them, and workers who struck for higher wages or other improvements in working conditions could claim reinstatement if they had not been replaced. The Wagner Act thus sought to end employers' blacklists, "yellow dog" contracts under which potential employees had to renounce union membership as a condition of employment, lockouts, dual unionism, the corporate hiring of private armies or armed thugs, spying, and various other antilabor tactics.

The new quasi-legislative, quasi-judicial National Labor Relations Board (NLRB) charged with administration of the Wagner Act was resurrected from the Supreme Court's devastation of Roosevelt's early New Deal legislation. The NLRB was created under the aegis of the National Industrial Recovery Act of 1933 (NIRA), itself designed to hasten economic recovery through the formulation of industrial-labor codes. The NIRA was declared unconstitutional by the Supreme Court's decision in the famed *Schechter* case two years later. The old NLRB, established specifically to ensure collective bargaining under the NIRA's section 7a, was abolished as well.

The tenacity of the chairman of the old NLRB, Senator Robert F. Wagner of New York, proved the main force behind the NLRB's re-creation. A German-American immigrant, Wagner had carved a brilliant career as a labor reformer, partly during Roosevelt's incumbency as governor, in New York State's roiling politics. Wagner brought the character and experience requisite to the launching of the new NLRB to a New Deal administration less uncaring than ignorant about the labor world and more concerned, at least before 1935, with engineering recovery through business.

Formation of the NLRB embodied a dawning comprehension of the complexities of the American economy. That comprehension was based on perceptions of the growing inseparability of intrastate and interstate commerce, and it therefore incorporated Wagner's and the administration's elastic definition of what constituted interstate commerce. This implicit loose construction afforded the NLRB's three directors their jurisdiction in overseeing and enforcing workers' rights to collective bargaining and prohibiting employers' unfair labor practices. These were the battlegrounds, as it transpired, on which the effectiveness and the constitutionality of the act were to be tested.

Impact of Event

Passage of the Wagner Act coincided with the massive unemployment of the Great Depression. Union membership, which in 1920 included 12 percent of the labor force, had eroded steadily thereafter, so seriously that by the advent of the Roosevelt Administration in 1933, unions could count only two million members, or 6.6 percent of the labor force. Several factors accounted for this decline. The conservative, employer-dominated governments and economy of the 1920's were characterized in spirit and deed by effective antilabor campaigns, sometimes masked as patriotic suppression of communism. Changes in the complexion of the industrial world also contributed. Shifting structural and technological patterns in basic industries such as railroads, steel, and coal mining, along with the spread of mass-production enterprises in the automotive, appliances, chemical, tire and rubber, oil, trucking, longshoring, meatpacking, and textile industries, led to a greater concentration of unskilled and largely nonunion workers. In addition, with 40 percent of American children completing high school by 1930, the educational level of the workforce was undergoing dramatic alteration, bringing with it predominantly urban visions of democracy and fresh perceptions of individual rights.

The traditional craft unionism that distinguished the American Federation of Labor (AFL), a federation of skilled workers' unions, seemed increasingly ill suited to the needs of the largely unskilled workers of the 1930's. In previous decades, unskilled workers had been all but precluded from joining the AFL crafts because of the nature of their occupations. AFL president William Green eventually did sanction inclusion of several industrial unions, which rapidly became the fastest growing in the AFL, but he did not aggressively recruit them. The outlook of the unskilled workers' leaders differed from that of the AFL. In opposition to the AFL's perception of government's role in the economy—basically an eschewal of any role at all—the leaders of the unskilled, in general, were far more enthusiastic than their skilled brethren in calls for governmental intervention on labor's behalf.

These were just a few of the critical differences dividing labor's house by the mid-1930's. Almost simultaneously with enactment of the Wagner Act, they grew more serious because of the emergence of the Congress of Industrial Organizations (CIO), dedicated to the recruitment of unskilled labor as well as to vigorous political activism. Subsequent antipathies between the CIO's leaders—among them the fiery United Mine Workers' chief, John L. Lewis—and the AFL's old guard, from whose camp the industrial unionists of the CIO had departed, left the labor movement as a whole without clear direction or coherent policy.

Beginning almost instantly upon its enactment and continuing through the next decade, the Wagner Act successfully promoted its major objective of relatively free collective bargaining. The proof lay in the rise of union membership. The three million unionists of 1933 swelled to more than fifteen million by 1946, more than 22 percent of the labor force. The vast majority of the labor force was composed of unskilled or semiskilled industrial workers, previously shunned by the AFL. More revealing than these overall figures, however, were union gains in manufacturing industries. Barely one-fifth of manufacturing workers were bargaining collectively in 1935, but more than two-thirds were doing so in 1946. The AFL claimed nine million members by the end of this expansion. The CIO's count came to an impressive six million members.

Behind these statistics of rising union membership lay thousands of decisions rendered by the NLRB. During the ten years following the reestablishment of the NLRB, fifty thousand union representation elections were held under its auspices, while judgments were rendered on more than forty-five thousand union complaints about practices unfair to labor.

Once unions were lawfully established, labor-management disputes no longer fell under the jurisdiction of the NLRB. The Wagner Act and NLRB nevertheless contributed significantly to removing violence from, and substituting democratic procedures for, the selection of workers' union representation and thus their right to collective bargaining.

On April 12, 1937, Chief Justice Charles Evans Hughes delivered the Supreme Court's majority decision in *National Labor Relations Board v. Jones & Laughlin Steel Corp.*, in essence proclaiming the Wagner Act constitutional. The act and the NLRB, along with "little Wagner Acts" in many states, were already engulfed in controversies. The NLRB was understaffed, underfunded, and ill prepared to cope with these disputes. With only a thousand employees, even with self-imposed restrictions on its business, it handled annually roughly seven thousand representational cases and fourteen thousand complaints on practices unfair to labor, which averaged a year and a half for resolution.

Operation of the NLRB fell under different interpretations. These differences arose from confusion among employers and unionists, complicated by their traditional animosities, and differences in interpretation of the act's jurisdictions and responsibilities. There were notable lapses in the drafting of the law. It said nothing, for example, about employer (rather than employee) petitions for union elections. The act likewise had no provisions for handling the harassment of one union by another, a serious matter given the sometimes heated competition for union membership by the mutually hostile AFL and CIO. What constituted a "bargaining unit" when industries or plants were divided between craft and industrial workers was unresolved. There were problems regarding whether bargaining should be by area, company, or plant. These problems and many more were made more vexatious both by immature union leadership and by inexperienced and resentful employers.

The heart of the Wagner Act's difficulties lay in its legal promotion of union activity and its prolabor bias. Official and popular sentiments soon shifted toward seeking greater balance between labor and management. Those sentiments led to amendment of the National Labor Relations Act in 1947 by the Taft-Hartley Act.

Bibliography

Galbraith, John Kenneth. *The New Industrial State.* Boston: Houghton Mifflin, 1967. This readable work covers unions from the Wagner Act through the early 1960's in chapters 23 and 24. Intelligent and insightful. Few notes and no bibliography, but a useful index.

Hughes, Jonathan R. T. *American Economy History.* 5th ed. Reading, Mass.: Addison-Wesley, 1998.

Millis, Harry, and Gordon E. Bloom. *From the Wagner Act to Taft-Hartley.* Chicago: University of Chicago Press, 1950. Readable scholarly analysis with good historical context on labor-government-employer interrelationships from the early 1930's to 1947. Notes, bibliography, good index.

Northrup, Herbert R., and Gordon E. Bloom. *Government and Labor: The Role of Government in Union-Management Relations.* Homewood, Ill.: Richard D. Irwin, 1963. Emphasizes key questions raised by the NLRA and NLRB in chapter 3. Notes, chapter bibliographies, notations of authors and cases cited, good index.

Richberg, Donald R. *Labor Union Monopoly.* Chicago: Henry Regnery, 1957. A scholarly view of the imbalances between unions and employers resulting from the Wagner Act and other New Deal reforms. Notes, bibliography, good index.

Schlesinger, Arthur M., Jr. *The Coming of the New Deal*. Vol. 2 in *The Age of Roosevelt*. Boston: Houghton Mifflin, 1958. Classic scholarly narrative of its subject with extensive, detailed discussion of pertinent politics and personalities associated with the Wagner Act and the NLRB. Wonderful reading. Detailed notes in lieu of bibliography. Extensive, valuable index.

Wilcox, Clair. *Public Policies Toward Business*. Homewood, Ill.: Richard D. Irwin, 1966. Clear, detailed, and authoritative. Worth reading in its entirety. Chapter 32 gives an excellent context for the NLRA and NLRB. Very useful indexes of cases, names, and subjects.

Clifton K. Yearley

Cross-References

The Railway Labor Act Provides for Mediation of Labor Disputes (1926); The Norris-LaGuardia Act Adds Strength to Labor Organizations (1932); The CIO Begins Unionizing Unskilled Workers (1935); Roosevelt Signs the Fair Labor Standards Act (1938); The Taft-Hartley Act Passes over Truman's Veto (1947); The AFL and CIO Merge (1955); The Landrum-Griffin Act Targets Union Corruption (1959).

THE SOCIAL SECURITY ACT PROVIDES BENEFITS FOR WORKERS

CATEGORY OF EVENT: Labor
TIME: August 14, 1935
LOCALE: Washington, D.C.

In passing the Social Security Act, the United States government took initial steps to ameliorate problems caused by old age, unemployment, and varied disabilities

Principal personages:
FRANKLIN D. ROOSEVELT (1882-1945), the president of the United States, 1933-1945
FRANCES PERKINS (1882-1965), a social reformer, the secretary of labor
EDWIN WITTE (1887-1960), a professor of economics and an authority on social insurance
ARTHUR ALTMEYER (1891-1972), the assistant secretary of labor

Summary of Event

The Social Security Act of 1935 established federally sponsored old-age pensions and unemployment insurance as well as providing categorical assistance to the needy aged, dependent children of low-income mothers, and the blind. The legislation was long in coming and was bitterly opposed. Although its framers were familiar with foreign social security programs, this act was shaped by domestic circumstances. The legislation's significance lies in its carving out of a new area of federal responsibility.

Western Europe initiated social insurance in 1854 with Austria's compulsory but limited program. In the 1880's, Germany, led by Chancellor Otto von Bismarck, launched a broad program embracing workers' accident, illness, and invalidity insurance as well as old-age pensions. Around the turn of the century, Denmark, England, and Scandinavia adopted social assistance programs, some financed by general revenues.

In the United States, limited steps were taken by a number of state governments. Between 1910 and 1915, thirty states enacted workers' compensation laws. By 1931, seventeen states and Alaska were providing assistance to the noninstitutionalized needy poor. By 1933, twenty-six states had adopted old-age pension programs, although in almost all cases financial aid was minimal.

Initial efforts at the federal level were motivated primarily by efficiency considerations. The Civil Service Act of 1920 established an impersonal mechanism, in place of reliance upon personal relationships, to retire older employees. The Railroad Retirement Act (1934) was enacted in response to the drastic downsizing of the industry that began in the 1920's. The Supreme Court struck down the legislation in May, 1935, contending that it did not achieve the goals of efficiency and safety in the conduct of interstate commerce.

Efforts to formulate a broader, federally sponsored safety net were thwarted by a longstanding preference for self-reliance and private philanthropy, the presumed linkage of long-term unemployment with personal frailties, and a commitment by virtually all the nation's economists to keeping government interference in business to a minimum. Inexpensive burial and disability insurance, coupled with home nursing services provided by several large insurers, seemed an adequate security program for working-class families.

The depth and duration of the Great Depression shattered deeply held beliefs. By 1932, one-fourth of the labor force was unemployed, and only fifteen percent of those employed were covered by retirement programs. In this changed environment, the moral underpinnings for social insurance legislation buoyed the growing conviction that only a national program could create an adequate safety net. Profound differences existed, however, concerning how far the net should extend, who should be included, and how it was to be financed.

The legislation's timing and character were affected by a range of seemingly radical proposals. Francis Townsend, a retired California physician, gained widespread support for his advocacy of a $200 monthly pension for all persons aged sixty and over, financed by a 2 percent sales tax. Senator Huey Long of Louisiana trumpeted a vague "share the wealth" scheme. Representative Ernest Lundeen of Minnesota introduced legislation establishing a national unemployment insurance system, to be financed by general tax revenues.

In June, 1934, President Franklin D. Roosevelt appointed, through executive order, a cabinet Committee on Economic Security, with Secretary of Labor Frances Perkins as chairperson. The committee was charged with the task of recommending legislation that would enhance individual economic security. The same executive order established an advisory council, representing diverse interest groups, and a technical board, composed of government specialists in social insurance and chaired by Arthur Altmeyer, the assistant secretary of labor. Economist Edwin Witte was named executive director of the entire project.

The Committee on Economic Security concurred with Roosevelt's belief that an acceptable program must be self-supporting and should not be viewed as a plan to provide adequate retirement income. Employees would be expected to accumulate some personal retirement funds. Aware of Supreme Court thinking in striking down the railroad retirement legislation, committee members relied on congressional taxing power as a means of funding the program. This would ensure constitutionality.

The committee's final report, submitted on January 15, 1935, recommended a multifaceted program to include compulsory old-age annuities, to be federally administered; a voluntary plan of old-age annuities; and an old-age assistance program, to be funded by federal grants to states. Also recommended was a federal-state program providing assistance to widows and children of deceased workers. A federal-state unemployment insurance plan was advocated, as was an extension of the public health service.

During public hearings held by the House of Representatives and the Senate, opposition to the proposed legislation was expressed by conservative groups, which warned of the destruction of individual initiative, and by liberal organizations, which contended that regressive taxation would be imposed on low-income workers who would gain inadequate benefits. In April, 1935, the House Ways and Means Committee reported out a bill, renamed the Social Security Act. It quickly passed the full House. Soon thereafter, a slightly different version passed the Senate. A conference committee reconciled differences, and President Roosevelt signed the bill into law on August 14, 1935.

The act did not include all the recommendations of the Committee on Economic Security. Omitted were the voluntary pension program and the proposal for a state-administered system of health insurance. The legislation covered only workers in commercial and industrial occupations, omitting government workers and the self-employed.

Impact of Event

The business community was sharply divided on major social security issues. Confronted with the more radical Long, Lundeen, and Townsend proposals, spokespeople for some industries rallied behind the Roosevelt Administration's measure. The advisory council included executives of large firms that lacked adequate pension programs; these executives perceived the advantages of a compulsory national system. Even as a supplement to private pensions, limited social security benefits would encourage employees to plan for retirement, making room for younger and potentially more productive workers. Moreover, retirement income would help stabilize the economy by providing a source of spending that was relatively constant over the business cycle. Chamber of Commerce spokespeople generally were favorable to the legislation, while representatives of the National Association of Manufacturers were opposed. The life and health insurance industry sponsored an amendment in the Senate that would permit the contracting out of private annuities. Opposition to this proposal centered on the conviction that insurers would skim off low-risk employees. The amendment failed in the Finance Committee but was introduced into the full Senate, strengthened by requiring that private annuity plans meet federal guidelines. The amendment was adopted but was lost at the conference committee level.

Overall, business interests played a major role in shaping the legislation. Secretary of Labor Perkins, Witte, and administration officials initially opposed old-age insurance. It came to the fore as a retirement measure favored by business interests. Businesspeople believed that productivity would be enhanced by annuities large enough to induce the retirement of older workers and would eliminate from the labor market women and children who sought employment as a means of supporting elderly relatives.

The Committee on Economic Security, sensitive to business concerns, resisted efforts to peg the normal retirement age above sixty-five. The act discouraged retirees from reentering the work force by placing a low limit on income that could be earned before pension benefits were reduced and by subjecting postretirement earnings to social security taxation.

After surviving attacks by the conservative press and by the 1936 Republican candidate for president, Alfred Landon, the Social Security Act was upheld by the Supreme Court on May 24, 1937. In the decades following its validation, many changes to the legislation took place. One constant feature has been the contributory character of the program, insisted upon by President Roosevelt, who feared that in its absence workers might lose entitlement to benefits. Employees, however, never possessed a legally enforceable annuity, and Congress time after time altered costs and benefits. Between 1944 and 1950, Congress authorized the use of general revenues to pay benefits if necessary. In 1977, a proposal to rely on general revenues during periods of high unemployment was rejected by Congress.

The first major change in the program took place in 1939 as a result of the rapid buildup of reserves, as contributions to the Social Security system exceeded benefits paid. Conservative legislators became alarmed by the prospect of a projected $47 billion surplus by 1980. They feared that availability of these funds would result in a government spending spree. Social Security Commissioner Altmeyer recommended expanding benefits. This solution, which sailed through Congress without significant debate, began pension payments in 1940 rather than in 1942, provided benefits to dependents and survivors, and enlarged the federal share of public assistance. Most significant, the system was converted from full reserve financing to a pay-as-you-go plan. Instead of funds being set aside to pay benefits later, current beneficiaries would have their benefits paid for by current contributions.

During the administration of Dwight D. Eisenhower, Social Security became irrevocably interwoven into the nation's social fabric. Health, Education, and Welfare Secretary Oveta Culp Hobby came to believe that because benefits were linked to earnings, Social Security did not undermine the free market system. Her successor, former Eastman Kodak executive Marion Folsom, was convinced that by integrating Social Security with private pensions, corporations could retire older workers more readily and thereby promote efficiency. During the 1950's, the proportion of persons aged sixty-five or older who were eligible for Social Security benefits rose from 25 percent to 70 percent. In 1956, the minimum retirement age for women was dropped to sixty-two. That amendment was supported by representatives of the depressed Southern textile industry. Five years later, the retirement age for male employees was lowered to sixty-two. Both women and men who retired before reaching the age of sixty-five received reduced benefits.

As part of the Great Society program during the Lyndon B. Johnson Administration, Medicare was added to the social security program. Medicare involved a compulsory hospital insurance plan as well as a voluntary program of supplementary medical insurance. Medicaid, a federal-state program for the medically indigent, was also enacted.

In 1969, the Social Security trust fund for the first time became part of the nation's unified budget rather than being accounted for separately. In years of trust fund surpluses, the true magnitude of the national debt was hidden. From 1935 until 1972, the federal-state system of old-age assistance and aid to the disabled remained structurally intact. In 1972, as part of the Richard M. Nixon Administration's family assistance plan, the Supplemental Security Income system initiated the federalization of that system. In 1979, a special provision gave divorced people the same protection as current spouses if they had been married for a minimum of ten years prior to divorce. This made the United States the only nation to pay benefits to former spouses.

Substantive changes to the system were advocated in the 1980's. Strong opposition arose to a proposed drastic reduction of benefits to people who retired at the age of sixty-two, and the proposal was dropped. Numerous cutbacks took place, especially to the Aid to Families with Dependent Children (AFDC) program. Student benefits for youths aged eighteen to twenty-one were phased out. A cap on disability benefits was established. In 1983, federal income taxation was imposed on half the Social Security benefits received by people with relatively high incomes. Self-employed persons were required to pay Social Security taxes equal to the combined employee-employer rate. The age at which full retirement benefits would be paid was raised in steps to sixty-seven, beginning in the year 2000.

The U.S. Social Security program, although becoming more comprehensive and closely coordinated than those of many other nations, remained highly controversial. As economic growth replaced equity as a prime macroeconomic goal, some analysts argued that the programs had become too costly to maintain and were counterproductive to business and to the nation because of adverse effects on employment and investment. By the mid-1960's, employers began preferring to pay overtime to existing employees rather than expanding the work force, because they did not have to pay into the Social Security system for workers who had exceeded an income threshold. By the 1970's, the compulsory nature of the system was being condemned by younger employees, who anticipated a long-term shortfall of reserves and feared that they would not get back in benefits what they put in as contributions. Some critics contended that the system needed simplification.

By the 1980's, the high cost and inadequate coverage of health insurance became a subject of growing concern, even among those convinced that the old-age pension program was in sound condition. The implementation of a more equitable, comprehensive, and cost-effective health delivery system emerged as the most significant social insurance issue.

Bibliography

Ball, Robert M. *Social Security, Today and Tomorrow*. New York: Columbia University Press, 1978. A former commissioner of Social Security under three presidents provides a rounded overview of the system. Insightful treatment of such key issues as whether women and minority groups are treated fairly and how Social Security and private pensions interact. Contains a select bibliography and a thorough index.

Bernstein, Irving. *A Caring Society: The New Deal, the Worker, and the Great Depression.* Boston: Houghton Mifflin, 1985. An extensively researched, well-written assessment of the 1930's from labor's vantage point. Includes a comprehensive discussion of the passage of the Social Security Act. Solid documentation and full index. Crafted by a leading labor historian, this is among the best single-volume studies of the period.

Graebner, William. *A History of Retirement: The Meaning and Function of an American Institution, 1885-1978.* New Haven, Conn.: Yale University Press, 1980. Graebner depicts Social Security as a function of pragmatic macroeconomic and business considerations. Use of Columbia University's trove of oral interviews led to new insights on the framing of the legislation. A scholarly, well-documented, interesting monograph.

Hughes, Jonathan R. T. *American Economy History.* 5th ed. Reading, Mass.: Addison-Wesley, 1998.

Nash, Gerald D., et al., eds. *Social Security: The First Half-Century.* Albuquerque: University of New Mexico Press, 1988. Contains the proceedings of a conference of the same name held in 1985 to commemorate the fiftieth anniversary of that landmark legislation and to evaluate its impact. Contains valuable discussion by some of the people who shaped the program and thoughtful essays comparing social security mechanisms of various nations. Appendix of a chronology of significant events in social security from 1935 to 1985.

Schottland, Charles I. *The Social Security Program in the United States.* 2d ed. New York: Appleton-Century-Crofts, 1970. A sound, succinct primer providing a survey of the evolution of the system. Notes and an index enhance its value to the general reader.

Jack Blicksilver

Cross-References

The U.S. Stock Market Crashes on Black Tuesday (1929); Johnson Signs the Medicare and Medicaid Amendments (1965); The Employee Retirement Income Security Act of 1974 Is Passed (1974).

THE BANKING ACT OF 1935 CENTRALIZES U.S. MONETARY CONTROL

CATEGORY OF EVENT: Finance
TIME: August 23, 1935
LOCALE: Washington, D.C.

By centralizing monetary control, the Banking Act of 1935 assured businesspeople of a more stable and predictable economic environment and allowed longer-range planning

Principal personages:
MARRINER ECCLES (1890-1977), a banker and Federal Reserve System official
CARTER GLASS (1858-1946), a congressman influential in passage of the Federal Reserve Act of 1913 and coauthor of the Glass-Steagall Act of 1932
BENJAMIN STRONG (1872-1928), the governor of the Federal Reserve Bank of New York, 1914-1928
EUGENE MEYER (1875-1959), the governor of the Federal Reserve Board, 1930-1933
EUGENE BLACK (1898-1992), the governor of the Federal Reserve Board for fifteen months in 1933 and 1934

Summary of Event

The Banking Act of 1935 (H.R. 7617) reorganized control of the U.S. monetary system, centralizing power in the hands of the Board of Governors of the Federal Reserve System and the Federal Open Market Committee. Prior to the act, each of the twelve Federal Reserve Banks that had been established by the Federal Reserve Act of 1913 had been freer to pursue policies of their own choosing.

This lack of central control had the potential to create chaotic business conditions. Businesspeople could not be sure what credit policies the Federal Reserve Banks would implement. As a result, an entrepreneur could not predict confidently whether his or her customers would face an economic upturn and easy credit in upcoming months or instead be discouraged from purchasing because of an economic downturn that might be allowed or encouraged by the local Federal Reserve Bank. Furthermore, a business could unexpectedly find itself at a competitive disadvantage in relation to a rival in another city if Federal Reserve Banks differed in their monetary policies. These types of uncertainties made business planning and forecasting difficult.

The Federal Reserve Act of 1913 had represented a desire to put knowledge of the economy and its monetary system to work. Its passage marked the first systematic attempt to influence the U.S. economy through monetary policy (governmental control of the national money supply and credit conditions). A committee of experts with specialized knowledge not commonly held by politicians would guide monetary policy. Concern about how to balance potential control of the monetary system for political purposes against domination of it by private banking interests led to a splitting of power between private bankers and the presidentially appointed Federal Reserve Board.

The Federal Reserve Board could indirectly change interest rates charged by banks or change the amount of money available to lend, by recommending to the twelve Federal Reserve Banks that they change the interest rate on loans they made to banks or by recommending purchases or sales of government bonds and bills. The Federal Reserve Board made few recommendations of either type during its first twenty years. Instead, the chief executive officers, or "governors," of the twelve Reserve Banks took independent control of monetary policy through the Governors Conference. That group made its own policy choices, then offered them to the Federal Reserve Board for ratification. The Federal Reserve Act of 1913 did not provide for this conference; its unauthorized action was indicative of private banks' reluctance to yield to central control.

In addition, the individual Federal Reserve Banks were free to ignore recommendations of the Federal Reserve Board. The New York Reserve Bank in particular acted independently. Its governor, Benjamin Strong, also acted as a powerful leader among the officials who set monetary policy for the system as a whole. Strong's death in 1928 left the system without commanding leadership. Following the 1929 stock market crash, the New York Reserve Bank favored buying government bonds from banks to provide purchasing power to the economy. It acted on this policy, but Strong's successor was unable to persuade the rest of the Federal Reserve System to follow along. The Depression might have been far less severe if he had.

Between the stock market crash and the banking holiday declared by President Franklin D. Roosevelt in 1933, the Federal Reserve Banks operated essentially independently, according to the beliefs of their own boards of directors. The Federal Reserve Board was weak and divided in opinion. The Open Market Investment Committee (an authorized body that replaced the Governors Conference in 1923), with one member from each Federal Reserve Bank, was similarly powerless. Each bank's representative came to meetings with directions from the bank's board of directors, and those banks rarely were unified in their goals. The decentralized control in the period from 1929 to 1933 led to monetary policy that has been described as inept and as possibly worsening the Depression.

The Banking Act of 1933 set up the Federal Open Market Committee (FOMC), as successor to the Open Market Investment Committee, to determine appropriate bond sales or purchases for the Federal Reserve System. The FOMC also had one member from each Reserve Bank. It instituted all policy actions, and the Federal Reserve Board had only the power to approve or disapprove. Reserve Banks remained free not to participate in any open market operations recommended by the FOMC.

System officials blamed inadequate powers, rather than misuse of powers, for their inability to stop the Depression's economic contraction and to prevent bank panics and failures. Furthermore, many system officials were willing to tolerate the bank failures, seeing them as proper punishment for poor management or excessive earlier speculation in financial markets. The failures were concentrated among smaller banks and those that were not members of the Federal Reserve System, so they were of relatively little interest to the larger banks with the most influence in the system. The larger banks, in fact, saw the failures as a way of shaking their small competitors out of the market.

In response to the behavior of the Federal Reserve System in the 1920's and early 1930's, Marriner Eccles, a banker and Treasury Department official, devised a plan to correct what he saw as flaws in the monetary control system. He and many others believed that better use of monetary policy could be a powerful tool to end the Depression. Some argued that improper use of monetary policy had exaggerated the economic downturn and that, therefore, less rather than more central control was indicated. Eccles, however, wanted to implement the powers of the Federal Reserve System more broadly and to establish conscious centralized control of the monetary system.

Eccles' proposals formed the basis for Title II of the Banking Act of

1935, which stirred strong debate in Congress. Senator Carter Glass, who had helped develop the Federal Reserve Act of 1913 and had coauthored the Glass-Steagall Act of 1932, particularly opposed changing the nature of the system. It was argued that a stronger Federal Reserve Board would become an arm of the political administration rather than providing independent judgment. These debates led to rewording the act to reduce control by the executive branch.

The act reorganized the central bodies of the Federal Reserve System. The Federal Reserve Board was renamed the Board of Governors of the Federal Reserve System, and the secretary of the treasury and comptroller of the currency were dropped from membership. Each of the board's seven members was to be appointed by the president, but their fourteen-year terms would overlap, so that no single presidential administration could appoint a majority. The FOMC was reconstituted to include all members of the Board of Governors and five presidents of Federal Reserve Banks. Those five positions would be filled by the twelve Reserve Bank presidents on a rotating basis. They were to give independent policy recommendations rather than being guided by their banks' boards of directors as in the past. Most important, each Reserve Bank was required to follow the policies recommended by the FOMC and not operate on its own.

The Board of Governors also gained the power to set reserve requirements, or the percentage of deposits that private banks in the system had to keep available to meet demands for withdrawals. The act left election of Reserve Bank presidents and vice presidents up to the banks' boards of directors but made those choices subject to approval by the Board of Governors. These main provisions of the Banking Act of 1935 took power from the individual Reserve Banks and centralized it within the Board of Governors and FOMC. Eccles, who had been made chair of the Federal Reserve Board late in November, 1934, was chosen to chair the new Board of Governors that replaced it.

Impact of Event

The most important impact of the Banking Act of 1935 was its message: In the future, there would be a centralized guiding hand behind U.S. monetary policy. Along with other New Deal reforms such as the establishment of the Federal Deposit Insurance Corporation (which the Banking Act of 1935 amended), the act helped to persuade the American business community that there would not be another Great Depression. Businesspeople could predict a more stable American economy in which the government promoted a steady course of growth, with neither excessive unemployment nor the opposite problem, high rates of inflation.

Businesspeople became relatively certain of being able to obtain bank credit for promising projects. Previously, they sometimes had faced bank loan officers who were unwilling to lend because they were uncertain about future national financial conditions and the availability of funds to their banks. Centralized and planned monetary control greatly reduced these uncertainties.

Although individual banks would still fail, depositors and borrowers could rely on the Federal Reserve System to prevent large-scale bank failures. Banks themselves could count on a steadier, more predictable monetary policy environment in which to conduct business. Centralization of power made it possible and profitable for businesses and especially financial speculators to monitor the FOMC and try to guess its policy decisions, which were kept secret for several weeks to avoid any disruptive effects on financial markets. A new job function of "Fed watcher" thus was created.

Formal centralization of control did not end debates concerning independence of the Federal Reserve System. Individual bankers still wanted influence within the system, and the Treasury Department was unwilling to relinquish control of the system completely. The Board of Governors agreed at first to cooperate with the Treasury by buying government bonds, as a means of keeping bond prices high to aid the financing of government operations. In 1936, the Board of Governors also exercised its new power to raise the required reserve rate. This acted to reduce the amount of money available to the financial system, more than offsetting the effects of bond purchases. The combined policy contributed to a minor recession in 1936 and 1937. Congress then proposed very specific guidelines for establishing monetary policy, leaving little room for discretion on the part of Federal Reserve System officials. The proposal was not made law, but system officials heeded the implicit warning to coordinate plans with other government agencies.

The Board of Governors and FOMC chose not to exercise their powers to any great degree during the 1930's, generally letting recovery from the Depression run its course. During World War II, the Reserve Banks agreed to cooperate with the Treasury's borrowing, buying Treasury bonds to maintain their price and keep interest rates low. As the war neared its end, however, the Treasury's desire to keep interest rates low conflicted with the FOMC's wish to restrain the growth of the money supply as a means of preventing inflation.

The Employment Act of 1946 stated that the government had a responsibility to use all of its tools in a coordinated fashion to maximize employment, production, and purchasing power. Implicitly, the act recognized that neither fiscal policy (use of government powers to tax and spend) nor monetary policy alone was powerful enough to control the U.S. economy. The FOMC continued to buy Treasury bond issues, but Federal Reserve System officials argued more strongly against the constraint that this cooperation imposed on their decisions. In March, 1951, an agreement was reached under which the FOMC was no longer responsible for supporting the price of Treasury bonds. That left the system without a clear and specific policy objective. The public had begun to believe in the power of monetary policy, so Federal Reserve System officials wanted to state clearly how that policy would be used.

An appropriate growth rate of the money supply was chosen as one objective. The FOMC would provide enough money to finance business expansion without causing inflation. The second objective was to vary credit conditions countercyclically, reducing credit availability during business expansions and allowing easier credit during contractions, as a means of offsetting business cycles. The Board of Governors and the FOMC began to exercise their powers of central control in a manner basically independent of political or private business interests.

Bibliography

Broaddus, Alfred. *A Primer on the Fed*. Richmond, Va.: Federal Reserve Bank of Richmond, 1988. This seventy-four-page booklet summarizes the structure and operation of the Federal Reserve System. A long section is devoted to describing actions of the system in the 1970's and early 1980's. Also offers case studies. Useful for understanding the background of the Federal Reserve System.

Clifford, Albert Jerome. *The Independence of the Federal Reserve System*. Philadelphia: University of Pennsylvania Press, 1965. Discusses the structural arrangement of the Federal Reserve System, including changes up to 1960. Valuable for its insights into debates concerning which public or private agencies should control the U.S. monetary system.

De Saint-Phalle, Thibaut. *The Federal Reserve: An Intentional Mystery*. New York: Praeger, 1985. Provides a history of the U.S. system of bank regulations, including those related to overseas bank holding companies and international lending. Written for a high school or undergraduate audience.

Friedman, Milton, and Anna Jacobson Schwartz. *A Monetary History of the United States, 1867-1960*. Princeton, N.J.: Princeton University Press, 1963. The authoritative study of the operation of the U.S. monetary system. Economists Friedman and Schwartz provide a narrative discussion of the use of monetary policy, illustrated with detailed statistics. The use of theory is advanced in places, but arguments are always summarized clearly. The authors' agenda is to prove the power of monetary policy; they devote more than one hundred pages to explaining how correct use of that policy could have prevented the Great Depression or at least minimized its effects.

Hughes, Jonathan R. T. *American Economy History.* 5th ed. Reading, Mass.: Addison-Wesley, 1998.

Krooss, Herman E., ed. *Documentary History of Banking and Currency in the United States.* 4 vols. New York: Chelsea House, 1969. Volume 4 in this set covers the time period from 1913 to 1968, including passage of the original Federal Reserve Act of 1913. Much of the text reprints banking laws, with some commentary on them that was written at the time of their passage. Also reprints presidential speeches and letters as well as court decisions.

Moore, Carl H. *The Federal Reserve System: A History of the First Seventy-five Years.* Jefferson, N.C.: McFarland, 1990. Highlights major events in the history of the Federal Reserve System, giving an overview of the issues faced by the system. Easy to read.

Patman, Wright. *The Federal Reserve System: A Study Prepared for the Use of the Joint Economic Committee, Congress of the United States.* Washington, D.C.: Government Printing Office, 1976. Chapter 9, "The Banking Act of 1935," gives a concise history of the political maneuvering behind passage of the act and rationales for its passage. Other chapters outline the history of the Federal Reserve System. Appendices contain letters and speeches by Patman concerning aspects of the U.S. banking system.

A. J. Sobczak

Cross-References

The Federal Reserve Act Creates a U.S. Central Bank (1913); The U.S. Stock Market Crashes on Black Tuesday (1929); The Banking Act of 1933 Reorganizes the American Banking System (1933); Congress Deregulates Banks and Savings and Loans (1980-1982); Bush Responds to the Savings and Loan Crisis (1989).

THE CIO BEGINS UNIONIZING UNSKILLED WORKERS

CATEGORY OF EVENT: Labor
TIME: November 9, 1935
LOCALE: The United States

The formation of the Congress of Industrial Organizations signaled the unionization of mass-production industries and their workers and labor's increasing confrontations with management

Principal personages:
JOHN L. LEWIS (1880-1969), an AFL official and leader of the break-away CIO unions
WILLIAM GREEN (1872-1952), the president of the AFL
PHILIP MURRAY (1886-1952), a leading figure in the CIO
SIDNEY HILLMAN (1887-1946), a CIO leader and head of the clothing workers
WALTER P. REUTHER (1907-1970), a CIO organizer and a leader of the autoworkers

Summary of Event

In the mid-1930's, the American Federation of Labor (AFL) was the oldest, largest, and most durable labor organization in the United States. Modestly begun in 1881 when a score of American and Canadian trade unions decided to federate, the AFL formally came into existence in Columbus, Ohio, in 1886, largely as a result of the efforts of Adolf Strasser, Samuel Gompers, and Peter McGuire. Strasser and Gompers, who more indelibly marked the character of the AFL than did the radical socialism of McGuire, were both foreign-born—Strasser in Germany, Gompers in Lon-

259

don. Both men were cigar makers by trade and both flirted with Marxism and other forms of socialism. Anomalously, their foreign birth engendered scant affection in them for most immigrant workers. Their cigarmaking skills diverted them from sympathies with unskilled workers. In the light of what they perceived to be the realities of the American workplace and the outlook of American workers, they swiftly jettisoned their socialism because it appeared impractical.

Gompers presided over the AFL from 1886 until his death in 1924, except during 1895. His like-minded successor, William Green, headed the union until 1952. The AFL remained a conservative federated organization of labor's elite, that is, of skilled workers. The strategies to which its leaders clung reflected lessons learned from their own experiences and from those of their constituent trades' rank-and-file workers. The nationwide unions that had preceded the AFL had all failed or were failing by 1886. Like the National Labor Union or the Knights of St. Crispin, both formed in the late 1860's, or the Knights of Labor, established in 1871, these earlier unions— in company with various "labor reform" political parties—had cast their nets too widely. They were actively and ambitiously political. They recruited unselectively—men and women, immigrants and native-born, black and white, skilled and unskilled workers, even employers and professionals. They were chronically short of funds, could ill-afford their strikes, and were ravaged by economic depressions. They were weakened, too, by the hostile actions of legislatures and courts and won few friends among the general public of a predominantly agricultural nation.

In contrast to such organizations, the AFL was officially nonpolitical and nonideological. It championed "bread-and-butter" or "business" unionism, concentrating on winning higher wages, shorter hours, and better working conditions. Its craft workers, mainly white and native-born or of northern European origin, resented competition from unskilled southern European immigrants and black workers, both of which groups tended to be willing to work for lower wages. Skilled workers had watched employers defeat unionization by exploiting the "babel of tongues" and diverse backgrounds common to unskilled workers and reckoned that inclusion of these workers in the AFL would prove disastrous. Furthermore, as skilled men (membership was overwhelmingly male), AFL members paid the higher dues that funded effective strikes: strikes of the essential workers whose walkouts sufficed to cripple industries. Within three decades, numbers confirmed the wisdom of such organizational strategies. By 1916, more than 2.1 million of America's 2.7 million trade unionists belonged to the AFL.

By 1935, the United States had changed dramatically but the AFL had not. The country had become overwhelmingly urban. A substantial portion of the workforce was engaged in manufacturing, at the vital core of which were relatively new mass-production industries with jobs filled largely by unskilled and almost entirely unorganized workers. Moreover, the administration of President Franklin D. Roosevelt, in a climate that warmed toward labor, witnessed the passage of impressive prolabor legislation. Accordingly, a fresh generation of AFL leaders recognized the limits of the old guard's successes. They were eager to seize the moment and organize the millions of unskilled mass-production workers whom older AFL officials mostly resented or hoped to ignore.

Clashes of personalities and perceptions climaxed on November 9, 1935, shortly after this long-rankling conflict erupted at the AFL's annual convention. John L. Lewis, a veteran leader of the United Mine Workers (UMW), convened a meeting of other dissidents at the Washington, D.C., headquarters of the UMW. Among those present were Philip Murray, leader of the International Ladies' Garment Workers' Union (ILGWU); Sidney Hillman, who led the Amalgamated Clothing Workers; Thomas McMahon, head of the United Textile Workers; Harvey Fremming, representing the Oil Field, Gas, and Refinery Workers of America; and leaders of the mine, mill, and smelter workers, and of the cap and millinery trades. With Lewis as chairman, they formed the Committee for Industrial Organization, an AFL committee the purpose of which was to unionize workers in mass-production and other industries on an industrial rather than a craft basis. Workers would be organized by entire plants and industries rather than on the basis of dozens of discrete trades or crafts within those plants or industries.

Declaring that the committee's objective was simply to grasp organizing opportunities on behalf of the AFL, Lewis and the dissidents disavowed any desire to foster "dual unionism" or to raid the parent body's unions for members. The committee's aim, Lewis and his colleagues asserted, was to inform unorganized mass-production workers of the advantages of industrial unionism without producing disharmony or chaos within the AFL. Nevertheless, Lewis resigned his AFL vice presidency late in November, 1935, despite political allurements dangled before him by AFL president Green.

Despairing of seeing sympathetic actions by the AFL executive committee, or by AFL membership at large at the annual convention, Lewis assumed the CIO's permanent chairmanship the same month. For the next two years, he and his minority of CIO brethren, still remaining within the AFL, fought procedural and constitutional roadblocks thrown up against them by Green and other AFL officials, in the meantime trading self-justifications, challenging motives, mutually citing lost opportunities, implying communist influences, and exchanging predictions of disaster. What labor historian Philip Taft described as the CIO's "road to suspension" proved to be a lengthy one filled with acrimonious outbursts alternating with peace conferences. The suspension of Lewis' UMW and (initially) nine CIO unions in other industries came on September 5, 1936. Their expulsion, along with exclusion of twenty CIO unions formed in the interim, was completed in 1938. Led by Lewis, the renamed Congress of Industrial Organizations then independently persisted in its challenge both to the AFL and to the captains and managers of major industries.

Impact of Event

Building around the half million members of John L. Lewis' UMW, the CIO, in important regards, was born strong. Its constituent unions, upon their suspension or expulsion from the AFL, carried away 982,000 members from the AFL, almost one-third of the AFL's strength. To these members were added the recruits gained by CIO organizers between the committee days of 1935 and separation in May, 1938. While CIO leaders were fighting their internecine battles within the AFL, they maintained their assiduous campaigns to bring industrial unionism to the unorganized, foremost to mass-production workers.

Lewis and his CIO officials and organizers were presented with an array of opportunities that were matched both by subtle and by violent opposition from powerful industrial leaders and managers. Across America's industrial terrain were millions of disgruntled nonunion employees, notably in the steel, automotive, rubber, chemical, electrical, aluminum, cement, meatpacking, textile, oil refining, shipbuilding, and long-haul truck transportation industries. As Walter P. Reuther demonstrated among autoworkers, these industries' workers were primed for CIO industrial unionism.

Beginning in the 1920's, some areas of these industries became riddled with "company" unions, management-sponsored unions designed to forestall organization of workers by bona fide labor unions. These "tame" unions may have included as many as 2.5 million members by 1935. The Roosevelt Administration's National Industrial Recovery Act (NIRA) of 1933, moreover, gave impetus to their growth. Ironically, Lewis, who was then regarded by many AFL officials as a conservative unionist (he was a staunch Republican as well), had participated in efforts to launch the NIRA, section 7a of which, in the name of industrial cooperation, opened the door officially to company unions.

Employers who merely established their own unions, however, chose a relatively moderate course in trying to prevent real unionization. A somewhat more sophisticated approach toward breaking union efforts was widely publicized by the National Association of Manufacturers. The so-called "Mohawk Formula" was applied most notably by the president of Republic Steel against the CIO's Steel Workers' Organizing Committee. The formula called for employer-conducted strike balloting in concert with branding union leaders as outsiders, radicals, or communists. Coordinated threats were directed toward local communities, warning that unionization would force industry to leave town. The hiring of strikebreakers was masked under the guise of back-to-work movements, and reopenings of formerly struck factories and mills were touted widely as rescue operations conducted by sensible workers.

Steel was among the major industries whose disgruntled workers the CIO targeted for unionizing during the late 1930's. (National Archives)

Convinced that basic American values were under assault, many employers used more obvious forms of coercion against unions, including resorting to overt violence. Despite passage in July, 1935, of the path-breaking prolabor National Labor Relations Act (the Wagner Act), which legally ensured labor's right to organize and to bargain collectively, three more years were to pass before any noticeable atrophy of industry's union-breaking tactics.

The establishment of the CIO, massive division within the labor movement between craft and industrial unionism, passage of the Wagner Act, and the nation's plunge by 1937 deeper into the Depression coincided with waves of antiunion violence. Daily news accounts and newsreels of bloody battles involving pickets or strikebreakers in steel, rubber, or automotive plants, for example, led many people to fear that the nation had sunk into insurrection or class warfare. The apparent stridency of union leaders, the militancy of organizing tactics, and the widespread suspicion that some CIO unions in particular were communist-inspired persuaded large sectors of the general public to sympathize with employers who hired and armed private guards. Such acquiescence also lent sanction to the deployment of police and troops by state and local authorities against union organizers, pickets, and strikers.

Although the Roosevelt Administration became more actively prolabor by the mid-1930's, the realities of management-labor relations continued to be harsh. During 1935 and 1936, forty-eight workers were killed on picket lines and more than ten thousand strikers were arrested. A wave of "sit-down" strikes featuring workers' occupation of employers' properties—a CIO tactic first tried on a large scale in an Akron, Ohio, Goodyear Tire & Rubber plant early in 1936—was especially unnerving to the property-conscious public and served to heighten antilabor sentiments. The Chicago Memorial Day Massacre of peacefully demonstrating striking CIO steelworkers by Chicago police in 1937 epitomized company, community, and police attacks on unionists.

Although the CIO's defeats in trying to organize smaller steel plants and the construction industry bared its vulnerabilities, the rise in its membership to 3.4 million by 1938 was more rapid than that ever before experienced by an American labor union. Large sectors of the nation's major industries, from automotive to coal mining to steel, were unionized by the CIO. Further, the CIO had developed what proved to be an increasingly effective political action committee. On balance, CIO victories cost the AFL little. Its leaders, stung into action by the "rebel" CIO, counted a membership of 4 million by 1939. Both federations were able to grow, mostly along the separate lines of craft versus industry and skilled versus unskilled workers. There were, however, many intense jurisdictional disputes as both federations tried to claim some newly forming unions.

Bibliography

Barnard, John. *Walter Reuther and the Rise of the Auto Workers*. Boston: Little, Brown, 1983. A fine summary written for lay readers. Provides an important vignette of mid-1930's CIO activity in a major industry. Bibliographical essay on sources and useful index.

Bernstein, Irving. *The Turbulent Years: A History of the American Worker, 1933-1941*. Boston: Houghton Mifflin, 1970. Excellent window into the subject. Clear, authoritative, and balanced narrative. Good notes, bibliography, and index.

Brooks, Thomas R. *Toil and Trouble: A History of American Labor*. 2d ed. New York: Delacorte Press, 1971. Colorful reading with good personality sketches. The author's prounion bias does not detract from a good general survey. No notes or bibliography. Useful index.

Fine, Sidney. *Sit-Down: The General Motors Strike of 1936-1937*. Ann Arbor: University of Michigan Press, 1963. A clear scholarly view of specific CIO battles with business and the community. Notes, bibliography, useful index. Exciting reading.

Hughes, Jonathan R. T. *American Economy History*. 5th ed. Reading, Mass.: Addison-Wesley, 1998.

Schlesinger, Arthur M., Jr. *The Coming of the New Deal*. Vol. 2 in *The Age of Roosevelt*. Boston: Houghton Mifflin, 1958. Wonderful for context on labor, government, and business in the mid-1930's. Detailed chapter notes, excellent index.

Stolberg, Benjamin. *The Story of the CIO*. New York: Viking Press, 1938. Good encapsulation of atmosphere and personalities affecting establishment of the CIO. A readable journalistic account, with some theory and some history. No notes or bibliography, but a good index.

Taft, Philip. *The A.F. of L. from the Death of Gompers to the Merger*. New York: Harper & Brothers, 1959. An invaluable study, though at times dense reading. The best work of its kind for understanding the AFL and CIO dissidents. Chapter notes, valuable index.

Clifton K. Yearley

Cross-References

The Norris-LaGuardia Act Adds Strength to Labor Organizations (1932); The National Industrial Recovery Act Is Passed (1933); The Wagner Act Promotes Union Organization (1935); Roosevelt Signs the Fair Labor Standards Act (1938); The AFL and CIO Merge (1955).

THE DC-3 OPENS A NEW ERA OF COMMERCIAL AIR TRAVEL

CATEGORIES OF EVENT: Transportation and new products
TIME: June 25, 1936
LOCALE: The United States

The Douglas DC-3 revolutionized air travel by providing passenger comfort and operating capabilities, together with profit-making potential, previously unavailable in the fledgling airline industry

Principal personages:

DONALD W. DOUGLAS (1892-1981), the founder of the Douglas Aircraft Company

JACK FRYE (1904-1959), the vice president of flight operations for Transcontinental & Western Air Lines

CHARLES A. LINDBERGH (1902-1974), the chief technical adviser for Transcontinental & Western Air Lines

W. E. PATTERSON (1899-1980), the president of United Air Lines

EDWARD (EDDIE) RICKENBACKER (1890-1973), the president of Eastern Air Lines

C. R. SMITH (1899-1990), the president of American Airlines

Summary of Event

The Air Mail Act of 1925 authorized the U.S. postmaster general to contract with any individual, firm, or corporation for the carriage of mail by aircraft between points designated by the postmaster general. This legislation signaled the beginning of what would become the airline industry. The Air Mail Act's first amendment (in 1926) changed the basis for payment to these contract mail carriers, but even with this change, which essentially amounted to subsidization, the young airlines frequently had difficulty in generating a profit. The carriers came to recognize that additional revenue was possible if aircraft could carry passengers in addition to mail. This demand eventually led to a larger aircraft, suitable for combined mail/ passenger service. The first generation of these aircraft could accommodate from two to six passengers, but soon, larger multiengine aircraft became operational, the most popular of which were the all-metal Ford trimotor and Fokker's wood and fabric trimotor, which used laminated plywood as the wing skin. It was this plywood wing that ultimately would lead to Donald W. Douglas' DC series.

In March, 1931, a Fokker trimotor owned by Transcontinental & Western Air Lines (TWA; became Trans World Airlines in 1950) crashed while en route from Kansas City to Wichita. One of the passengers aboard was Knute Rockne, Notre Dame's famous and beloved football coach, whose death was mourned nationwide. Public pressure began to mount on the Department of Commerce as the news media became increasingly strident in calling for public release of information on the cause of the accident, particularly since Rockne had been one of the passengers. Ultimately, the Department of Commerce concluded not only that the accident was traceable to the Fokker's wooden wing structure but also that all Fokker F-10's should be grounded temporarily while inspections and structural fixes were made. Publicity surrounding the accident turned public opinion against Fokker's trimotors, forcing TWA to depend solely on its Ford trimotors. The airline's vice president of flight operations, Jack Frye, recognized that a more modern aircraft type was needed as soon as possible.

Frye visited Seattle in an attempt to obtain some of Boeing Aircraft's new B-247 models. The B-247 was a ten-passenger, streamlined, all-metal airplane that Boeing thought would revolutionize air travel. The first sixty B-247's, two years worth of production, were destined for United Air Lines, an affiliated company then under the Boeing umbrella. Frye and his engineers, with technical advice from Charles A. Lindbergh, then proceeded to develop a set of specifications for a trimotored transport, and proposals were solicited from a number of aircraft manufacturing companies, the smallest of which was Donald Douglas' company in Santa Monica, California.

Douglas' engineers, after studying TWA's specifications, determined that they could meet the stringent requirements with a twin-engine airplane by using new design applications as well as new, more powerful engines then being developed by both the Wright Aeronautical Company and Pratt & Whitney. Eleven months after receiving the specifications, Douglas' first version of this new generation of aircraft, the twelve-passenger Douglas

Commercial-1 (DC-1) made its first flight. Even before the plane's delivery to TWA, the airline was asking for design changes that would, among other things, increase the DC-1's capacity by two passengers. TWA quickly ordered twenty-five of this new model, the DC-2. Douglas began work on the new version immediately after flight tests had been completed on the DC-1, and in May, 1934, TWA took delivery of its first DC-2.

One of the earliest DC-2's was delivered to KLM, the Royal Dutch Airline, and almost immediately was entered in the MacRobertson Trophy Race, the London-to-Melbourne Derby. Finishing second to a British twin-engine fighter aircraft and well ahead of a Boeing B-247 in this contest, even while carrying a few passengers, helped firmly establish the DC-2 in the traveling public's mind as the fastest and most reliable passenger aircraft yet made.

As the number of carriers ordering the DC-2 continued to grow, Douglas' engineers began working with specifications developed by American Airlines for an aircraft with sleeping berths that could provide American's passengers with overnight transcontinental sleeper service. Stretching and enlarging of the DC-2 created a new aircraft, the DC-3. Because of its combination of operating performance, passenger comfort, and operating costs, the DC-3 quickly became the most widely used passenger airplane in the world. C. R. Smith, president of American Airlines, commenting on his company's high regard for the DC-3, said that it was "the first airplane in the world that could make money just by hauling passengers."

Impact of Event

In the years following the Army's around-the-world flight in 1924 with Douglas-built airplanes, the company continued designing and building mostly military aircraft, but in 1931 TWA's accident in Kansas ironically served to revolutionize air travel by presenting Douglas with an opportunity to enter the commercial aircraft market. TWA's need was for a new type of aircraft that could exceed the performance capabilities of the Boeing B-247, about to be introduced by its chief competitor, United Air Lines. The B-247 gave United a definite competitive advantage over TWA, with its older and slower trimotors, but that advantage lasted only for little more than one year.

On August 22, 1932, Jack Frye, seeking a new and competitive airplane for TWA, solicited proposals by sending letters containing the airline's detailed specifications to six aircraft manufacturing companies. Donald Douglas later would refer to Frye's letter as the "birth certificate of the modern airliner."

Douglas and his engineering staff, having decided that they could produce an aircraft capable of meeting or exceeding each of TWA's design and performance specifications, submitted a proposal to TWA, and a contract was signed on September 20, 1932, for the first airplane, at a cost of $125,000, with a one-year option for up to sixty additional planes priced at $58,000 each. TWA later admitted to Douglas that obtaining financing for the purchase had been difficult. Bankers, it seems, doubted that an aircraft could be built that would meet all of TWA's specifications.

The DC-1 first flew on July 1, 1933. It could operate at 180 miles per hour while carrying twelve passengers. On the other hand, United's Boeing B-247, the pride of its fleet, could carry only ten passengers while cruising at 165 miles per hour. At TWA's insistence, Douglas immediately started making refinements to the DC-1, and orders began coming in for this improved model, the DC-2. Within two years, the DC-2 had evolved into the larger and more powerful DC-3, capable of carrying twenty-one passengers at 195 miles per hour. The DC-3 would continue as the workhorse of the world's airlines through World War II and into the early postwar years.

In February, 1934, President Franklin D. Roosevelt abruptly canceled all existing airmail contracts and transferred airmail operations to the Army Air Corps. The service, hampered by continuing and worsening budgetary reductions, was anxious to demonstrate its capabilities to Congress and the American public. Tragically, during the Army's four months of air mail operation, there were sixty-six crashes and twelve fatalities, three of which occurred as Army pilots were en route to their assigned origination points.

As the Army was preparing to fly the mail, the DC-1 was used to demonstrate the capabilities of airlines and their new aircraft. In a highly publicized demonstration flight only hours before the Army was to take over airmail carriage, Jack Frye of TWA and Eastern's Eddie Rickenbacker flew the DC-1 from Burbank Air Terminal in California to Newark, New Jersey, in slightly more than thirteen elapsed hours, with two refueling stops, at Kansas City, Missouri, and Columbus, Ohio. The flight's success did much to convince the American public of the efficiency and capability of the nation's airlines.

Although airmail contracts were again awarded to private carriers, effective June 1, the Roosevelt Administration's change of heart resulted not from the February DC-1 demonstration flight of Frye and Rickenbacker but instead from growing public displeasure with the Army's obvious inability to sustain the airmail operation with its inexperienced pilots flying virtually obsolete aircraft. Contractually, the airlines had been receiving from 42 to 54 cents per mile for airmail carriage, but the cost to the taxpayer of the Army's operation was put at $2.21 per mile, an unacceptable difference.

In June, with the contract situation resolved and airlines again carrying the mail, TWA began operating DC-2's on its overnight service from Newark to Los Angeles, with intermediate stops at Chicago, Kansas City, and Albuquerque. At the same time, American Airlines, on its overnight transcontinental service, was operating a sleeper version of the Curtiss Condor, a twelve- to fifteen-passenger, twin-engine airplane that was the last bi-wing air transport in commercial service in the United States. After TWA quickly gained a competitive edge with its DC-2's, American began looking for a replacement aircraft for the Condor, one capable of carrying a greater payload at a faster speed and at lower operating costs. American's search began and ended at Douglas Aircraft.

With American's order for an upgraded version of the DC-2 that could accommodate sleeper berths, Douglas realized that this new model, the Douglas Sleeper Transport (DST), virtually would be a new airplane. The fuselage, enlarged to accommodate sleeper berths, could be fitted with twenty-one seats, and this new, larger version's operating performance still handily exceeded that of the two-year-old DC-2's.

Although Douglas' development costs for its DC-3 series reached $400,000, prospects for sales of this series were such that the company was not overly concerned. American Airlines was so pleased at the combination of passenger comfort, performance, and operating costs that over the next few years, at a cost of $110,000 per plane, its aircraft fleet gradually was converted exclusively to DC-3's. This revolutionary airplane's payload capacity, gross weight, and operating performance exceeded those of any other aircraft then in commercial operation.

The DC-3 became an instant success with the airlines and their passengers. Although the DC-2 had proven successful, Douglas decided to terminate further production when it became evident that the DC-3 would outperform its predecessor rather significantly, and at lower operating costs. Up to that point, Douglas had built a total of 191 DC-2's, the company recouping all of its development costs with the 75th aircraft. The success of the DC series caused Boeing to terminate its B-247 line at seventy-five aircraft. William Boeing's revolutionary new transport had been in production for less than three years.

In the meantime, a provision of the 1934 Air Mail Act prohibited any interlocking of airlines with aircraft manufacturing companies, a practice common up to that time. As a result, United Air Lines was freed of dependence on Boeing as its principal aircraft supplier, and United's new president, W. E. Patterson, immediately contacted Douglas. United's primary transport, the Boeing B-247, was no match for the DC-3, either competitively from a passenger standpoint or operationally from a performance and cost standpoint. Patterson realized that he needed to upgrade United's fleet quickly, to the point that over the next few years United became almost exclusively a DC-3 airline. Eastern Air Lines quickly followed suit. It was becoming obvious to the entire industry that this new Douglas transport truly was revolutionizing air travel throughout the world.

American Airlines, the first operator of the new DC-3 series, began taking delivery of both versions in mid-1936, putting its first DC-3, a sleeper version, into regular line service on June 25, 1936. Most aviation chroniclers consider that day to have marked the beginning of a new era in air transportation. The end finally was at hand for airline operations that had been delivering, at best, only marginal profits on an irregular basis.

The DC-3, together with its predecessor, the DC-2, proved so popular with the traveling public that within the first calendar year following the DC-3's introduction and first flight, one million passengers had flown on scheduled airlines in the United States. This total would grow significantly each year after doubling within two years to exceed two million in 1939.

Douglas originally had estimated a total sales volume of 50 DC-3's, but because of the airline's popularity with travelers and operators alike, a total of 803 eventually were built. In addition, almost 10,400 military versions of the DC-3 saw service during World War II as the C-47.

The DC-3 revolutionized commercial air travel throughout the world. Its well-deserved reputation for reliability and safety attracted more and more people to air travel. Within two years of the first DC-3 commercial flight, a significant industry milestone was reached when, for the first time, passenger revenues exceeded airmail revenues. From an airline standpoint, the DC-3 offered a virtually unbeatable combination of revenue potential and low operating costs. It is little wonder that by 1939, 90 percent of the world's airlines were using the Douglas DC-3, a plane that unquestionably changed airline travel forever.

Bibliography

Glines, Carroll V., and Wendell F. Moseley. *The DC-3: The Story of a Fabulous Airplane*. Philadelphia: J. B. Lippincott, 1966. An excellent account of the DC-3's evolution, although much more emphasis is placed on its military service in World War II than on its commercial airline role.

Holden, Henry M. *The Boeing 247: The First Modern Commercial Airplane*. Blue Ridge Summit, Pa.: TAB Books, 1991. Interesting account of the development of the DC-3's primary competitor, Boeing's B-247, and the DC-3's effect on Boeing and its pride and joy.

Johnson, Robert E. *Airway One*. Chicago: United Air Lines, 1974. Written by a longtime member of United Air Lines' top management, this is one of the better corporate narratives. Includes an interesting look at United's developmental years and its changeover from a Boeing B-247 airline to a DC-3 airline.

Kane, Robert M. *Air Transportation.* 11th ed. Dubuque, Iowa: Kendall/ Hunt, 1993. Primarily a college-level aviation textbook. Includes some interesting information on the early airline period and the evolution of the DC-3.

Morrison, Wilbur H. *Donald W. Douglas: A Heart with Wings.* Ames: Iowa State University Press, 1991. An excellent account of the DC-3's development, seen as one of the landmark accomplishments of this aviation pioneer.

Pisano, Dominick A. "The Crash That Killed Knute Rockne." *Air & Space Smithsonian* 6 (December, 1991): 88. A fascinating narrative of the accident that would lead TWA to request proposals for a new airplane that ultimately would become the revolutionary DC-3.

James D. Matthews

Cross-References

Ford Implements Assembly Line Production (1913); The Panama Canal Opens (1914); Truman Orders the Seizure of Railways (1946); Carter Signs the Airline Deregulation Act (1978).

ROOSEVELT SIGNS THE FAIR LABOR STANDARDS ACT

CATEGORY OF EVENT: Labor
TIME: June 25, 1938
LOCALE: Washington, D.C.

A Depression measure, the federal Fair Labor Standards Act stipulated minimum wages and maximum hours of work for employees of firms engaged in interstate commerce

Principal personages:

FRANKLIN D. ROOSEVELT (1882-1945), the president of the United States, 1933-1945

FRANCES PERKINS (1880-1965), a former social worker who as secretary of labor supported the act

HARLAN FISKE STONE (1872-1946), the chief justice who rendered the Supreme Court's first decision on the act

WILLIAM GREEN (1873-1952), the president of the American Federation of Labor

THOMAS JAMES WALSH (1859-1933), a U.S. senator who fought for the abolition of child labor

Summary of Event

Enacted into federal law on June 25, 1938, the Fair Labor Standards Act (FLSA) was part of a package of reform legislation characterizing the so-called "Second New Deal" of President Franklin D. Roosevelt that began with his landslide reelection in 1936. It applied to all businesses that were engaged in or that affected interstate commerce. Article I, section 8 of the U.S. Constitution, the "commerce clause," provided the legal grounds

273

granting federal jurisdiction to effectuate the act. Because the U.S. Supreme Court had begun giving broad construction to what was meant by interstate commerce (as it did in decisions regarding the Wagner Act, for example), the Roosevelt Administration believed it would have wide latitude in applying the act.

The Fair Labor Standards Act placed a floor under wages and a ceiling over hours for those workers covered by it. Initially, it established a minimum wage of forty cents an hour, with provisions for subsequent increases, and mandated a maximum forty-hour workweek. To smooth the act's implementation, the provisions for both wages and hours were to be phased into effect over eight years. The act also placed national authority behind the abolition of child labor. The labor of children under sixteen years of age was forbidden, and persons under eighteen years of age were prohibited from working in hazardous occupations, including mining. In its original form, however, a number of occupations were exempted from the FLSA's coverage, notably farm laborers, professional workers, and domestic servants, although these exemptions would be altered in time. The original bill before Congress envisaged a special board to administer the law. In subsequent years, however, oversight of the act fell to the Department of Labor's Employment Standards Administration.

President Roosevelt had given little thought to placing his political prestige behind a wages and hours bill until 1937. In efforts to combat the Depression, the National Industrial Recovery Act of 1933 (NIRA), sponsored by Roosevelt during his "First New Deal," sought to increase purchasing power by establishing minimum wages among the NIRA's participating businesses and industries. Along with several other major pieces of early New Deal legislation, however, the NIRA was declared unconstitutional by the Supreme Court.

By 1935, however, prolabor legislation and support for the incomes of disadvantaged groups were popular in Congress. The Guffey Coal Act of 1935 and the Merchant Marine Act of 1936, for example, each contained provisions to limit hours and raise wages. The institution of Social Security in 1935 was still another attempt to raise the incomes of disadvantaged groups. The National Labor Relations Act (Wagner Act) of 1935 threw federal protection around union organization and collective bargaining. The principles of a wages and hours bill were further vindicated in 1936 with congressional passage of the Walsh-Healy Government Contracts Act. Guided through Congress chiefly by Montana's Democratic Senator Thomas James Walsh, long an enemy of child labor, the act mandated that a prevailing minimum wage, as determined by the secretary of labor, was to be paid to workers on all jobs performed under federal contracts worth more than $10,000. Work hours were limited to eight hours per day, and the labor of boys under the age of sixteen and girls under the age of eighteen was prohibited.

Even with these enactments in the mid-1930's, the United States continued to differ from other advanced economies in regard to promulgating national standards for wages and hours. The American version of laissez-faire economics was deeply rooted in an endemic individualism coupled with a widespread fear of peacetime government intervention. Consequently, the Roosevelt Administration faced serious difficulties in persuading Congress to pass the Fair Labor Standards Act.

These difficulties were compounded by Roosevelt's shift into a spirited campaign of reform following his 1936 reelection. The president was eager to defuse his growing popular opposition and restore the essence of several key programs of his first administration that had been held to be unconstitutional by the Supreme Court. He was also faced with a secondary economic depression that threatened to be as deep as the one that he had inherited in 1933.

After initial rebuffs by Congress, the bill that became the Fair Labor Standards Act was introduced to the special congressional session called by Roosevelt in November, 1937. The bill was backed by the president's message to the nation that a self-respecting democracy "can plead no justification for . . . child labor, no economic reason for chiseling workers' wages or stretching workers' hours." Hugo L. Black, then a senator from Alabama and later a Supreme Court justice, had sponsored an earlier wages and hours bill. He chaired the joint congressional committees charged with conducting hearings on the bill. Backing his effort were socially conscious Progressives such as Secretary of Labor Frances Perkins, Leon Henderson, and White House aides Thomas Corcoran and Benjamin Cohen.

Opposition to the bill was

Associate Justice Harlan Fiske Stone wrote the Supreme Court's first decision on the Fair Labor Standards Act. (Harvard Law Art Collection)

275

intense. Critics branded the measure as fascist. The Chamber of Commerce and the National Association of Manufacturers (NAM) denounced the bill on both economic and constitutional grounds. Reflecting Southern textile and lumber interests, Southern congressmen fought bitterly against prospective federal interference in or regulation of their industries. Nor was organized labor of one mind. The American Federation of Labor (AFL) and its president, William Green, seeking important changes in the bill, temporarily joined the NAM in opposition, while the Congress of Industrial Organizations (CIO) under John L. Lewis was split on the measure. A Gallup Poll indicated that most Americans, from the North and the South, favored the bill, as did many Northern industries that competed with the low-wage, long-hour employment of Southern workers. Amid such divisions, many of the bill's original features were dropped or amended. On June 13, 1938, the House passed the bill by a 291 to 97 vote. The Senate accepted it without a recorded vote. Roosevelt signed the FLSA on June 25, and it became effective on October 24.

Impact of Event

The FLSA reflected many debilitating and limiting congressional compromises, although over subsequent years amendments would remedy a number of these deficiencies. Leading economists in 1938 reckoned that in its original form the act covered fewer than eleven million workers, less than 25 percent of the employed labor force. Administration officials estimated that when the act took effect, nearly 300,000 workers covered by it were earning less than twenty-five cents an hour and 1.3 million workers normally labored more than forty-four hours a week. The national standard of a forty-hour work week did not arrive until 1940.

The long battle to abolish child labor was also far from over. Entry into employment was restricted to those aged sixteen and over, and the act's administrators could raise that age to eighteen for work in hazardous or unhealthy industries. Administrators could lower the age of employment to fourteen, however, in nonmanufacturing and mining industries in some cases. In addition, the act's coverage did not extend to agriculture, personal services, street trades, or retailing, which collectively were the largest employers of children.

The act proved to be the last of the Second New Deal's major reform measures. It was also a popular law. A 1939 Gallup Poll showed that 71 percent of the country favored it, and it therefore came as a political blessing to an embattled President Roosevelt. The president's own view of the measure was that it constituted "the most far-reaching and the most far-sighted program for the benefit of the workers ever adopted."

One purpose of the law was to secure better terms of employment for workers than they could secure acting alone. It undoubtedly raised wages for the lowest paid employees, particularly in the South. These included workers in sawmills, canneries, cigar factories, and textile mills. Depending on the degree of enforcement of the act, which generally was low, it shortened the hours of work where abuses were greatest. Its general effects varied widely, from very positive to negative, depending on a variety of factors including product prices, the extent of unionization and collective bargaining, and the state of the economy. Unions eventually applauded it because it curtailed competition from underpaid workers. The act also excluded from legal employment many people who wished to work, by putting their wages above what employers were willing to pay.

The last word on the act was that of the Supreme Court. Until 1937, major New Deal programs had been almost systematically eviscerated by the Court. This had led President Roosevelt to launch an attempt to pack the Court with his own appointees, a legal, if unpopular, method of changing the Court's conservative complexion by appointing additional justices. Politically, this unfolded as a battle that Roosevelt lost but a war—as a result of events beyond his control—that he won. Amid the controversy, five incumbent justices had either died or retired before the constitutionality of the FLSA came before the Court in 1941. Five new, ostensibly liberal, justices had been appointed by Roosevelt to replace them. As a consequence, when redrafted, several major New Deal programs that earlier had been killed by the Court passed the test of constitutionality before the substantially reconstituted Court. Labor observers thought it a foregone conclusion that the FLSA would find Supreme Court approval, but at the time, the Roosevelt Administration was not overly optimistic.

The test of the Fair Labor Standards Act came before the Supreme Court as *United States v. Darby Lumber Company* in 1941. The Darby Lumber Company bought timber, transported it to its mill, and manufactured it into finished lumber, entirely within the state of Georgia. Its finished lumber, however, was thereafter shipped out of state, thereby entering interstate commerce. By FLSA criteria, Darby's employees, who earned less than twenty-five cents an hour and who worked more than forty-four hours a week, were underpaid and overworked. Moreover, the company kept no records, as the Labor Department discovered when it tried to bring Darby into compliance with the FLSA. Darby's rejoinder was that the FLSA was unconstitutional insofar as it sought to regulate manufacturing taking place entirely inside Georgia. A Georgia district court agreed with this reasoning. On appeal, the case went before the Supreme Court.

At the request of Chief Justice Charles Evans Hughes, Justice Harlan

Fiske Stone was asked to write the Court's opinion, principally because Hughes deemed it to be a "great" case and because it involved issues that long had concerned Stone. Stone's opinion sought first to reassert the absolute nature of congressional power over interstate commerce. In effect, this was designed to return the Court to the sweeping mandate it received from Chief Justice John Marshall in *Gibbons v. Ogden* in 1824, a position that had been eroded by Supreme Court decisions such as *Hammer v. Dagenhart* in 1918 that separated actual manufacturing activities from the stream of interstate commerce. Stone declared that congressional authority over interstate commerce, on the contrary, was "complete in itself . . . and acknowledges no limitations other than are prescribed by the Constitution." That power, he argued, was not susceptible to modification by states. He granted that although manufacturing was not commerce, the shipment of manufactured goods outside a state was commerce and thus fell under national authority.

In order to restore federal power over the regulation of child labor, Stone made his second assertion, namely that congressional power to regulate child labor was "plenary." Such power was not limited to child labor in hazardous or unhealthy occupations. On both points and contrary to Darby's plea, the Supreme Court was unanimous. The Fair Labor Standards Act survived its constitutional test and gained additional strength from Stone's reaffirmation of Congress's complete authority over interstate commerce.

Bibliography

Babson, Steve. *The Unfinished Struggle: Turning Points in American Labor, 1877-Present.* Lanham, Md.: Rowman & Littlefield, 1999.

Bernstein, Irving. *A Caring Society: The New Deal, the Worker, and the Great Depression.* Boston: Houghton Mifflin, 1985. Clearly and sensitively written by a leading labor historian. Although there is a pro-New Deal bias, Bernstein maintains a critical balance. Chapter 5 deals specifically with the FLSA in one of the rare extensive discussions of the act outside federal documents. For context and details, the work should be read in its entirety.

Douglas, Paul H., and Joseph Hackman. "The Fair Labor Standards Act of 1938 I." *Political Science Quarterly* 53 (December, 1938): 491-515.

_____. "The Fair Labor Standards Act of 1938 II." *Political Science Quarterly* 54 (March, 1939): 29-55. A distinguished economist and a labor expert assess the immediate impact of the FLSA on the work force. Clear and concise. Very useful, although it must be supplemented for details of the act's effects on child labor.

Felt, Jeremy P. "The Child Labor Provision of the Fair Labor Standards Act." *Labor History* 11 (Fall, 1970): 477-481. One of the clearer scholarly assessments of the subject in concise journal form. Examines three decades of the act's child labor provisions at work.

Hughes, Jonathan R. T. *American Economy History.* 5th ed. Reading, Mass.: Addison-Wesley, 1998.

Mason, Alpheus Thomas. *Harlan Fiske Stone: Pillar of the Law.* New York: Viking Press, 1956. Mason has produced several fine biographies, of which this is one. Stone was an important justice whose views changed during the troubled Depression-New Deal years. The index is useful in locating Stone's opinions on interstate commerce and child labor.

Rauch, Basil. *The History of the New Deal.* New York: Capricorn Books, 1963. A fine summary of the New Deal by an important historian. A sympathetic political portrait, it records work of Roosevelt's "brain trust" in writing and fighting for the president's legislation. The FLSA is treated as part of a complex political picture in chapter 13.

Wilcox, Claire. *Public Policies Toward Business.* 3d ed. Homewood, Ill.: Richard D. Irwin, 1966. Excellent and authoritative review of the subject. Chapter 32 deals with the FLSA in the context of previous domestic and foreign legislation on wages and hours. Provides an overview of expanding government controls over economic and social life.

Clifton K. Yearley

Cross-References

The Supreme Court Strikes Down a Maximum Hours Law (1905); The Supreme Court Rules Against Minimum Wage Laws (1923); The National Industrial Recovery Act Is Passed (1933); The Wagner Act Promotes Union Organization (1935); The Social Security Act Provides Benefits for Workers (1935); Congress Passes the Equal Pay Act (1963).

THE 1939 WORLD'S FAIR INTRODUCES REGULAR U.S. TELEVISION SERVICE

CATEGORY OF EVENT: New products
TIME: April 30, 1939
LOCALE: New York, New York

The National Broadcasting Company coverage of the New York World's Fair opening began weekly television scheduling

Principal personages:

DAVID SARNOFF (1891-1971), the president of Radio Corporation of America

FRANKLIN D. ROOSEVELT (1882-1945), the thirty-second president of the United States, whose speech opening the World's Fair was the first talk by a president to be televised

PHILO T. FARNSWORTH (1906-1971), the developer of the cathode ray tube, the basis of the video viewing screen

VLADIMIR ZWORYKIN (1889-1982), the developer of the orthicon tube, the basis of the television camera

Summary of Event

Regularly scheduled U.S. television began on April 30, 1939, when President Franklin D. Roosevelt opened the New York World's Fair. The fair, billed as "The World of Tomorrow," featured futuristic designs, such as the Perisphere, a round globe in which visitors were carried up giant escalators to a revolving platform to look down on a model city of tomorrow. The six-hundred-foot pointed Trylon symbolized the aspirations of humankind. The fair, which attracted forty-five million visitors, advertised United States industry. It implicitly challenged the military might of Nazi

280

Germany, which had recently rejected President Roosevelt's plan to guarantee ten years of peace in Europe.

The president's speech stressed his desire for peace but emphasized the unity of Americans in times of threat. The speech climaxed a parade in which nearly twenty-thousand servicemen took part. The speech was the first presidential address to be televised. It was followed with speeches by New York Governor Herbert H. Lehman, New York City Mayor Fiorello La Guardia, and Fair President Grover A. Whalen. This telecast, lasting more than three hours, marked a personal victory for David Sarnoff, president of the Radio Corporation of America (RCA) since 1930.

On April 20, 1939, ten days before the official fair opening, Sarnoff dedicated the fair's RCA Exhibit Building, which would offer most visitors their first exposure to television. Sarnoff spoke before a television camera while several hundred people viewed him on receivers inside the building and at the RCA Building in Manhattan. Sarnoff announced that this marked the birth of a new art in America, one that would eventually transform society. He foresaw television's use for entertainment and education as well as its impact on the American economy.

Television broadcasting theoretically had been possible since Paul Nipkow of Germany had patented a system in 1884. Scottish inventor John Logie Baird developed the first workable apparatus in 1924 and gave his first public demonstration in London in 1926. His system was adopted by Germany in 1929. By 1939, German government stations provided programming five evenings a week. British television service began in 1936. These first systems, however, depended on awkward and complex mechanical devices that produced shadowy, low-definition images. Visually pleasing images depended on the replacement of the mechanical system by an all-electronic system. Philo T. Farnsworth had devised such a system by the age of eighteen. He formed his own company, then later worked for Philco. In 1930, he patented the scanner that became the basis of modern television tubes. The first public demonstration of his electronic system was given in Philadelphia in 1934. Vladimir Zworykin, whose inventions led to the modern television camera, became RCA's director of electronic research; he first demonstrated his iconoscope in 1924.

World War I had shown the need for an American communications technology independent of foreign powers and foreign ownership. With government sanction, RCA was chartered on October 17, 1919, absorbing the American Marconi Company, the pioneering wireless company that had originated in England, and eliminating its international affiliations. With stock exchanges and cross-licensing among affiliates that included General Electric, Westinghouse, American Telephone and Telegraph, and United

Fruit, RCA held a virtual monopoly on patents for radio transmitting and receiving devices. In 1915, Sarnoff had accurately forecast the development of radio for home use. In an April, 1923, memo to the RCA board of directors, Sarnoff first forecast similar growth for television. In 1931, Sarnoff's National Broadcasting Company (NBC) televised New York Mayor Jimmy Walker and a variety of entertainment acts, including George Gershwin playing the piano. William Paley, head of the Columbia Broadcasting System (CBS), NBC's only competition, established two experimental stations in 1931, but RCA's investment in television research gave it a commanding position.

Development, however, was crippled by the stock market crash of 1929 and the Great Depression. Although the formation of RCA had been supported by the government, the Depression created strong opposition to big business, and the Justice Department brought an antitrust suit against RCA. The suit was not settled until 1932.

Increasing competition brought the need for broadcasting standards. In 1934, Congress passed the Communications Act, which created the Federal Communications Commission (FCC), with power to regulate all communications service. If television sets were to be sold, the FCC had to mandate uniform standards. Lawsuits, scandals, investigations, and appeals to the commission delayed commercial development. At the height of the Depression, however, few Americans could have paid the $200 to $1,000 prices of the sets available, at a time when $1,000 would purchase a new car.

In 1938, Sarnoff announced that RCA would offer television sets for sale in time for the opening of the New York World's Fair, but it was estimated that only about two hundred sets had been purchased in the metropolitan New York area, primarily by industry professionals and the curious well-to-do. Two NBC television vans were at the fair, one handling the pickup and the other relaying signals to the transmitter atop the Empire State Building. Cameras telecast the grounds and crowds. Fairgoers learned that studio shows would be televised from Radio City on Wednesdays and Fridays, between 8 and 9 P.M. Telecasts from the fair would be broadcast on Wednesday, Thursday, and Friday afternoons.

Impact of Event

The immediate, but temporary, effect of the World's Fair broadcast and publicity was a proliferation of television broadcasts. On May 17, 1939, NBC televised a Princeton University/Columbia University baseball game, billed as the world's first televised sporting event. On August 26, NBC telecast a professional baseball game between the Brooklyn Dodgers and the Cincinnati Reds at Brooklyn's Ebbets Field. NBC broadcasts from

Radio City featured cooking demonstrations, opera, and comedy, all live. A fashion show was broadcast from the Waldorf-Astoria Hotel, and there were broadcasts of the crowds at the 1939 New York premiere of *Gone with the Wind*. A dramatization of Robert Louis Stevenson's *Treasure Island* was televised, as was a seventy-minute feature film, *Young and Beautiful*. In October, 1939, NBC screened Edwin S. Porter's classic silent film *The Great Train Robbery* (1903). This limited programming lasted through 1939 and 1940.

By mid-1939, RCA was marketing four models of television sets, and at least sixteen other manufacturers were in the market, including Philco, which had sponsored much of Farnsworth's research; General Electric; and Westinghouse. Set owners were encouraged to mail in their programming preferences; these indicated that sports would be an audience favorite. RCA then began a crash program to turn out additional mobile transmitter units. Studios for other major markets in Washington D.C., Philadelphia, and Chicago were prepared, linked through coaxial cables. The first such linkage in the United States was between New York and Philadelphia in 1936. Television stations similarly proliferated and by May, 1940, twenty-three stations were broadcasting.

In 1940, the Federal Communications Commission was divided as to whether television was ready for commercial broadcasting standards. The industry itself was not in agreement. Some companies, including RCA, DuMont, and Philco, argued that television could not yet offer enough programming to justify commercial operation and that standardization at that time would freeze development at a level below its potential. In April, 1941, transmission standards were finally adopted by the FCC. Commercial operations were approved effective July 1, and two New York stations, NBC and CBS affiliates, went into operation. New York station WNBT began broadcasting to an estimated forty-seven hundred television set owners and began regular news broadcasting with commentator Lowell Thomas. By the end of that year, the first commercial on television, financed by Bulova watch manufacturers, had been aired. In December, with the bombing of Pearl Harbor and the entrance of the United States into World War II, commercial development was halted while American industry was retooled for wartime production.

When Allied victory was ensured, RCA reopened its television studio on April 10, 1944. CBS reopened on May 5. At the war's end in 1945, nine part-time and partly commercial television stations were on the air, reaching about seventy-five hundred set owners in the New York, Philadelphia, and Schenectady, New York, areas. Although newspapers did not yet print schedules and viewers could not know when programming would be available, NBC broadcast four nights a week by late 1944, generally *The Gillette Cavalcade of Sports*, while CBS featured a radio game show transferred to television, *Missus Goes A'Shopping*, on two nights a week.

With such meager programming, only about five thousand sets were produced in 1946, but that number increased to 160,000 in 1947. During prime time hours, the four networks that by then existed—American Broadcasting Company (ABC), CBS, NBC, and DuMont—could still provide only about ten hours of programming a week. Sporting events were featured, with boxing and wrestling especially popular. Bars and taverns were among the principal purchasers of sets. In late 1948, it was estimated that only 10 percent of the population had even seen a television show.

Modern programming essentially began in 1947, with such shows as the *Kraft Television Theatre*, a live-drama program that presented 650 plays in about eleven years. In 1947, too, the first popular children's shows were featured: *The Howdy Doody Show* and *Kukla, Fran, and Ollie*. The most important development came in 1948, when the William Morris talent agency ran an advertisement in *Variety*, saying that vaudeville was back. This was the announcement of the *Texaco Star Theater*, which premiered on June 8, on NBC. It had been a radio variety show. With Milton Berle, Henny Youngman, and Morey Amsterdam, all vaudeville performers, as hosts, the show brought to television names and faces that previously could only be heard on radio or seen occasionally in movies. CBS followed with Ed Sullivan's *Toast of the Town*. By fall, all four networks were regularly broadcasting prime time programming. In the spring of 1948, industry experts estimated that of the 300,000 sets in operation, more than half were in public places; a year later, 940,000 homes had television receivers. By 1949, production of sets had jumped to 3,000,000.

Bibliography

Abramson, Albert. *The History of Television, 1880 to 1941*. Jefferson, N.C.: McFarland, 1987. Contains compact and comprehensive chapters on technological developments between 1671 and 1900 that led to television, in language generally accessible to nonspecialists. Later chapters are more technical. Includes developments outside the United States generally ignored in American television histories, such as the 1930's development of television in Japan and London television service between 1936 and 1939.

Barnouw, Erik. *Tube of Plenty: The Evolution of American Television*. Rev. ed. New York: Oxford University Press, 1982. The most readable of the general surveys of television development, this is a condensation and updating of Barnouw's three-volume set, *A History of Broadcasting in the United States*, published between 1966 and 1970.

Bilby, Kenneth. *The General: David Sarnoff and the Rise of the Communications Industry.* New York: Harper & Row, 1986. A comprehensive study of Sarnoff in the context of his industry. This is a relatively unbiased account by a former RCA executive and associate of Sarnoff. It covers the full range of Sarnoff's career and gives a more superficial account of RCA after Sarnoff. Includes a useful bibliography.

Everson, George. *The Story of Television: The Life of Philo T. Farnsworth.* New York: Norton, 1949. This uncritical biography was written by a man who, recognizing the young Farnsworth's ability, helped him find funding for his research laboratory. It emphasizes the rags-to-riches odyssey of Farnsworth from farm boy to internationally known inventor but provides material unavailable elsewhere.

Geddes, Keith, and Gordon Bussey. *The Setmakers: A History of the Radio and Television Industry.* London: British Radio and Electronic Equipment Manufacturers' Association, 1991. Although concerned with the British industry, this book gives examples of model design and advertisement unavailable elsewhere, especially for the early years of radio and television. The text illustrates European and British developments generally overlooked by American historians. Excellent illustrations.

Goldstein, Norm. *Associated Press: The History of Television.* Avenal, N.J.: Outlet Book Company, 1991. The best-illustrated history of television. The text is unquestionably the easiest to read of those listed here; unfortunately, after the initial chapters, Goldstein tends to ignore international events and technological developments, so that this is primarily a history of American television.

Lichty, Lawrence W., and Malachi C. Topping, comps. *American Broadcasting: A Source Book on the History of Radio and Television.* New York: Hastings House, 1975. Part of the Studies in Public Communication Series, this volume collects a variety of articles under the topics "Technical," "Stations," "Networks," "Economics," "Employment," "Programming," "Audiences," and "Regulation." The contents range widely, from an article on Jack Benny to a history of the American Marconi Company. Almost all articles are comprehensible to a general audience.

Lyons, Eugene. *David Sarnoff.* New York: Harper & Row, 1966. Although this biography is less objective and critical than others cited here and was written during Sarnoff's lifetime, it is easily read. The author, Sarnoff's cousin, provides considerable material about Sarnoff's family, his early poverty and pursuit of a career, and his rise from office boy to executive.

Sarnoff, David. *Looking Ahead: The Papers of David Sarnoff.* New York: McGraw-Hill, 1968. Collects Sarnoff's most important speeches and communications from 1914 to 1967, arranged under such categories as "Wireless Communications," "Radio Broadcasting," "Black-and-White Television," and "The Communications Revolution." Includes the 1915 memo forecasting household entertainment through radio and the similar prediction for television of 1923. Most papers are abridged.

Sobel, Robert. *RCA*. New York: Stein & Day, 1986. Written in a wooden style, but gives a comprehensive picture of the development of RCA from its origins in the American Marconi Company to the time of writing. Includes charts containing information on finances, ownership, and production. Extensive and valuable bibliography.

Betty Richardson

Cross-References

Station KDKA Introduces Commercial Radio Broadcasting (1920); The A. C. Nielsen Company Pioneers in Marketing and Media Research (1923); Congress Establishes the Federal Communications Commission (1934); The U.S. Government Bans Cigarette Ads on Broadcast Media (1970); Cable Television Rises to Challenge Network Television (mid-1990's).

ROOSEVELT SIGNS THE EMERGENCY PRICE CONTROL ACT

CATEGORY OF EVENT: Government and business
TIME: January 30, 1942
LOCALE: Washington, D.C.

Adoption of the Emergency Price Control Act gave the Office of Price Administration the power to control prices of civilian goods and rents during World War II

Principal personages:

FRANKLIN D. ROOSEVELT (1882-1945), the president of the United States, 1933-1945

LEON HENDERSON (b. 1895), the first administrator of the Office of Price Administration and Civilian Supply

WILLIAM S. KNUDSEN (1879-1948), the director-general of the Office of Production Management

PRENTISS M. BROWN (1889-1973), the administrator of the Office of Price Administration, January to October, 1943

JAMES F. BYRNES (1879-1972), the head of the Office of Economic Stabilization, 1942-1943, and of the Office of War Mobilization, 1943-1945

CHESTER BOWLES (1901-1986), the administrator of the Office of Price Administration, 1943-1946

PAUL PORTER (1904-1975), the last administrator of the Office of Price Administration, formerly a New Deal lawyer and chairman of the Federal Communications Commission

HARRY S TRUMAN (1884-1972), the president of the United States, 1945-1953, who fought a losing battle to retain price controls during the postwar transition to a peace economy

Summary of Event

As the American military buildup in the face of the threat from the Axis Powers accelerated in the spring of 1940, the United States began to face shortages of critical materials. Shortages raised difficult and politically sensitive questions concerning the proportion of the nation's resources to reserve for civilian use and how to allocate the available supplies fairly. The problem was aggravated because government spending on defense was placing large amounts of cash into the hands of consumers. The United States spent an estimated $288 billion to fight World War II, compared to the $9 billion annual federal budget in 1940. Disposable personal income (income after taxes) rose from $92 billion to $151 billion during the war, while the supply of civilian goods and services (measured in constant dollars) increased only from $77.6 billion to $95.4 billion. With so much money pursuing a limited supply of goods, the government became concerned with preventing runaway inflation that could wreck the economy.

The federal government followed a complex of strategies to keep inflation under control. Higher taxes imposed by the Revenue Act of 1942 soaked up part of the increased consumer purchasing power. Expanded sales of Series E government savings bonds to individuals similarly took out of circulation money that otherwise would have gone to purchase goods and services. Another weapon was the wage stabilization program administered by the National War Labor Board, which was established in January, 1942, to settle labor disputes in war industries. The Office of Price Administration, however, constituted the linchpin in the battle against inflation.

President Franklin D. Roosevelt established the Office of Price Administration and Civilian Supply (OPACS) by executive order on April 11, 1941. The OPACS was given a dual responsibility. It was to prevent inflationary price increases and to stimulate provision of the necessary supply of materials and commodities required for civilian use, in such a manner as not to conflict with military defense needs. Concurrently, it was to ensure the "equitable distribution" of that supply among competing civilian demands. Roosevelt appointed as OPACS administrator Leon Henderson, an economist who had risen from director of the Research and Planning Division of the National Recovery Administration to become one of the most influential New Deal leaders. In 1939, Roosevelt had appointed Henderson to the Securities and Exchange Commission. An outspoken champion of competition, opponent of monopoly, and defender of consumers, Henderson was temperamentally and ideologically at odds with the business executives who were brought to Washington, D.C., to mobilize the

288

economy for the impending war. Roosevelt aggravated the situation by his typical practice of dividing responsibility and leaving blurred the lines of authority among different officials.

Henderson perceived a duty to act as spokesman for civilian needs. He accordingly came into bitter conflict with William S. Knudsen in the spring of 1941 over control of the priority system for the allocation of scarce materials. Knudsen, a former General Motors executive, as director-general of the Office of Production Management (OPM) was responsible for expanding military production. Roosevelt's establishment of the Supply Priorities and Allocations Board (SPAB) in August, 1941, under former Sears, Roebuck and Company executive Donald M. Nelson placed that control in the hands of those giving military demands top priority. With the establishment of the SPAB, the functions of the OPACS in the allocation of materials among competing civilian users were transferred to the OPM. The result was the administrative separation of price control from production control. The OPACS was renamed the Office of Price Administration (OPA).

Rising prices accompanying the defense buildup shifted the focus of Henderson's attention to the problem of inflation. The OPA lacked effective power to halt the spiral of rising prices, and the inflation rate reached 2 percent per month by the end of 1941. Although Roosevelt asked Congress in July, 1941, for prompt action on price stabilization, the lawmakers dragged their feet until after Pearl Harbor. The Emergency Price Control Act, which Roosevelt signed into law on January 30, 1942, authorized the OPA to set maximum prices and to establish rent controls in areas in which defense activity had affected rent levels. Because Henderson thought some price increases to be necessary as incentives to expand production, he delayed acting under this new authority until late April. The OPA then issued its first General Maximum Price Regulation, requiring that sellers charge no more than the highest price charged in March, 1942. This move slowed down, but failed to halt, the rise in the cost of living.

The regulation worked satisfactorily for standardized articles but did not do so for products such as clothing, for which manufacturers and sellers could hide price increases through changes in style, quality, or packaging. The biggest loophole, however, was the provision that the congressional farm bloc wrote into the Emergency Price Control Act barring the imposition of price ceilings on farm products until their prices reached 110 percent of "parity," a level that would put product prices where farmers believed they ought to be. With most farm products thus excluded from price controls, food prices increased 11 percent during 1942.

Impact of Event

The conflict over allocation of resources between military and civilian needs resurfaced in the so-called "feasibility" dispute that reached its climax in the fall of 1942. Henderson took the lead in attacking the armed services for exaggerating their supply needs at the expense of the civilian economy. The immediate dispute was resolved by a compromise whereby the military program was cut back through extending scheduled delivery dates farther into the future. The military won the larger battle. In October, 1942, Roosevelt established the Office of Economic Stabilization under James F. Byrnes, formerly a senator from South Carolina and Supreme Court justice, to take charge of wage and price stabilization.

Because of his political skills, his contacts in Congress, and Roosevelt's confidence, Byrnes was able to expand his control over all matters relating to the economy. That control was formalized by the creation in May, 1943, of the new Office of War Mobilization, which was to coordinate the activities of the different war agencies. With Byrnes in charge, the armed services had the upper hand when questions arose about military versus civilian needs. At the same time, the military services successfully resisted the imposition of OPA price ceilings on the purchase of military supplies. In the fall of 1942, Henderson had to agree to exempt "strictly military goods" from maximum price controls in return for a promise by the services to try to hold down prices and the profits of suppliers. Although this exemption did not apply to materials going into military end products, approximately two-thirds of the War Department's prime contracts were outside OPA control.

The OPA was more successful in maintaining price ceilings on consumer goods. Faced with a continued rise in the cost of living resulting from exemption of most farm products from the Emergency Maximum Price Regulation, Roosevelt in September, 1942, warned Congress that unless the lawmakers voted to rectify the situation, he would act himself on the basis of his war powers. After a bitter struggle, Congress approved the Anti-Inflation Act of October, 1942, giving Roosevelt most of what he wanted. The legislation authorized the president to freeze wages and salaries, prices (including those of agricultural products), and rents at their levels on September 15. Roosevelt proceeded immediately to institute freezes. The cost of living, however, continued to rise. By April, 1943, prices were on average 6.2 percent above the September 15 level, with food prices rising even more. The OPA came under increasing pressure from producer groups and their congressional allies to relax price controls, and from labor unions for higher wages. The turning point in the battle against inflation came on April 8, 1943, when Roosevelt ordered the economic stabilization agencies to "hold the line" against further price and wage increases. He followed this order with governmental seizure of coal mines to break a miners' strike for higher wages. The OPA simultaneously launched an aggressive campaign to roll back food prices. That campaign culminated in a 10 percent reduction in the retail prices of meat, coffee, and butter.

Along with price and rent controls, the OPA adopted a system of rationing for particularly scarce commodities. The purposes of rationing were to combat inflation by preventing a bidding war for scarce goods, to ensure equitable distribution, and to give priority to military needs by restricting consumer demand. Rationing began at the end of December, 1941, with automobile tires as the first rationed good. A severe rubber shortage had resulted from the Japanese seizure of Southeast Asia. Rationing was extended to sugar, coffee, and gasoline in 1942. Rationing was instituted in 1943 for meats, fats and oils, butter, cheese, and processed foods. Shoes were added later. At the peak of rationing, the OPA administered thirteen rationing programs. Rationed goods still represented only one-seventh of total consumer expenditures.

There were two types of rationing. One—applied, for example, to gasoline and rubber tires—involved a priority system under which different quotas were allotted on the basis of need. Equal rations for all were the rule, with few exceptions. The second type of rationing, the point system, was a scheme whereby a whole family of items (such as meats, fish, cheese, and butter) was lumped together, with each item in the family given a point value. Consumers were allotted a certain number of points per month and were free to spend those points as they wished. The OPA exercised control at the final stage of the distribution chain. Retailers would collect ration coupons or stamps from their customers and had to give them to their suppliers before they could get a new supply of the article. Administration at the consumer level was delegated to approximately fifty-six hundred local rationing boards. This arrangement had important political advantages, as the boards were made up of respected and influential members of the local community. The accompanying price was lack of uniformity across the country.

From the first, the OPA was a center of political infighting. As was the norm under Roosevelt, rival bureaucrats maneuvered to expand their empires. Thus Henderson clashed with Secretary of the Interior Harold L. Ickes, the petroleum administrator, over gasoline rationing, and with War Food Administrator Chester C. Davis over food rationing. Patronage-hungry politicians strove to control appointments to OPA positions. A host of rival interests jockeyed for favored treatment. Henderson's vocal championship of consumers against pressure groups from business, agriculture, and labor antagonized producer groups and the conservative coalition of Southern Democrats and Republicans in Congress. In December, 1942, Henderson resigned, officially for reasons of health; he appears to have been pushed out by Roosevelt because he had become too much of a political liability. Roosevelt replaced Henderson as OPA administrator in January, 1943, with Prentiss M. Brown, a Democratic senator from Michigan who had just been defeated for reelection partly because of his support for agricultural price controls. Brown was succeeded in October, 1943, by former advertising executive Chester Bowles. In February, 1946, New Deal lawyer and Federal Communications Commission chairman Paul Porter became the last OPA administrator.

The OPA did not work perfectly. There were numerous cases of evasion of price controls and rationing. Landlords in areas where housing was scarce, for example, often demanded an under-the-table payoff before renting an apartment. There was a large black market in such goods as coffee and soap. Because of the time and difficulties involved, the OPA rarely instituted criminal prosecutions of violators; its major enforcement tool was a court injunction to prevent further illegal sales. Mistakes in the handling of rationing were a major contributor to the OPA's unpopularity. The introduction of rationing for sugar and coffee was accompanied by what many thought was excessively restrictive and pointless bureaucracy and regulation. Even worse, the OPA had by 1944 issued food rationing coupons far in excess of available supplies. A survey in late fall showed that consumers had an average of 2.8 months of unused food coupons. When the temporarily successful German counterattack in the Battle of the Bulge at the end of 1944 threatened to further cut supplies, authorities canceled the unused coupons despite their previous pledge that no such action would be taken. The OPA was largely successful in keeping consumer prices under control. Living costs had increased by almost two-thirds from 1914 to the end of World War I. In contrast, the cost of living rose only by approximately 28 percent from 1940 to the end of World War II. Most of that increase came before adoption of the Anti-Inflation Act of October, 1942. Living costs increased less than 2 percent during the last two years of the war. Perhaps most important, most Americans enjoyed a higher standard of living at the war's end than they had before it began.

The end of the war led to a bitter struggle over continuation of the OPA. The new president, Harry S Truman, backed Bowles in his plan for a gradual relaxation of wartime controls over prices, wages, and scarce commodities to smooth the transition to a peacetime economy. On the day after the surrender of Japan, the OPA ended rationing of gasoline, fuel oil, and processed foods. By the end of 1945, only sugar remained under rationing. During late 1945 and early 1946, the OPA was able to control price increases, but inflationary pressures were gaining momentum. Consumers were buying in black markets, labor unions were pushing for wage hikes, and manufacturers and farmers had joined with Republican leaders in Congress to demand an end to all controls. A battle raged through the spring of 1946 over extension of the OPA. A conservative coalition of Republicans and Southern Democrats passed through Congress in late June, 1946, a price control bill extending the OPA for one year but drastically cutting its powers and commanding it to decontrol prices "as rapidly as possible." Instead of acquiescing, Truman vetoed the bill on June 29 and allowed price controls to expire on July 1.

Prices rose sharply, while shortages of meat, sugar, electrical appliances, housing, and automobiles continued. In late July, Congress approved a second bill extending price and rent controls for one year. Truman reluctantly accepted it, but the damage had been done. The new measure was even weaker and more confusing than the one that Truman had vetoed. Republican speakers and advertisements during the election campaign in the fall of 1946 made the confusion and failure in the price control program a major theme. One incident was particularly damaging to the Truman Administration and the Democrats. When the OPA restored price ceilings on meat in August, 1946, farmers withdrew their cattle from the market to force a change in policy. While shoppers waited in vain for meat, Republicans seized on the shortage as a campaign issue. After the Republicans won control of both houses of Congress, Truman gave up the fight. He ended all wage and price controls, except those on rents, sugar, and rice, on November 9, 1946. The OPA began to wind up its affairs a month later.

Bibliography

Bowles, Chester. *Promises to Keep: My Years in Public Life, 1941-1969.* New York: Harper & Row, 1971. An autobiography concerning his years of public service. Extensive account of Bowles's struggles as OPA administrator.

Chandler, Lester V. *Inflation in the United States, 1940-1948.* New York: Harper & Brothers, 1951. An analysis of the forces responsible for inflation during and following World War II. Emphasizes the role of government fiscal and monetary policies.

Chandler, Lester V., and Donald H. Wallace, eds. *Economic Mobilization and Stabilization: Selected Materials on the Economics of War and Defense.* New York: Henry Holt, 1951. An anthology of materials treating problems of economic mobilization and stabilization during wartime, drawing heavily on the experience of the United States in World

War II. Part 4, "Direct Stabilization Controls in Wartime," focuses on the OPA's price control and rationing policies.

Harris, Seymour. *Price and Related Controls in the United States*. New York: McGraw-Hill, 1945. A sympathetic detailed account of OPA price and rent controls by an economist who served with the agency.

Hughes, Jonathan R. T. *American Economy History*. 5th ed. Reading, Mass.: Addison-Wesley, 1998.

Mansfield, Harvey C., et al. *A Short History of OPA*. Washington, D.C.: Office of Temporary Controls, OPA, 1948. The indispensable official history of the OPA, written by a team headed by one of the country's leading experts in public administration.

Polenberg, Richard. *War and Society: The United States, 1941-1945*. Philadelphia: J. B. Lippincott, 1972. An excellent survey of all aspects of the American home front during World War II. Includes a brief but perceptive account of the struggle for economic stabilization.

Rockoff, Hugh. *Drastic Measures: A History of Wage and Price Controls in the United States*. Cambridge, England: Cambridge University Press, 1984. A comprehensive history of efforts to control wages and prices. Compares the United States' experiences in World War I, World War II, and the Korean War.

Somers, Herman M. *Presidential Agency: OWMR, the Office of War Mobilization and Reconversion*. Cambridge, Mass.: Harvard University Press, 1950. An excellent account of James F. Byrnes's coordination and direction of the wartime government management of the economy.

U.S. Bureau of the Budget. *The United States at War*. Washington, D.C.: Government Printing Office, 1946. This official history is a comprehensive survey of the wartime government management of the economy.

John Braeman

Cross-References

The Banking Act of 1935 Centralizes U.S. Monetary Control (1935); Roosevelt Signs the Fair Labor Standards Act (1938); Truman Orders the Seizure of Railways (1946); Congress Passes the Equal Pay Act (1963).

THE UNITED STATES BEGINS THE BRACERO PROGRAM

CATEGORY OF EVENT: Labor
TIME: August 4, 1942
LOCALE: Washington, D.C.

Initiated as a war measure to ensure adequate agricultural labor supplies during World War II, the bracero program was continued until 1964, when it was terminated on the basis of alleged negative influences on the employment of domestic workers

Principal personages:
WILLARD WIRTZ (1912-   ), the secretary of labor who allowed the bracero program to expire in 1964
CLAUDE R. WICKARD (1893-1967), the secretary of agriculture, 1940-1945
WILLIAM R. POAGE (1899-1987), a congressman who cosponsored Public Law 78
ALLEN J. ELLENDER (1890-1972), a U.S. senator who cosponsored Public Law 78

Summary of Event

The bracero program for importation of Mexican labor importation into the United States was begun in 1942 in response to the rising complaints of southwestern farmers and railroad shippers of a severe agricultural labor shortage. Agriculturalists argued that the military draft, along with high-paying defense-industry jobs, had drawn large numbers of agricultural workers away from farms at the very time that uninterrupted agricultural production was needed for military success. Without foreign contract labor,

295

they concluded, food shortages were inevitable. Although many economists, most notably Conrad Taeuber, head agricultural economist of the Bureau of Agricultural Economics, disagreed with this view of the agricultural labor market, the Franklin D. Roosevelt Administration responded to pressure and opened negotiations with Mexico for temporary contract laborers.

Mexico's initial response, however, was negative. Mexican officials sharply reminded the United States of the long and exploitive history of U.S. relations with Mexican workers. During the Great Depression, the United States had forcibly returned hundreds of thousands of Mexican laborers to Mexico in an effort to protect the jobs of American citizens. Unless the United States was willing to accede to a host of procedural safeguards for these temporary workers, Mexico was unwilling to allow its citizens to cross the border. These safeguards included having individual contracts written in Spanish, each with guarantees to pay living expenses and to provide adequate shelter and transportation costs while a worker was in transit. Workers were further protected from all discriminatory acts and were not subject to the U.S. military draft. Wages were to be set at an annually determined "prevailing wage" based on the locality in which the laborer was to be employed. Most important, these contracts were between the Mexican and U.S. governments, not the worker and employer. The idea was that the U.S. government, as the primary contractor, would "sublease" the workers' contracts to farmers. This meant that the U.S. government held the ultimate responsibility for ensuring that the contracts' provisions were upheld. It also gave the Mexican government the power to limit the number of workers allowed into the United States if discriminatory practices occurred or if contracts were violated.

Under pressure to act, President Roosevelt agreed to these concessions and, on August 4, 1942, signed an executive agreement initiating the bracero program. Roosevelt drew his authority to initiate the program from the Immigration Act of 1917. Although it specifically prohibited contract agricultural workers, that act allowed the commissioner general of immigration and the secretary of labor to admit otherwise inadmissible persons. Roosevelt then assigned the Farm Security Administration (FSA) of the Department of Agriculture the responsibility to administer the program.

From the start, the program was controversial. Farmers disliked the restrictions imposed on them by the program, particularly the wage provisions, which they saw as a first step toward universal wage regulations for agriculture. They also distrusted the FSA, which they believed was generally in opposition to farmers. At the same time, labor disliked the program as run by the FSA because of its lax rules as to the setting of the "prevailing wage." Ideally, the "prevailing wage" in a region was to be set by the market. Where labor is scarce, wages should rise. Only where labor shortages existed after wages rose were braceros to be allowed. In practice, however, the FSA allowed farmers to set the "prevailing wage" at the beginning of the growing season, and if this wage was inadequate to attract enough domestic workers, the farmers were allowed to bring in braceros.

In April, 1943, dissatisfaction with the FSA resulted in passage of Public Law 45, in which Congress gave its approval to the bracero program. In doing so, however, Congress significantly reshaped the operation of the program. First, it removed the FSA as administrator of the program, giving this authority to the Cooperative Extension Service (CES). This presumably was done to satisfy the complaints of large growers about the FSA. The CES was also a part of the Department of Agriculture, but unlike the FSA it was historically allied with large growers and shippers. In addition, the wage and working condition provisions of the original executive order were not included in Public Law 45. Although the government would still hold contracts with individual braceros, it would not have the power to demand the application of a "prevailing wage." Instead, the power to set wages was, in effect, returned to farmers. In practice, farmers had always had the power to set wages; this law merely formalized the process.

Following the end of World War II, the original justification for the bracero program ended. On December 31, 1947, so too did the executive agreement between the United States and Mexico. Public Law 45, however, remained on the statute books, authorizing the use of braceros if the U.S. government wished it. Harry S Truman's administration did. On February 21, 1948, a new labor importation agreement was concluded with Mexico. In following years, similar annual agreements would be signed. The post-1948 agreements also drew their authority from the 1917 Immigration Act. There were, however, a few significant differences between the new agreements and those from wartime. The U.S. government would no longer be the employer of record for braceros. Instead, individual growers or growers' associations contracted directly with Mexico for bracero workers. This meant that the government was no longer legally responsible for the fulfillment of bracero contracts.

This provision of the post-1948 agreements was to bring a further change in the bracero program in 1951. Angered over repeated violations of contract provisions by U.S. farmers, and empowered by the growing demand for immigrant labor resulting from the Korean War, the Mexican government demanded that the U.S. government reacquire control over bracero contracts. Congress responded on July 12 with Public Law 78, which returned the bracero program to a government-to-government basis and thus placed the responsibility for guaranteeing that the provisions of bracero contracts were met directly on the U.S. government. With this change in place, the postwar bracero program was complete. It continued unchanged until 1964.

The reformism of the New Frontier and the Great Society finally killed the bracero program. Both the John F. Kennedy and Lyndon B. Johnson administrations thought that braceros cost American workers jobs and permitted farmers to keep agricultural wages low. Without braceros, the reasoning went, farmers would have to raise wages to get enough workers to pick their crops. In 1961, President Kennedy ordered Secretary of Labor Arthur Goldberg to look into ways to protect domestic workers. Goldberg's successor, Willard Wirtz, recommended that the program, which came up for renewal in 1964, not be renewed. On December 31, 1964, the bracero labor importation program was allowed to expire.

Impact of Event

There is little doubt that the bracero program had effects on the agricultural sector of the United States both during and after World War II. By the end of 1947, when the first bracero program ended, some 220,000 workers had been recruited under the program. In the years following, the annual number of braceros working on U.S. farms ranged between 50,000 and 350,000. This many contract laborers could not help having an impact both on the agricultural output of the nation and on working conditions in the agricultural sector. It is difficult to say, however, how significant their impact was.

During World War II, for example, braceros made up only a part of the total number of Mexican laborers working on U.S. farms. In reaction to Texas' historic discrimination against Hispanic people, Mexico refused to contract any braceros to Texas for the first five years of the program. This meant that Texas farmers had to use either domestic laborers or illegal immigrant workers. Many Texas farmers chose illegal workers, even after Mexico allowed braceros to contract in Texas.

Following the war, the use of illegal workers by many U.S. farmers, in preference to both braceros and domestic laborers, continued. During the mid-1950's, the immigration enforcement mechanism became overloaded. Tens or even hundreds of thousands of illegal immigrants were deported every year. They made up only a fraction of the "wetbacks" (a term then used in legal documents) actually working on U.S. farms. Only with "Operation Wetback," a multidepartment, multiyear effort by the U.S. and Mexican governments to halt the flow of illegal immigrants northward, did the number of such laborers working on U.S. farms decrease, and then only temporarily.

Given the large number of illegal workers on U.S. farms during the period in which the bracero program operated, it is difficult to argue that the bracero program had any significant effect in raising agricultural wages. In fact, the opposite seems more plausible. Wartime problems with the "prevailing wage" system got worse following the war, when contracting powers were placed directly in the hands of farmers. The return of the U.S. government as official contractor of braceros after 1951 did not bring much effective change in the wage-reducing effects of the bracero program. Throughout the period, agricultural wages remained low in comparison to those in other sectors of the economy.

As late as 1964, the Mexican government continued its support of the bracero concept. It believed that the program provided significant protections to Mexican workers in the United States that would be absent without a formal agreement. It also worked to improve relations between the United States and Mexico and helped to improve working conditions on U.S. farms for both Mexican and domestic workers. The program also helped keep the already troublesome problem of illegal immigration from getting worse. Following the end of the program in 1964, the number of illegal Mexican workers increased. The flood would continue to grow well into the 1980's.

Bibliography

Craig, Richard. *The Bracero Program: Interest Groups and Foreign Policy.* Austin: University of Texas Press, 1971. Examines the various interests pushing for the bracero program and the reasons why it changed over time.

Galarza, Ernesto. *Merchants of Labor: The Mexican Bracero Story.* Charlotte, N.C.: McNally and Loftin, 1964. An account of the operation of the bracero program in California from 1942 to 1960. Offers an early evaluation of the program's operations and effectiveness. One of few book-length examinations of the bracero program. A good place to start a study of the bracero program.

Garcia, Juan Ramon. *Operation Wetback: The Mass Deportation of Mexican Undocumented Workers in 1954.* Westport, Conn.: Greenwood Press, 1980. Examines the problem of undocumented Mexican workers in the 1950's. Useful as a background to the later parts of the bracero program.

Hawley, Ellis W. "The Politics of the Mexican Labor Issue, 1950-1965." In *Mexican Workers in the United States: Historical and Political Perspectives*, edited by George C. Kiser and Martha Woody Kiser. Albuquerque: University of New Mexico Press, 1979. The best account of the politics behind the bracero program in the 1950's. Explains why the program was continued throughout the decade and why it was ended in 1964. The volume contains other important essays. See especially the short sum-mary of the second bracero period on pages 67-71.

Kirstein, Peter. *Anglo over Bracero: A History of the Mexican Worker in the United States from Roosevelt to Nixon.* San Francisco, Calif.: R and E Research Associates, 1977. An essential survey of U.S. policy toward Mexican laborers, both legal and illegal. Provides useful background and details about the bracero program.

Pfeiffer, David G. "The Bracero Program in Mexico." In *Mexican Workers in the United States: Historical and Political Perspectives*, edited by George C. Kiser and Martha Woody Kiser. Albuquerque: University of New Mexico Press, 1979. Describes the Mexican side in organizing and running the bracero program.

Scruggs, Otey M. "Texas and the Bracero Program, 1942-1947." In *Mexican Workers in the United States: Historical and Political Perspectives*, edited by George C. Kiser and Martha Woody Kiser. Albuquerque: University of New Mexico Press, 1979. Discusses the operation of the bracero program during World War II. Stresses the limited nature of this program for Texas. Explains the opposition of many farmers to the bracero program and shows many of the efforts of farmers to undermine the program's effectiveness.

Charles Zelden

Cross-References

Roosevelt Signs the Fair Labor Standards Act (1938); Roosevelt Signs the Emergency Price Control Act (1942); Eisenhower Begins the Food for Peace Program (1954); Congress Passes the Equal Pay Act (1963); The North American Free Trade Agreement Goes into Effect (1994).